Soviet Foreign Policy
1962–1973

ROBIN EDMONDS

Soviet Foreign Policy
1962-1973

THE PARADOX OF
SUPER POWER

OXFORD UNIVERSITY PRESS
London   Oxford   New York

OXFORD UNIVERSITY PRESS

London   Oxford   New York
Glasgow   Toronto   Melbourne   Wellington
Cape Town   Ibadan   Nairobi   Dar es Salaam   Lusaka   Addis Ababa
Delhi   Bombay   Calcutta   Madras   Karachi   Lahore   Dacca
Kuala Lumpur   Singapore   Hong Kong   Tokyo

To the memory of
C. H. K. E.

PREFACE

This book is indebted to a large number of people, both in Britain and abroad: to my colleagues in the Glasgow University Department of Politics and Institute of Soviet and Eastern European Studies, for the help and advice that they offered me during my time as visiting Research Fellow at the University—particularly Professor Alec Nove, Professor William Mackenzie, Professor Allen Potter, Dr. Vladimir Kusin, Dr. Christopher Mason, and Dr. Stephen White; to Lord Zuckerman, Sir Duncan Wilson, Mrs. Enid Balint, and Mr. Malcolm Mackintosh, all of whom read the whole manuscript and will, I hope, find in the book a reflection of their benevolent but unsparing criticisms; to Mr. Raymond Hyatt, for the maps; to Sir Edgar Williams, for reading the proofs; to Mrs. Jean Beverly, for typing the manuscript, with the help of Miss Carole Curtis, Miss Patricia Key, and Miss Charlotte Thompson; and to Sir Ronald and Lady Orr-Ewing, a corner of whose house provided the perfect setting for writing a book.

Long as it is, this list leaves unmentioned the many others whom I have consulted over the past year. Moreover, the book would never have been written if the Foreign and Commonwealth Office had not given me sabbatical leave and the University of Glasgow had not offered me both a Visiting Fellowship and a research grant that enabled me to exchange views on the spot with a wide range of those concerned with this field of international relations in the United States, France, and the Federal Republic of Germany. To all of them I am deeply grateful. Needless to say, the Office, the University, and all those who have helped over the past year are in no way responsible for the views expressed in the book, which are my own.

The dedication is to my Father, who taught me how to write.

Cardross
Port of Menteith
1974

CONTENTS

SELECTIVE CHRONOLOGY OF
INTERNATIONAL EVENTS

1956	February:	XXth CPSU Congress: Khrushchev denounces Stalin
	October:	Second Arab-Israeli War (the Suez invasion); Hungarian revolt; Polish 'October revolution'
1957	October:	First *sputnik*; Sino-Soviet nuclear agreement
	November:	Mao Tse-tung's speech in Moscow
1958		Year of the Chinese Great Leap Forward
1959	June:	Sino-Soviet nuclear agreement rescinded by Soviet Government
	September:	Khrushchev's visit to USA
	September–October:	Khrushchev's visit to China
1960	May:	U-2 incident; abortive summit meeting in Paris
	July:	Recall of Soviet experts from China
1961	April:	Invasion of Cuba: the Bay of Pigs fiasco
	June:	Meeting of Kennedy and Khrushchev in Vienna; beginning of second Berlin crisis
1962	October:	Cuban missile crisis; Sino-Indian war
1963	July:	CPSU Open Letter on Sino-Soviet dispute
	August:	Partial Nuclear Test Ban Treaty signed in Moscow
1964	August:	Tonkin Gulf incident, followed by joint Congressional Resolution on Vietnam
	October:	Fall of Khrushchev, replaced by collective Soviet leadership; explosion of first Chinese nuclear device
1965	February:	Kosygin visits Hanoi; US bombing of North Vietnam begins
	September:	Soviet Economic Reform; beginning of Chinese Cultural Revolution
1966	January:	Kosygin mediates between India and Pakistan at Tashkent
1967	June:	Third Arab-Israeli war
	November:	Security Council Resolution 242 on Arab-Israeli dispute
1968	January:	Dubček becomes First Secretary of Czechoslovak Communist Party
	July:	Nuclear Non-Proliferation Treaty signed; end of Chinese Cultural Revolution
	August:	Invasion of Czechoslovakia
1969		Year of Soviet-US numerical strategic nuclear parity
	March:	Sino-Soviet border clash
	July:	First withdrawal of US troops from Vietnam
	September:	Meeting of Soviet and Chinese Prime Ministers in Peking
	October:	Brandt elected Federal German Chancellor
	November:	Soviet and US SALT delegations meet in Helsinki

	December:	Soviet-German talks begin in Moscow; Berlin talks proposed by Three Allied Powers; first moves towards multilateral European negotiations; CPSU Central Committee convened to discuss economic problems
1970	January	Soviet military intervention in Egypt
	March:	Ratification of Non-Proliferation Treaty by Great Britain, US, and USSR
	August:	Signature of Soviet-German Moscow Treaty; Egyptian-Israeli cease-fire
	September:	Allende elected President of Chile
1971	March-April:	XXIVth CPSU Congress adopts Programme of Peace
	July:	Announcement of US President's acceptance of invitation to visit China
	August:	The dollar declared inconvertible into gold
1971	September:	Quadripartite Agreement on Berlin signed
	October:	Nixon invited to Moscow
	December:	Indo-Pakistan war; Republic of China takes seat in UN
1972	February:	Nixon's visit to China
	May:	Nixon's visit to USSR; signature of first Soviet-US summit agreements; Quadripartite Berlin Agreement brought into force
	July:	Soviet troops withdrawn from Egypt, at Egyptian request
	August:	Last US combat troops withdrawn from Vietnam
	December:	Basic Treaty between the two Germanies signed
1973	January:	Britain, Denmark, and Ireland enter the European Economic Community; Vietnam cease-fire agreement signed in Paris
	April:	CPSU Central Committee approves Brezhnev foreign policy and changes in Politburo
	May:	Brezhnev visits Bonn
	June:	Brezhnev visits US; Agreement on Prevention of Nuclear War signed
	September:	*Coup d'état* in Chile; Geneva Conference on Security and Cooperation opens
	October:	Fourth Arab-Israeli War; Vienna talks on mutual reduction of forces and armaments in Europe open
	December:	World oil prices quadrupled
1974		Year of the Energy Crisis
	February:	Solzhenitsyn exiled
	May:	Indian explosion of a nuclear device
	June–July:	Third Soviet-American summit meeting
	July–August:	Cyprus crisis
	August:	Resignation of President Nixon, succeeded by Vice-President Ford
	October:	Kissinger's visit to Moscow; announcement of forthcoming working meeting between Brezhnev and Ford at Vladivostok

ABBREVIATIONS

ABM	Anti-ballistic missile
ASM	Air-to-surface missile
ASW	Anti-submarine warfare
CCP	Chinese Communist Party
CENTO	Central Treaty Organization
COMECON	Council for Mutual Economic Cooperation
CPSU	Communist Party of the Soviet Union
CSCE	European Conference on Security and Cooperation (the ordering of initials derives from the French translation)
DDR/GDR	East Germany (German Democratic Republic)
EEC	European Economic Community
FBS	Forward based system
FRG	West Germany (Federal Republic of Germany)
GATT	General Agreement on Trade and Tariffs
GNP	Gross National Product
ICBM	Intercontinental ballistic missile
IISS	International Institute for Strategic Studies
IMF	International Monetary Fund
IRBM	Intermediate range ballistic missile
MAD	Mutually assured destruction
MARV	Manoeuvrable re-entry vehicle
MBFR	Mutual and Balanced Force Reductions (the title finally agreed was Mutual Force Reductions and Associated Measures)
MFN	Most favoured nation
MIRV	Multiple independently targetable re-entry vehicle
MRBM	Medium range ballistic missile
MRV	Multiple re-entry vehicle
NATO	North Atlantic Treaty Organization
OECD	Organization for Economic Cooperation and Development

SALT   Strategic Arms Limitation Talks
SAM   Surface-to-air missile
SLBM   Submarine launched ballistic missile
SSBN   Ballistic missile submarine, nuclear
UNCTAD   United Nations Commission on Trade and Development

Note

Billion is used here as meaning a thousand million.

Soviet Foreign Policy
1962–1973

1

INTRODUCTION

In 1962 the Soviet Union and the United States suddenly found themselves on the brink of thermonuclear war. Had this war been fought, such historians as survived the holocaust would have recorded as its immediate cause each side's perception of the other's intentions regarding a Caribbean island whose revolutionary leader had recently professed himself a Marxist-Leninist.* The more perceptive among these historians, mindful of the belief of one of the two principal actors in the drama enacted during this seminal crisis, that the mysterious 'essence of ultimate decision remains impenetrable to the observer—often, indeed to the decider himself . . .',[1] would have added that the real reasons for the conflict lay much deeper, in the relationship between the two countries as it had developed since the end of the Second World War, during which they had been the senior partners in the Grand Alliance. The date on which the cold war was declared and Europe was split in two is debatable: perhaps 2 July 1947, when Molotov broke off negotiations in Paris, announcing that the Soviet Union would not take part in the Marshall Plan for the European Recovery Programme.[2] But there can be no question when the cold war came closest to becoming, literally, a hot war: 22 October 1962, the day on which the presence of Soviet ballistic missiles in Cuba was revealed to the world, and the six days that followed until Khrushchev announced his decision to withdraw them.

* Lenin would hardly have recognized Fidel Castro as a disciple, although he might well have seen him, in traditional Russian terms, as a left-wing Social Revolutionary. Fidel Castro, who came to power as a radical, reforming *caudillo*, made his famous profession of Marxist–Leninist faith in a television broadcast three years later on 1 December 1961.

A decade later, although the Soviet Union and the United States each remained at the head of opposing alliances, the cold war was over. Again, there is no exact date for its conclusion, but as good as any is 22 June 1973, when the Soviet-American Agreement on the Prevention of Nuclear War[3] was signed in Washington, then being visited by the General-Secretary of the Communist Party of the Soviet Union (CPSU) for the first time since the brief armistice in the cold war marked by Khrushchev's visit in 1959. And again, this transformation of the Soviet-American relationship did not come out of the blue, but took several years to develop. That their relationship has undergone a radical change is beyond dispute. But the crucial question remains, what exactly is it that has changed and why? Is it Soviet as well as American foreign policy that has altered; or is it only American foreign policy, reacting to what Soviet observers of the international scene regard as a change in the 'correlation of forces'* in favour of the Soviet Union?

Defenders of the second view can point to the absence of any change in the doctrine of Soviet foreign policy as it has been formulated ever since 1956. (The one exception—the expansion of the concept of peaceful coexistence—will be examined in a later chapter.) The official History of Soviet Foreign Policy describes the policy's four basic tasks as:

1. To secure, together with the other socialist countries, favourable conditions for the building of socialism and communism;
2. To strengthen the unity and solidarity of the socialist countries, their friendship and brotherhood;
3. To support the national-liberation movement and to effect all-round cooperation with the young, developing countries.
4. Consistently to uphold the principle of peaceful coexistence of states with different social systems, to offer decisive resistance to the aggressive forces of imperialism, and to save mankind from a new world war.[4]

This formulation follows word for word the resolution on foreign policy approved by the XXIIIrd Congress of the CPSU in March 1966, which was repeated in turn by Leonid Brezhnev in his opening speech at the XXIVth Congress five years later.[5] To this formulation must be added two important riders. One is Lenin's statement that 'the deepest roots both of the international and of the external policy of our state are

---

* The Marxist concept of this correlation is of something inherently unstable, which it is the task of the statesman to turn to his country's advantage, with the aid of the forces of history—an important difference from the traditional Western concept of the balance of power, designed to preserve international stability.

determined by the economic interests . . . of the ruling classes of our state':[6] the policy pursued by the Soviet Government abroad is a reflection and an extension of its policy at home. The other rider is the belief, also propounded in the Official History,[7] that the danger of war, including the danger of a Third World War, will continue as long as imperialism exists: peaceful coexistence is therefore a form of the Marxist class struggle. This belief was implicit in an article on strategic arms limitation published in *Pravda* on the eve of Brezhnev's visit to the United States in 1973, which reminded readers of his statement made six months earlier at the celebration of the fiftieth anniversary of the Soviet Union:

The . . . class struggle of the two systems . . . in the sphere of economics, politics and, it goes without saying, ideology, will be continued . . . The world outlook and the aims of socialism are opposed and irreconcilable. But we shall ensure that this inevitable struggle is transferred to a channel which does not threaten wars, dangerous conflicts, and an uncontrolled arms race.[8]

True, there was a change in the conduct of foreign policy in 1964, when the present Soviet leadership took over from Khrushchev. But, at any rate at the outset, the way in which they described the difference between themselves and the man whom they had removed from power was primarily one of style or posture: their own approach they commended as that of prudent managers. As Brezhnev put it in a definition of Soviet foreign policy in a speech delivered to the Central Committee of the CPSU on 29 September 1965: 'we are striving to make our diplomacy active and thrusting, while at the same time showing flexibility and circumspection'.[9] Nevertheless, the doctrinal continuity of Soviet foreign policy from 1956 to 1973 has been remarkable.

The West, and particularly Western Europe, faces a bleak prospect if Soviet apologists are right in contending that for over seventeen years Soviet foreign policy has remained immutable, and that the only change is that the rest of the world, notably the United States, has had to adjust itself to an altered strategic power balance—at the moment, Soviet-American, but ultimately a triangular balance between China, the Soviet Union, and the United States. This view is not supported by the facts. The invasion of Czechoslovakia certainly demonstrated the paramount importance to the Soviet leadership of the first and second of the basic tasks of their foreign policy. But as for the third task (support of national-liberation movements), the Soviet Union gave North Vietnam enough help—and no more than that—both to keep it on its feet and to

maintain Soviet influence in Indo-China against the Chinese; in Chile, the
Soviet Union made no attempt to repeat its Cuban experience; Soviet
commitment to this task is taken with a pinch of salt by Egyptians; and it
is ridiculed by the Chinese Communist Party (CCP).[10] Above all, since
1972/3 the Leninist* principle of peaceful coexistence has been given an
interpretation that goes far beyond anything ever suggested by Lenin
(who described it to the VIIIth CPSU Congress as inconceivable over a
long period of time). In short, although Soviet foreign policy may have
remained unaltered on paper for nearly twenty years, in fact a gap has
developed between its theory and its practice. For a Marxist, there can
be no difference between theory and practice. In non-Marxist terms
such a difference may be regarded as a conflict that cannot be tolerated
indefinitely.

Is there another, tenable explanation of the contrast between the
events of October 1962 and those of October 1973? The greatest
achievement of the Soviet leadership since the fall of Khrushchev has
been the Soviet Union's attainment of parity with the United States.
Khrushchev's claim to this parity was proved hollow by the Cuban
missile crisis. Under the flexible and circumspect management of his
successors, however, the Soviet Union is today universally acknowledged to be a super-power, co-equal with its old adversary in the cold
war, the United States. The relationship between the two super-powers
is complex and ambivalent; and it has so far eluded attempts to define
it in a single word or phrase. The word super-power is not part of the
Soviet vocabulary; on the occasions when it is used, it appears in inverted
commas; and Brezhnev brushed the term aside at his meeting with
United States Senators in June 1973.[11] The reason for this modesty is
partly the pejorative significance that the word has acquired in the
political vocabulary of the Chinese, who disclaim any intention of
aspiring to super-power status themselves. Instead, the Soviet Union is
described as one of 'the two nuclear giants' or, in the History of Soviet
Foreign Policy, as 'one of the greatest world powers, without whose
participation not a single international problem can be solved':[12] a
definition which foreshadowed Brezhnev's statement, during his television broadcast in the United States in June 1973, that the economic
and military power of the two countries invested them with a special

* Although peaceful coexistence is the invariable phrase in contemporary
Soviet usage, Lenin himself spoke rather of peaceful cohabitation (*mirnoe
sozhitel'stvo*)—see, for example, *Collected Works*, English edition, vol. 40, p. 145;
vol. 41, pp. 132–3; and vol. 45, pp. 327–44.

responsibility for the preservation of universal peace and the prevention of war.[13]

It is instructive to compare Brezhnev's statement with the plea for collaboration between the super-powers made nearly thirty years earlier by William Fox, who first coined the term 'super-power' and attempted its first definition (a great power, whose armed force is so mobile that it can be deployed in any strategic theatre, as opposed to a great power whose interests and influence are confined to a single regional theatre[14]). This definition, made before Hiroshima and Nagasaki, holds good today, when the central strategic fact underlying the world power structure is the nuclear armoury of the super-powers. It is this armoury, combined with the expanded Soviet conventional military forces, both at sea and in the air, that has at last entitled the Soviet Union to its global role. Yet in the process of achieving this goal, the Soviet Union, like the United States, has become in many ways the prisoner of its power, which it must control, and of its responsibility, which it must seek to define. Today both the Soviet Union and the United States possess what American theorists have defined as the capacity for mutually assured destruction (MAD). Although Soviet theorists have never officially accepted the MAD concept (that each super-power, even after an all-out first-strike attack on its strategic forces, would still be capable of inflicting an unacceptable degree of retaliatory damage on the other), both the Soviet Union and the United States now have at least one vital interest in common: not to destroy each other—an interest shared by most of the bystanders, who would be destroyed as well if the two super-powers were to come to thermonuclear blows.

At first sight, the determination simply not to destroy may appear a negative concept. But it implies a determination to survive; and the logic of strategic nuclear power is so inexorable, that sooner or later the relationship between two super-powers—however much they may pursue their rivalry in other, less dangerous fields—must become positive. If we examine the history of the past eleven years, we shall find that this is indeed what has come about between the Soviet Union and the United States, culminating in the twenty bilateral agreements signed between them during 1972–3: a paradox which, before the nuclear age, would have been inconceivable for Lenin, which in its first years Stalin could not understand, and which Khrushchev only partly perceived.

By a further paradox, at the end of the 1960s, just as the Soviet leadership finally scaled the peak of super-power status that they had expended so much national effort to reach, they found themselves confronted with a dilemma at home, which was both economic and political. The Soviet economy had reached a point in its development where it could not meet both the demands of the defence sector and the aspirations of the consumer except on one of two alternative conditions: either a root and branch reform of the Soviet system or a massive importation of Western technology, capital, and in the end, management techniques. In accordance with the doctrine of the class struggle, while the former alternative was inconceivable, the latter was acceptable, as the lesser of two ideological evils, provided Western imports did not infect the Soviet Union with the germ of alien political ideas—a proviso that necessitated a sharp tightening of ideological discipline in the Soviet Union in the 1970s. On the other hand, voices of dissent were raised in the Soviet Union, proclaiming the eternal truth that material progress and the liberty of the human spirit are indivisible. Among these voices the most authoritative urged the West not to give the Soviet Union economic help unless intellectual freedom were assured within its boundaries, at the very moment when promises of such help were forthcoming from the Soviet Union's traditional enemies—Germany and Japan—and from its principal adversary in the cold war—the United States, with which Brezhnev was now seeking a permanent relationship. These voices found a response in the West, both among those who believed that the Soviet Union should be helped only in return for political changes within that country, and among those who believed that such help would serve only to enable the Soviet Union to maintain and extend its military might.

This book is an attempt first, to reappraise Soviet foreign policy as it has been conducted in practice between October 1962 and October 1973, and in particular to study the evolution of the special relations now existing between the two super-powers; then, in the light of this evolution, to consider how these relations may develop further, over the next ten years; and in conclusion, to suggest how this development may affect Western Europe. It is hoped that this will throw some light on a third paradox: the gap between the theory and the practice of Soviet foreign policy, and the related question—what is the determining force that motivates the men who formulate and carry out this policy?

A professional diplomat writing history should bear in mind de Tocqueville's observation:

men of letters who have written history without taking part in public affairs . . . are always inclined to find general causes . . . politicians who have concerned themselves with producing events without thinking about them ... living in the midst of disconnected daily facts, are prone to imagine that everything is attributable to particular incidents, and that the wires that they pull are the same as those that move the world. It is to be presumed that both are equally deceived.[15]

By allowing an equal weight in his scales both to particular incidents and to general causes, a wise historian may, with the advantage of hindsight, be able to penetrate Kennedy's 'mystery of ultimate decision', and to describe not only what really happened but why it happened in the way that it did. Can the tools of modern political science developed over the past quarter of a century help him in his task, particularly in assessing what de Tocqueville called general causes? In answering this question a distinction must be drawn between the study of the past, the present, and the future. In studying the past, provided that all the evidence is available (for example, governmental archives open to the public, private memoirs published), the historian may be able to learn something extra[16] by applying, among other methods of analysis, quantitative and scientific methods to the full range of the facts that he has assembled. Their value is doubtful when applied to the study of the immediate past, where all the evidence cannot yet be obtained, or of the present; and still more so if they are used in an attempt to construct a productive conceptual model of the future of international relations, since these are the product of a complex interplay of variables, which are not susceptible to treatment by the disturbance factor in a mathematical model. Indeed, as an eminent British scientist has observed in a criticism of abstract strategic analysis, these variables are 'of so qualitative a nature that no one could attribute numerical values to them.'[17]

Why is it that so much intellectual effort devoted since the Second World War to this form of analysis has helped us so little to understand the history of our times?[18] (For example, in the strategic field, games theory, though fascinating at first sight, becomes unmanageable when applied to a contest between more than two players; and in the political field, the astringent approach sought by structural functionalism ends by calling to mind Roy Campbell's: 'you use the snaffle and the rein all right, but where's the bloody horse?'). The reason is surely that history describes, and seeks to explain, the conduct of human beings, acting individually as well as in groups; and there is no instrument that can understand human beings better than the human mind.

Thucydides' approach to history was influenced by the medical theory of his day; he was a contemporary of Hippocrates. In my view, the scientific discipline which should most influence the modern historian, especially if he is studying the present and the recent past, is medicine. What the modern physician must do above all, if he is to make an accurate diagnosis and a successful prognosis, is to listen to the patient with a trained ear. The best service that the historian of our times can render is, so far as possible, to allow events to speak for themselves, in the hope that a comparison of what these events teach him with the lessons of the past may enable him to try to identify some of the parameters of the future. Such an approach to history is especially appropriate to a study of Soviet policy, because in the Soviet Union hard evidence is often lacking, and what is said and written, when studied in isolation from what actually happens, may be deceptive. Listening to the events of history is as difficult for the historian as listening to the patient is for the physician; the historian of a state inspired by a dialectical philosophy can best understand it if he observes closely what its rulers do; and if he observes a conflict between their thought and their actions, he must draw his own conclusions as best he can. This book will seek to observe events dispassionately, but as though from the Kremlin—a difficult task, because the Politburo of the CPSU, the supreme decision-making body in the Soviet Union and the hub of the lobbies that make up the Soviet élite, is not given to indiscretion. Moreover, its decisions on foreign policy are not based only on information and advice from the Soviet Ministry of Foreign Affairs. Other important bodies which submit to the Politburo views that are by definition closed to the outside observer, are the foreign departments of the Party's central apparatus and the foreign directorate of the KGB.[19] As if to emphasize the limitations of the Foreign Ministry, only one Soviet Foreign Minister—Vyacheslav Molotov—had been a member of the Politburo until April 1973, when Andrei Gromyko (who had succeeded Molotov as Foreign Minister in 1957)[20] became the first professional diplomat to enter it.

It has been well said that where the Soviet Union is concerned, there are no degrees of knowledge, only degrees of ignorance. Our knowledge of the years 1962–73 is indeed still fragmentary. But there are by now enough substantial fragments of evidence to make possible the work of reconstructing, as a coherent whole, the foreign policy of the Soviet Union during the period of its evolution from great power to super-power.

NOTES

1. J. F. Kennedy, in the foreword to Theodore C. Sorensen, *Decision-Making in the White House*, Columbia University Press, New York, 1963, p. xi.
2. In *Expansion and Coexistence*, Secker and Warburg, London, 1968, pp. 432 ff, Adam Ulam makes a good case for regarding this as the opening of the cold war. (The Soviet Government subsequently obliged Czechoslovakia, not yet a member of the Soviet bloc, to follow suit.) Soviet historians might prefer March 1947, when the Truman Doctrine was announced. Certainly the great divide must be set somewhere in 1947.
3. Text in *The Times*, 23 June 1973.
4. *Istoriya Vneshnei Politiki SSSR*, Moscow, 1971, edited by Ponomarev, Gromyko, and Khvostov, vol. 2, p. 486. The distinction between 'building socialism' and 'building communism' is that only the Soviet Union is regarded by Soviet theorists as having reached the latter stage of development (as was announced by Khrushchev in 1961).
5. L. I. Brezhnev, *Leninskim Kursom*, Moscow, 1972, vol. 3, p. 196. An even more recent, and identical, formulation is given by *Diplomatiya Sotsializma*, Moscow, 1973, p. 17.
6. V. I. Lenin, *Complete Collected Works*, Fifth Russian edition, vol. 36, p. 327, Moscow, 1962. This quotation comes from Lenin's report on Soviet foreign policy of 14 May 1918. (All other quotations from Lenin's *Collected Works* are taken from the English edition.)
7. Op. cit., vol. 2, p. 485.
8. *Pravda*, 5 June 1973.
9. Ibid., 30 September 1965.
10. Soviet treatment of Allende is discussed in chapter 12. For the Egyptian attitude towards the Soviet commitment to their country, see, for example, Sadat's speeches reported in *The Times* of 26 July 1973 and 19 April 1974, and his interview with *Al Ahram* reported by the Associated Press in the *International Herald Tribune*, 30/31 March 1974. For a recent statement of Chinese policy towards the Third World, and of Chinese criticism of Soviet policy towards the latter, see David Bonavia's article 'China Takes a New View of the World', *The Times*, 22 April 1974.
11. *Pravda*, 21 June 1973.
12. The first description is quoted from *Krasnaya Zvezda*, 9 July 1974. The second is from op.cit., vol. 2, p. 480.
13. *The Times*, 25 June 1973.
14. W. T. R. Fox, *The Super-Powers—their responsibility for peace*, Yale Institute of International Studies, 1944, pp. 20–1.
15. Alexis de Tocqueville, quoted on the fly-leaf of Graham Allison, *Essence of Decision: Explaining the Cuban Missile Crisis*, Little, Brown, Boston, 1971.
16. It is as well not to expect too much. Cf. Harold Guetzkow's remark (quoted by Nigel Forward in *The Field of Nations*, Macmillan, London, 1971) that 'if the use of quantitative methods and scientific analysis were to bring about an improvement of five per cent in the performance of nations in their relations with one another, he for one would be well pleased'.
17. Solly Zuckerman, *Scientists at War*, Harper and Row, New York, 1966, p. 25.
18. So far as Soviet studies are concerned, the title of a chapter in a book of American essays on Soviet foreign policy—'Ten Theories in Search of Reality'—is significantly disheartening: see *Process and Power in Soviet Foreign Policy*, edited by Vernon Aspaturian, Little, Brown, Boston, 1971,

ch. III, pp. 290 ff. But an interesting, if controversial, application of quantitative methodology to the past has recently been carried out by R. W. Fogel and S. L. Engerman in their two-volume reappraisal of American slavery: *Time on the Cross*, Little, Brown, Boston, 1974.

19. The KGB, or Committee for State Security, is the lineal descendant of the *Cheka*, the 'Extraordinary Commission for combating counter-revolution, speculation, sabotage and malfeasance in office', formed in 1917 on Lenin's order. The KGB's activities abroad are not invariably directed against Western interests: a notable exception to the rule was the important part played by Fomin at the decisive moment of the Cuban missile crisis (Allison, op.cit., p. 220).

20. Gromyko was Ambassador in Washington before the end of the Second World War. The nearest Western parallel to his long experience of diplomacy is that of David Bruce, although he has never held ministerial office.

PART ONE

Khrushchev's Foreign Policy: The Years of Adventure

2
THE THEORY

There is a long tradition in Soviet politics (of which Stalin himself took full advantage) of stealing the Whigs' clothes while they are bathing. In March 1954, seven months after he had announced the Soviet thermonuclear bomb, Georgyi Malenkov warned the Soviet people that a new world war fought with contemporary weapons would mean the destruction of world civilization.[1] It is clear that had Malenkov remained in power, he would have pursued a foreign policy designed to allow the Soviet consumer, at long last, a fair share of his country's economic resources. Khrushchev ousted Malenkov with a return to the long-standing priority of heavy industry, on which the modernization of the Soviet Armed Forces depended; and he at once increased the defence budget. Yet by 1964 he had become an advocate of minimum nuclear deterrence, at loggerheads with both the 'steel-eaters' and the military, having taken the first steps towards an accommodation with the United States.

In the process Khrushchev transformed Soviet foreign policy. During Stalin's last years, not only as dictator of the Soviet Union but also as the acknowledged[2] leader of the Sino-Soviet bloc, even though he referred to the principle of peaceful coexistence (for example, in the *Economic Problems of Socialism*, the year before his death), the image of the Soviet Union's relationship with the non-communist world which he projected was that of a besieged camp, with Europe as its citadel. Khrushchev staked out a new political claim for the Soviet Union (no longer seen as besieged by the West, but the latter's challenger throughout the world), while at the same time seeking an understanding with the United States, based on the premise that the Soviet Union was already its equal, with the prospect of superiority, economic and military in sight.

This new policy had to be based on an ideological reformulation, which was approved by the XXth Party Congress, held in February 1956. At this historic meeting, in parallel with his destruction of the Stalinist idol, Khrushchev introduced three major changes, two of which are reflected in the third and fourth basic tasks of Soviet foreign policy. First, he laid a fresh emphasis on the principle of peaceful co-existence between communist and non-communist countries. This was no longer seen as a temporary phenomenon. Although imperialism was perceived as being as aggressive as ever, the socialist commonwealth was now held to be strong enough to make war avoidable. This change, coupled with his second innovation—that a country's transition to socialism could be carried out by peaceful means—paved the way for Khrushchev's visit to the United States in 1959 (the 'spirit of Camp David') and the non-summit in Paris the following year. Thirdly, he propounded a new approach to the Third World. For Stalin, a country such as India was governed by bourgeois, who as such deserved no support from the communist states. Khrushchev, on the contrary, saw Soviet championship of countries that had recently won their independence from the colonial powers, or were seeking independence, as part of the Soviet Union's new global role. These countries, and the United Nations—where they were soon to form the majority—were perceived in a new light. The visits which Khrushchev and Bulganin made in 1955 to India, Burma, and Afghanistan marked the beginning both of the Soviet foreign aid programme and of the Soviet Union's special relationship with India, while the arms deal with Egypt in the same year was the first to be concluded as part of a new policy of military aid to non-communist countries. It has been estimated that by the time of Khrushchev's fall, about 3 billion dollars worth of arms had been supplied to thirteen such countries in the preceding decade, amounting to nearly half the total of all Soviet economic aid to underdeveloped countries in the same period.[3]

Although the doctrines of peaceful coexistence and of peaceful transition to socialism, against the background of the 'thaw' within the Soviet Union, made Khrushchev appear at first sight easier for the West to deal with than Stalin had been, his new policy towards the Third World brought his country to the brink of nuclear war. For Khrushchev's foreign policy to succeed, two projections into the future—one economic and the other technological—had to be fulfilled. According to the first, announced by Khrushchev at the XXIInd Party Congress in October 1961, not only would the Soviet Union enter the phase of communism by 1980; in twenty years it would overtake the per capita standard of living of any capitalist country, and specifically reach 80 per cent above the 1960 American standard of living.[4] (By the time Khrushchev died, Japan was already in sight of overhauling his country as the world's second greatest industrial power.) The second projection arose from the successful launching of the first *sputnik* in September 1957. Whether Khrushchev really believed that the initial Soviet success in rocket technology would enable him to deploy intercontinental ballistic missiles (ICBMs) swiftly enough to achieve strategic nuclear parity with the United States is a matter for speculation.

It has been argued[5] that the successive Soviet boasts made between 1957 and 1962 should be regarded as bluff: these ranged from Tass's statement in August 1957 that it was 'now possible to send missiles to any part of the world', through Khrushchev's own claim, made to the Supreme Soviet in January 1960, that the Soviet Union by then had enough nuclear weapons and rockets to wipe out any country or countries that attacked the Soviet Union or other socialist states, to Malinovsky's statement in January 1962, that approximate nuclear parity existed between the Soviet Union and the United States.[6] It is questionable whether the public debate on the 'missile gap'[7] that these boasts provoked in the United States really affected the pace of the six strategic nuclear Research and Development programmes already being carried out by the three US armed services in the fifties. The momentum of these immense, crash programmes was by that time so great that by 1962 the result would probably have been the same in any case: a large number of American ICBMs and *Polaris* submarines confronting a much inferior Soviet strategic nuclear force. Be that as it may, the possibility that the Soviet Union was indeed carrying out an effective crash programme of first generation ICBMs (in reality their design was one of extreme awkwardness) succeeded only in spurring on the Administration to greater efforts with their ICBMs and their *Polaris* submarines. In 1960 the first *Atlas* ballistic missile units became operational and the first *Titan* less than two years later, followed by the first *Minuteman* missiles towards the end of 1962; and the first *Polaris* missiles were deployed at sea in November 1960.[8] These American successes were such that in the autumn of 1962 Khrushchev resorted to a gambler's throw.

Khrushchev's changes in the doctrine of Soviet foreign policy,

coupled with his claim for Soviet ballistic missile technology, contributed to the great schism in the communist world, which became public
the year before his fall. Although both sides trace the origins of the Sino-
Soviet dispute to 1957, the Chinese leaders seem unlikely ever to have
forgiven the Russians for their ambivalent attitude to their cause from
the 1920s onwards. Given the growing divergence in their economic and
social policies, it is hard to see how the Soviet Union and China could
have remained allies for long. Nevertheless, Khrushchev's impetuous
nature, his conduct of the dispute by public abuse, and his attempt to
have Chinese doctrines condemned by the majority of the international
communist movement may well have loomed large in the minds of his
colleagues when they finally decided to remove him from power.

Lenin's remark that 'abuse in politics often covers up the utter lack
of ideological content, the helplessness, and the impotence of the
abuser'[9] recalls the great schism between the Western and Eastern
branches of Christianity, which offers the closest historical parallel with
the Sino-Soviet dispute. Seen in retrospect, the Christian schism does
indeed appear to have had remarkably little theological content. Yet the
Sino-Soviet dispute has from the outset been a conflict of ideas, not
simply of national interests stemming from a secular difference of
cultural tradition. The ideological framework of the dispute may be
summarized as follows.[10] Having—in Soviet eyes—accepted, at the
XXth Congress, the CPSU's line on de-Stalinization, peaceful coexistence, and the peaceful transition to socialism, the Chinese afterwards opposed it. Basing themselves on the Maoist concept of contradictions within socialist society, the Chinese argued that revisionism,
not dogmatism,[11] was the greater threat to the unity of the Sino-Soviet
bloc, identifying the former first with Yugoslavia, and from 1963 onwards, with the Soviet Union itself. In their view therefore the CPSU
had forfeited the position of head of the international communist
movement. The CPSU responded by attacking the CCP as the expo-
nent of dogmatism, and claimed that the class struggle had been virtually
completed in the Soviet Union, where some relaxation was permissible.
The Chinese alleged that bourgeois elements within the Soviet Union
were increasing; and they regarded the picture of collectivist affluence
painted by the XXIInd Congress as imitating the United States. For
the Chinese, the commune experiment, together with the Great Leap
Forward, showed them as pioneers, outstripping the Russians, on the
path to pure communism; for the Russians, it discredited communism
because it required a control over individual liberty even stricter than

that which they themselves were in the process of discarding. The Russians maintained that the decisive event in world politics was the establishment of the world communist system, whose combined strength would expand communism by peaceful means. The Chinese replied that the imperialists would yield to force, if pressed, and that the tide was already running in favour of the communist movement.

Historically, the first duty of a Chinese Emperor was always the defence of the Empire. It was open to the Chinese Communists to choose to remain under the Soviet nuclear umbrella, which would have implied both an agreed policy over a wide range and a continuing trust in Soviet willingness to treat a threat to China as a threat to the Soviet Union. But their price for accepting this protection, and therefore opting out of the nuclear club themselves, was a more forward Soviet foreign policy than even the globalist Khrushchev could dare to contemplate. The fundamental differences between the Soviet and Chinese views of the nuclear issue were made plain by Mao Tse-tung in the speech which he delivered at the meeting of communist parties held in Moscow in November 1957 to celebrate the fortieth anniversary of the Russian Revolution. The full text has never been published, but it was on that occasion that Mao described the East wind as prevailing over the West, repeated his assessment of the United States as a paper tiger, and spoke of the millions of socialists who would survive a nuclear holocaust, which would leave imperialism razed to the ground.* At that moment Khrushchev was struggling to restore the unity of the world communist movement, in the wake of the Hungarian and Polish revolts of the preceding year. Perhaps therefore it was by way of compromise that he then granted Mao an agreement on new technology for national defence, which according to the Chinese version included the provision of a sample atomic bomb and the know-how for its manufacture.

The exact extent of defence cooperation between the two countries is uncertain.[12] In any event, according to the Chinese, 'the leadership of the CPSU put forward unreasonable demands designed to put China under Soviet control. These unreasonable demands were rightly and

* This historic speech, which must have chilled the blood of Mao's Soviet listeners, was summarized in the course of *Pravda*'s major survey of Chinese foreign policy on 26 August 1973 as a 'declaration that, for the sake of the achievement of a specific political goal, it is possible to sacrifice half mankind'. It is reconstructed, from published extracts, in ch. VIII of John Gittings's *Survey of the Sino-Soviet Dispute 1963–67*, Oxford University Press, 1968. Quotations for these years of the Sino–Soviet dispute are drawn from this comprehensive collection of polemical documents unless otherwise stated.

16

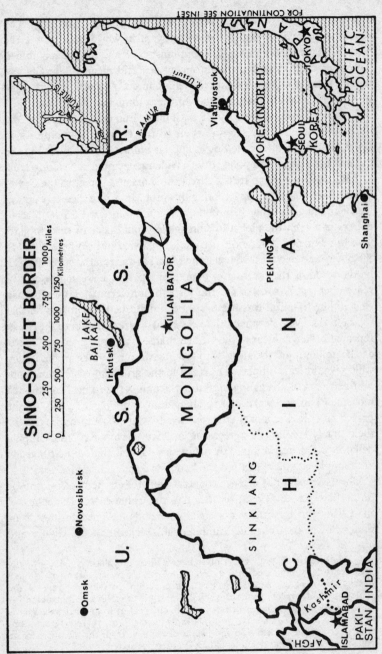

SINO-SOVIET BORDER

firmly rejected by the Chinese Government.' This disagreement on defence policy came to a head in 1958, simultaneously with that on internal policy; the Chinese Great Leap Forward, openly denounced by Khrushchev, reached its peak in the autumn. Thus the Sino-Soviet bloc, whose titanic potential mesmerized the West, really lasted little more than eight years, from the Sino-Soviet Treaty of 1950 until 1958, the year in which the two major communist powers set out on their separate ways. As additional grievances in that year, the Chinese could also point to the inadequacy of Soviet support during the Matsu-Quemoy crisis, and to the solution of the Jordan-Lebanon crisis. They saw the latter as an example of collusion between the governments of the Soviet Union and the United States, since Khrushchev's proposal was for a summit meeting of the Powers, which was to include India, but exclude China. In January 1959, Khrushchev proposed an atom-free zone in the Far East and the whole Pacific Ocean, which Chou En-lai at first endorsed; but later he added the condition that this should apply to all countries bordering the Pacific. In June 1959 (coinciding with Khrushchev's visit to the United States) the Soviet Government revoked the 1957 atomic agreement and, according to the Chinese, refused to supply the sample. In August, the Chinese Defence Minister was dismissed. A year later Soviet specialists of all kinds working in China were recalled.

Within the world communist movement, the first break between the Soviet Union and China took place in June 1960 at the Romanian Communist Party Congress, where Khrushchev (fresh from the failure of the Paris summit meeting) clashed with the Chinese delegate. The watershed was reached at the meeting of eighty-one communist parties held in Moscow in December 1960, where in another confrontation Albania supported China up to the hilt, while the Indonesian, North Korean, and North Vietnamese delegates remained neutral, although inclined towards the Chinese. In October 1961, at the XXIInd Congress of the CPSU, to which Albania had not been invited, Khrushchev attacked Albania—and implicitly China—for opposing the line agreed at the XXth Congress. Chou En-lai protested, walked out, laid a wreath on the tomb of Stalin (whose body was removed a few days later from the Lenin Mausoleum), and then left Moscow. Only two thirds of the parties represented at the Congress endorsed the attack on Albania; all the Asians remained silent. In the following year, when by a remarkable (but genuine) coincidence the Sino-Indian border war broke out two days before the Cuban missile crisis began, the two communist governments for a few days lent each other moral support. But by 5 November

1962 the Chinese had begun to criticize the Soviet withdrawal of missiles from Cuba, and the Russians had reverted to their earlier attitude of neutrality towards the Sino-Indian dispute, urging the need for a negotiated settlement and continuing to provide military aid to India. Following the events in Moscow a year earlier, it was only a short step for the Sino-Soviet dispute to become both direct and overt, as it did in 1963, and for China to claim leadership of the world communist movement.

Seen from Moscow, the last straw came in March 1963, when—as if the ideological and defence aspects of the Sino-Soviet dispute were not enough—a third dimension was added to it by the publication of the Chinese territorial claims against the Soviet Union.[13] The Chinese Government then declared that the nineteenth-century treaties of Aigun, Peking, and Ili were 'unequal', in the sense that the Tsarist Government of those days, as part of its expansionist policy in Asia, had taken advantage of Chinese weakness (as did other European Powers). The treaties were described in a *People's Daily* editorial of 8 March as raising outstanding issues; these should be settled peacefully through negotiations; until the time for such negotiations was ripe, the Chinese Government was prepared to maintain the *status quo*. From subsequent statements by both sides, it appeared that the Chinese wished to renegotiate the entire Sino-Soviet frontier—some 4,000 miles—although they were willing to accept the existing treaties as a basis for negotiations, provided that the Russians accepted their 'inequality'. For their part, the Russians denied the concept of inequality —a Russian Tsar was no worse than a Chinese Emperor—and were prepared only to make certain sections of the frontier more precise (much of it has never been delimited).

Under the terms of the Aigun and Peking treaties, the Russian Empire incorporated within its boundaries all the territory north of the Amur river and east of the Ussuri river, which was previously under Chinese suzerainty and today constitutes the Soviet Maritime Province in the Far East. The Ili treaty ceded part of Chinese Sinkiang (then Turkestan) to Russia, where it now forms part of the Kazakhstan Soviet Republic in Central Asia. But the 1,540,000 square kilometres of Chinese territory annexed by the Tsarist Government were not all that was called in question by the Chinese Government a century later. The Sino-Soviet Treaty of 1950 (also perhaps unequal, but in a different sense) had confirmed the independence of Outer Mongolia. Four years later Mao Tse-tung re-opened this question with Khrushchev. That he

had done so was revealed by Mao in July 1964, when he was reported by
the Japanese press as having taken the opportunity of the visit of a
Japanese Socialist Party delegation to back the Japanese claim for the
return of the Kurile Islands, and even to criticize other Soviet post-war
territorial acquisitions from Romania, Poland, and Finland.

No Soviet Government could fail to take seriously the claims of
March 1963 (let alone the rest). The Soviet Union is the biggest land-
owner in Asia; and east of the Urals it is inhabited by some 60 million
people, most of whom are not Slavs. The Soviet press gave publicity to
the Chinese territorial claims, including the question of the status of
Mongolia. A year later *Pravda* published a mammoth report by
Mikhail Suslov to a plenary meeting of the CPSU Central Committee
on 'The Struggle of the Communist Party of the Soviet Union for the
Unity of the International Communist Movement'. Dated 14 February
1964, its publication was delayed for nearly two months while the
Romanian Communist Party attempted mediation (one of the first
signs of Romania's independent foreign policy). The report was the
bitterest and most comprehensive attack yet made by the Russians
against the Chinese, whose deviation was described as *petit bourgeois*,
nationalistic, and neo-Trotskyite, hard on the heels of a personal attack
in the Chinese press on Khrushchev as the arch-revisionist. It was
rumoured in Moscow that Suslov's report was not his own work; that
whole passages were written by a member of Khrushchev's personal
staff; and that Suslov agreed to accept authorship on condition that the
report would not be published.[14] If true, this would explain why he was
credited in October 1964, with organizing the removal of Khrushchev,
who by that time had lost his colleagues' confidence in his conduct of
Soviet policy both at home and abroad.

NOTES

1. *Pravda*, 13 March 1954. For an analysis of the differences between Malenkov and Khrushchev at that time, see J. M. Mackintosh, *Strategy and Tactics of Soviet Foreign Policy*, Oxford University Press, London, 1962, pp. 88 ff.
2. Marshal Tito alone dissenting, from 1948 onwards.
3. Thomas W. Wolfe, *Soviet Power and Europe, 1945–70*, Johns Hopkins Press, Baltimore, 1970, p. 130.
4. Quoted in *Problems of Communism*, vol. XI, no. 1 (Jan.–Feb. 1962), p. 40.
5. A. L. Horelick and M. Rush, *Strategic Power and Soviet Foreign Policy*, University of Chicago Press, 1966, pp. 36–120.
6. Ibid., pp. 42, 58, and 88 respectively. Khrushchev also allegedly remarked

that he had been obliged to hold down the megatonnage of one of the Soviet nuclear test explosions in the Arctic because it might have 'broken all the windows of Moscow': see Solly Zuckerman, op. cit., pp. 59–60.

7. In fact it was a 'space gap', rather than a 'missile gap', and even this was more apparent than real: see Herbert York, *Race to Oblivion*, Simon and Schuster, New York, 1970, pp. 109–12, and 144–6, and—for American R and D in the fifties—pp. 83 ff.

8. Ibid., p. 127 for Soviet ICBM design, and pp. 94–101 for the dates of deployment of American ICBMs.

9. This remark, taken from Lenin's article 'The Political Significance of Abuse' was quoted in a Chinese statement in the *People's Daily*, 13 September 1963: see William E. Griffith, *The Sino-Soviet Rift*, Allen and Unwin, London, 1964, p. 423.

10. See Zbigniew Brzezinski, *The Soviet Bloc*, Harvard University Press, Cambridge, Mass., 1967, pp. 399 ff.

11. In Western terms these may roughly be regarded as schools of Marxist thought representing liberal and conservative communism.

12. At the very least, the Soviet Government must have supplied the Chinese Government with the technology required to construct a plant for enriching uranium. See Gittings, op. cit., pp. 102–5, and Harry Gelber, 'Nuclear Weapons and Chinese Policy', *Adelphi Papers* no. 99, IISS, 1973, p. 13.

13. Gittings, op. cit., pp. 158–61 ff., contains a concise summary.

14. Michel Tatu, *Power in the Kremlin*, Collins, London, 1965, p. 367. Suslov's report, like the 'Open letter' of 1963 (see chapter 3), covered seven pages of *Pravda*.

3

THE ADVENTURES

During his years of secret ideological combat with the Chinese, Khrushchev stood in urgent need of a diplomatic victory over the West to prove his point. He tried in Europe, over Berlin; in Africa, over Egypt and the Congo; and finally on the Americans' own doorstep, in the Caribbean. The Berlin crisis lasted off and on for nearly four years from November 1958, when Khrushchev suddenly declared that the Soviet Government no longer recognized its obligations under the Potsdam Agreement, in particular those affecting Berlin. It had only one consequence of far-reaching importance: the erection of the Berlin Wall in August 1961. The Egyptian arms deal, together with the subsequent financing of the Aswan Dam, was a success. But in the Congo, after it became independent in 1960, the Soviet Union backed two successive losers—Lumumba and Gizenga. Khrushchev may have calculated that even though he lost in the Congo itself, this was compensated for by the influence that the Soviet Union began to win in Africa as a whole (hence the university in Moscow named after Lumumba). But the Congo affair led him into a quarrel with the United Nations Secretary-General, Hammarskjöld, whom Khrushchev accused of arbitrary and lawless behaviour. On 23 September 1960 Khrushchev addressed personally the special emergency General Assembly, calling on Hammarskjöld to resign and proposing instead his *troika* arrangement, whereby the office of Secretary-General was to be converted into a commission of three men, one representing the Western bloc, one the Soviet bloc, and one the neutrals. This proposal made little headway. Having declared in the following February that it would no longer recognize Hammarskjöld as an official of the United Nations, the Soviet Government was spared further embarrassment by his death in an air crash seven months later. Khrushchev's performance at the General Assembly was memorable for his shoe-banging during Harold Macmillan's speech: an incident which did not put the British Prime Minister off his stride but was no doubt chalked up by Khrushchev's opponents at home as *nekul'turnyi* behaviour, unbecoming to a Soviet statesman.*

The Cuban missile crisis

No Soviet Government has pursued the third of the four basic tasks of foreign policy listed in the first chapter to such extremes as did Khrushchev over Cuba. There is by now little doubt what happened during the fourteen days of this crisis, which lasted from 14 to 28 October 1962. Nor is there any lack of evidence about the American handling of the crisis or about American motives. But the precise nature of Soviet motives both before and during the crisis are a matter for speculation and are likely to remain so until much more Soviet and Cuban evidence is made public.

Of these fourteen days, three really matter. On 14 October, incontrovertible photographic proof of the presence of Soviet nuclear missiles in Cuba was submitted to the US President. On 22 October, after eight days of agonized debate with his closest advisers, Kennedy announced the presence of the missiles in an address to the American nation, and he imposed a naval quarantine (a word that he had personally substituted for the original 'blockade') of all offensive military equipment under shipment to Cuba. Kennedy described the quarantine as an initial step and declared that any nuclear missile launched from Cuba against any nation in the Western hemisphere would be regarded as an attack by the Soviet Union on the United States, requiring a full retaliatory response upon the Soviet Union. Finally, on 28 October, after an exchange of ten personal messages between Kennedy and Khrushchev (in two of which—those of 26 and 27 October—Khrushchev suggested the outlines of a compromise), Khrushchev announced publicly that a new order had been issued 'to dismantle the weapons, which you describe as offensive, and to crate and return them to the Soviet Union', and expressed his respect and trust for Kennedy's statement, in a message sent on the previous day, that 'no attack would

---

* According to a well-placed eye-witness, Khrushchev had both his shoes on at the time. *Nekul'turnyi*, literally 'uncultured', is the Soviet word for 'uncouth', 'boorish', 'ill-mannered'.

be made on Cuba and that no invasion would take place—not only on the part of the United States, but also on the part of the other countries of the Western hemisphere'.

That Khrushchev backed down in the face of American determination is not surprising. What is uncertain is why he decided to instal nuclear missiles in Cuba at all. At first the Soviet attitude towards the Cuban Revolution had been cautious. But from 17 April 1961 onwards —when the CIA-sponsored landing of Cuban exiles at the Bay of Pigs was repulsed—events moved swiftly. In June a Soviet-Cuban communiqué acknowledged Cuba's free choice of 'the road of socialist development'; in July Castro announced the formation of a new political party, whose creed was unmistakably proclaimed when five months later he declared 'I am a Marxist-Leninist, and I shall be a Marxist-Leninist until the last day of my life';[1] and thereafter the Soviet Government, whatever its earlier doubts about the orthodoxy of Cuban communism, had no choice but to admit Cuba to the socialist bloc, a decision which was made formally apparent at the May Day celebrations in Moscow. (One Albania was enough.) An exposed member of the socialist bloc, even though not a member of the Warsaw Pact, was bound to look to Moscow to ensure its physical survival. Moscow could not therefore afford to ignore any danger, however remote, to Cuba at a moment when the lunatic fringe in the United States was clamouring for a second attack on Cuba of a different kind from the Bay of Pigs fiasco. Yet it is a fact of history that Kennedy had no intention whatever of repeating the mistake of 1961; and Khrushchev himself in his 'Friday Letter' to Kennedy of 26 October 1962* recorded that he had regarded with respect the explanation for the Bay of Pigs affair which Kennedy had offered him at their meeting in Vienna shortly afterwards (namely, that the invasion had been a mistake). Yet the same letter stated emphatically that it was only the constant threat of armed aggression which hung over Cuba that prompted the despatch of Soviet nuclear missiles to the island. Did Khrushchev believe in this threat? We cannot altogether exclude the possibility that the Soviet

* The full text in translation of this famous letter, together with the other nine exchanged during the Cuban missile crisis, was at last published in November 1973, in the *State Department Bulletin*, vol. 69, no. 1795, pp. 643–5. The style leaves no possible doubt of its authorship. It differs in significant respects from previous attempts to reconstruct it, e.g. Allison, op. cit., pp. 221–3. Allison's book, although published before the full text of all the letters was available, remains the most complete exposition of the facts of the crisis as known from American sources; and unless otherwise stated, facts mentioned in the present section of this chapter are derived from it.

Government was misinformed.[2] Today, thanks to the hot line and to the expertise in Soviet-American relations built up over the past decade both in the Soviet Ministry of Foreign Affairs and the Soviet Institute for the USA (not to mention the Kremlin), such a misreading of American presidential intentions would scarcely be possible. In 1962 perhaps it was—just. But even if it was, it remains as obvious today as it must have been then that if the Soviet aim was only to deter an American attack on Cuba, it could have been achieved simply by stationing on the island 20,000 Soviet troops, equipped not with nuclear but with conventional weapons: a close symmetry with the Western presence in Berlin.[3]

The risks that Khrushchev ran were so high in 1962 that the only explanation which does justice to his undoubted intelligence, and also squares with Castro's own evidence, is that he decided that the risks were worth running because the prize was far greater than the security of Cuba, important though this had become to Soviet national interests. This prize was nothing less than to establish a strategic balance with the United States, which would make possible an accommodation between the Soviet Union and the United States across the board, leading not only to a settlement of the Berlin problem but also to the prevention of either West Germany or China from acquiring nuclear weapons—a diplomatic triumph of such brilliance that no one in the Soviet Union would ever have dared to challenge Khrushchev's personal leadership again.[4] The other possible explanations are: first, bad professional advice from the Soviet military; second, the possibility that Khrushchev's assessment of Kennedy's character, formed at the time of the Bay of Pigs and at their meeting in Vienna the previous year, was wrong; third, a false deduction by Khrushchev from the Suez crisis six years earlier that atomic blackmail always paid; and fourth, that by the time Kennedy issued his first, unmistakable warning, in early September, Khrushchev decided that it was too late to put the Cuban missile operation into reverse, and that he might as well be hung for a sheep as for a lamb.

For the first of these four explanations there is no evidence: if anything, it points the other way, in that Marshal K. S. Moskalenko, a Deputy Defence Minister, was relieved of his command of the Strategic Missile Forces in April 1962, about the time when contingency planning of the Cuban operation was presumably in its initial stage.[5] The reason for Moskalenko's removal is unknown, but it does not require much imagination to guess the likely reaction of the commander of this Soviet force when asked to commit part of it to a strategic theatre where, without almost inconceivable luck, it risked either destruction or capture by the American forces only ninety miles away. As for the second explanation, Khrushchev may well have hoped to frighten Kennedy, whom he perhaps regarded as a brash young man, and to establish a personal ascendancy over him at Vienna. Yet the detailed accounts of this difficult meeting given by three American eye-witnesses record only plain speaking, with no ground given on either side.[6] One records[7] that the President's greatest concern before his meeting with Khrushchev was that it might create another spirit of Camp David; and Kennedy's parting words to Khrushchev were not those of a broken man—'it's going to be a cold winter'[8] (he was referring to Khrushchev's ultimatum about West Berlin). What did happen,[9] was that Kennedy's private briefings of the press were 'so grim, while Khrushchev in public appeared so cheerful, that a legend soon arose that Vienna had been a traumatic, shattering experience, that Khrushchev had bullied and browbeaten the President, and that Kennedy was depressed and disheartened'. But this was a legend, and although Khrushchev may have helped to create it, it was not something in which he himself had any reason to believe. Finally, Khrushchev could hardly have convinced himself that it was his own atom-rattling, rather than the United States Government's sustained pressure, that obliged the British and French Governments to halt their Suez operation in November 1956, or that he lacked the authority to take voluntarily in September 1962 a decision that he was compelled to take six weeks later. This is surely a case of the simplest explanation being the best: Khrushchev was a man who played for the highest possible stakes; and on this occasion he miscalculated the odds.

For Khrushchev's Cuban plan to succeed, the United States had to be confronted, without warning, by the presence of a Soviet nuclear force in Cuba—already operational and manned by some 20,000 Soviet troops, in sites protected by surface-to-air missiles—consisting of twenty-four medium range and twelve intermediate range ballistic missile launchers, together with some forty Ilyushin-28 jet bombers capable of carrying nuclear weapons. The range of the former launchers was 1,000 and that of the latter 2,000 nautical miles. The exact number of IRBM launchers planned seems uncertain; none arrived, although their sites were constructed. Certainly, had the plan succeeded, it would have given the Soviet Union extra strategic deterrence on the cheap, by comparison with the cost of bringing Soviet intercontinental and

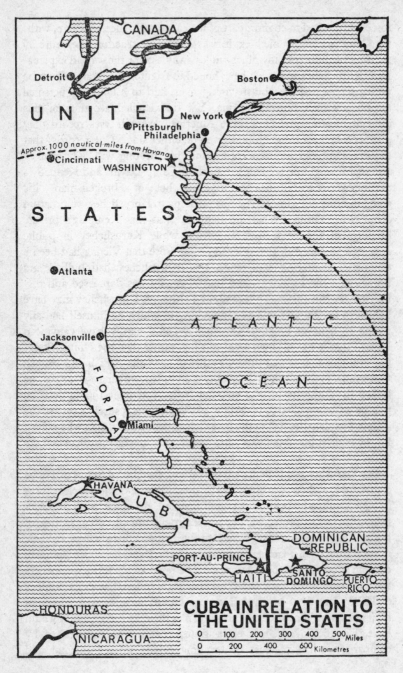

CANADA

Detroit

Boston

U N I T E D   New York
●Pittsburgh
Philadelphia

Approx. 1000 nautical miles from Havana
●Cincinnati
WASHINGTON

S T A T E S

●Atlanta

A T L A N T I C

Jacksonville

F L O R I D A

O C E A N

●Miami

★HAVANA   C U B A

DOMINICAN
REPUBLIC

PORT-AU-PRINCE
HAITI   SANTO
DOMINGO   PUERTO
RICO

HONDURAS

CUBA IN RELATION TO
THE UNITED STATES

NICARAGUA
0   100   200   300   400   500 Miles
0   200   400   600 Kilometres

submarine-launched ballistic missiles up to the American level; and the number of minutes' warning of oncoming missiles received by the Americans would have been greatly reduced. But even so, this would still not have given the Soviet Union anything resembling superiority. At the time of the crisis not only did the United States have about 144 missiles launched from *Polaris* submarines, as well as 294 ICBMs,[10] but the Caribbean was an area in which the United States possessed complete superiority in conventional weapons—at sea, in the air, and on land (during the crisis, a force of some 200,000 men was assembled in Florida). It can only be assumed that Khrushchev relied on everything going his way: that Cuba would be covered by ten-tenths cloud during the critical phase, that if the missiles were discovered, Kennedy (in the heat of a Congressional election) would dither, and that once he had decided on a course of action, it would be opposed by the United States' allies both in the Organization of American States and in NATO. Not one of these conditions was fulfilled—quite the reverse in each case. Granted what must have been known in Moscow about the performance of U-2 reconnaissance aircraft, from the one shot down over the Soviet Union in 1960, it is hard to see how the arrival of the missiles could have been expected to escape the notice of these aircraft, which overflew the island regularly, once American suspicions had been aroused. Moreover, the risks of the Soviet operation were increased still further by the number of mistakes made in its execution—for example, no attempt was made to camouflage the missile sites.[11]

Nor was there any lack of formal warning from the American side. On 4 September the White House issued a statement that 'the gravest issues would arise' if offensive ground-to-ground missiles were installed in Cuba'. On 12 September, four days after the first ship carrying Soviet missiles had docked in Cuba, *Pravda* published a governmental statement denying the need for the Soviet Union to 'set up in any other country—Cuba, for instance—the weapons it has for repelling aggression, for a retaliatory blow' and asserting that the power of Soviet nuclear weapons and missiles was such that there was no need to find sites for them beyond the boundaries of the Soviet Union. On the following day Kennedy himself repeated the warning of 4 September. Yet, according to all American sources, Khrushchev proceeded to give Kennedy the lie direct about the presence of the missiles in Cuba: speaking himself to the US Ambassador on 16 October—the day on which the photographic evidence of their presence was first submitted to the President—and via Gromyko to the President two days later. Whatever was said or left unsaid on these two occasions, as late as 25 October, *Izvestiya* observed that it was unnecessary to recall that both the Soviet Union and Cuba had recently emphasized that no offensive weapons and no long-range nuclear missiles were deployed on the island; and the next day two *Pravda* correspondents in Massachusetts described the allegation about the sudden appearance of Soviet nuclear long-range rockets in Cuba as a fantasy that did not inspire confidence among well-informed Americans.

From a crisis which, according to all the rules, should have ruined him, Khrushchev extricated himself with skill, by portraying himself as the world's peacemaker. In this he was helped by Kennedy, whose commitment not to invade Cuba cost him nothing, although it was sound as a means of saving Khrushchev's face. But it was paper-thin for the Chinese, who later accused the Soviet leadership of the double error of 'adventurism' and 'capitulationism' and enquired whether what had been done in the name of defending the Cuban Revolution was not in reality political gambling.[12] How do Soviet writers see their country's part in the crisis? Although there is nothing on the Soviet side of the Cuban equation remotely resembling Western analyses[13] in depth of the factors that made up its American side, what Soviet evidence there is should not be ignored. On one point all Soviet sources are unanimous: it was 'a damned nice thing'.[14] Making no precise mention of the missiles, which are referred to only as 'a series of new measures intended to strengthen Cuba's capacity for defence', the History of Soviet Foreign Policy describes the crisis as 'the most acute, in all the post-war years, which put mankind face to face with the threat of world-wide thermonuclear catastrophe'. There can be no quarrel with this verdict, which reflects the thought that (as the personal messages to Kennedy make clear) was in the forefront of Khrushchev's mind during the latter days of the crisis, which must have been as hard to manage in Moscow as it was in Washington. Western historians have tended to forget that during this crisis, Khrushchev had to contend not only with Kennedy's messages but also with Castro's. According to Khrushchev's subsequent report to the Supreme Soviet,[15] it was on the morning of 27 October that the Soviet Government became convinced, among other things, by telegrams from Havana 'displaying extreme alarm, which was well founded', that Cuba would be invaded within two or three days.*

The nearest approach to a Soviet explanation of why Khrushchev led with his chin consists of two articles published in 1971,[16] by Anatolyi

---

* This assessment was, as we know from American sources, correct.

Gromyko, son of the Soviet Foreign Minister, on the Caribbean crisis ('or, as they still sometimes call it in the West, especially in the USA, the "Cuban Missile Crisis" '). The articles draw mostly on American sources, but the first is notable for a lengthy account of the author's father's interview with Kennedy on 18 October, which in general counters the accusation that the Soviet Foreign Minister misled the President and in particular criticizes Robert Kennedy's account[17] of the interview as tendentious. The titles of the articles are themselves instructive: the first is 'The Instigation of the Caribbean Crisis by the Government of the USA' and the second is 'The Diplomatic Efforts of the USSR to Solve the Crisis'.

It is central to the argument of these articles that in 1962 it was the aim of the US Government's Cuban policy to prepare secretly a fresh attack against the island. The U-2 flights (which more than any other single factor wrecked Khrushchev's plan) are therefore portrayed as offensive, not defensive, in intention. But the accuracy of the deductions drawn in Washington from the critical U-2 flight of 14 October is in no way disputed: 'medium-range rockets' were indeed delivered to Cuba, for defensive purposes. American sources are quoted as proving that the presence of Soviet missiles in Cuba did not alter the strategic balance of power between the USSR and the USA, which the writer describes as based primarily on intercontinental strategic rockets. As Robert McNamara, then Defence Secretary, remarked during the crisis, 'it makes no great difference whether you are killed by a missile from the Soviet Union or from Cuba'. The conclusion is drawn that the Administration was governed more by political than by military considerations.

In his interview with the President on 18 October the Soviet Foreign Minister is said to have informed Kennedy unequivocally that since the governments of the USSR and Cuba feared a military attack on Cuba, the Soviet Union could not remain inactive, but that Soviet help to Cuba 'contributed only to its defensive capacity and to the strengthening of its economy'; Soviet specialists' training of Cubans in the handling of weapons intended for the defence of their country was a threat to no one. It is granted that the President read out to Gromyko, at the end of their talk, the text of his declaration of 4 September; but since Kennedy did not once raise directly the question of the presence in Cuba of Soviet missiles, he could not be given an answer. The tables are then turned, by accusing the President of deluding the Soviet side about his intentions, and this leads to the conclusion that it is enough to ask why the diplomatic representatives of the USSR were obliged to inform the United States Government in advance of these or other defensive measures, taken for the protection of a friendly state, while the USA never supplied the Soviet Union with information about the supply of arms to its own allies. The contention that if only Kennedy had put a straight question about the missiles to Gromyko, he would have got a straight answer, is not as odd as it sounds: the interpretation of 'interesting silences'* forms an integral part of Soviet diplomatic style.

The second theme that runs through both these articles is that if only the President had sought an 'elucidation of the situation' through diplomatic channels before embarking on a course as dangerous as a naval blockade—let alone the attack on Cuba recommended by the hawks among his advisers—the crisis would never have arisen. The only credit given to Kennedy is that he stood his ground against right-wing pressure. It is the Soviet Government that, according to the second article, played the decisive part in ensuring that events were brought under control. Khrushchev is nowhere mentioned by name, but his letter of 26 October is credited with suggesting the compromise formula which settled the crisis—correctly, although the recently published text makes it clear that the letter did not propose the compromise in precise terms, which were spelled out more clearly in Khrushchev's 'Saturday' letter of 27 October, this time linked with the suggested deal over American bases in Turkey.† Robert Kennedy is also correctly accused of omitting from his account the Soviet warning which accompanied this suggestion, namely that if the naval quarantine was intended as the first step towards war, then the Soviet Union would have no alternative but to accept the challenge.[18] This posture is twice described in the article as one of firmness coupled with flexibility, a phrase also used in the History of Soviet Foreign Policy. But the most important message that these two articles were intended to convey was this: in 1962 there would have been no crisis at all if at an early enough stage the US Government had been willing to treat the Soviet Government as its equal and to settle the problem bilaterally at the highest level. What they could not say was that in 1962 the Soviet Union was still far from achieving parity with the United States.

---

* Jane Austen, Emma, ch. XV, in which Mr. Elton says to Miss Woodhouse: 'Allow me to interpret this interesting silence. It confesses that you have long understood me.'

† The second letter, though it caused confusion and dismay in Washington, did not, in my view, formally contradict the first, nor is there any marked difference in tone between the two.

The temporary détente

Khrushchev survived this error of Himalayan proportions for two years. The remainder of his time in office was a period of relative *détente* between the Soviet Union and the West. Khrushchev allowed the Berlin crisis to fade away. In June 1963, in a major speech addressed to the American University, Kennedy called the cold war in question; the Soviet press published the text in full. Within a year following the crisis, the hot line was set up between Moscow and Washington, designed to eliminate the time factor in crisis management that had complicated the messages exchanged in October 1962; Great Britain, the Soviet Union, and the United States signed the partial Nuclear Test Ban Treaty in Moscow; at the United Nations it was agreed not to put into outer space 'any objects carrying nuclear weapons or any other kinds of weapons of mass destruction'. (This was to be embodied in treaty form in January 1967.) Other signs of the times were the dropping of the *troika* idea; the cessation of Soviet jamming of Western broadcasts; and the Soviet-American pledge to reduce the production of fissionable material for nuclear weapons. Why did Khrushchev not go further along the road towards a Nuclear Non-Proliferation Treaty, the conclusion of which would surely have been as much a national interest for the Soviet Union then as it was five years later? Perhaps he was held back by internal opposition to *détente*; or by Chinese criticism; or both.[19] The eruption of the territorial aspects of the Sino-Soviet dispute in March 1963 was bad enough, but the Nuclear Test Ban Treaty coincided with the final parting of the ways between the Soviet Union and China in July of that year. The three-power negotiations in Moscow before the signing of this document, rightly regarded at the time as a landmark in post-war history, opened simultaneously with an eleventh-hour attempt by the Russians and the Chinese to settle their differences through bilateral talks, also held in Moscow. The Soviet Central Committee's 'Open letter to Party organizations and all communists of the Soviet Union' published in *Pravda* on 14 July—the day before the Test Ban talks opened—provided the Soviet public with their first full account of their country's quarrel with China. Nearly 20,000 words in length, it included the vivid phrase: 'the nuclear bomb does not adhere to the class principle—it destroys everybody who falls within range of its devastating force'.[20] The Sino-Soviet talks were adjourned *sine die* on 20 July, just before the Test Ban Treaty was signed.

Meanwhile, having failed to attain parity with the United States on

the cheap, Khrushchev fell back on the Malenkov concept of minimum
nuclear deterrence. True, he had steadily increased the deployment,
mostly in the western USSR, of a force of medium and intermediate
range ballistic missile launchers targeted on Western Europe, which by
1964 levelled off at around 700. These served the purpose of a deterrent
to Western European countries, but not the United States. Intercontinentally, the Soviet Union remained greatly inferior to the United
States: in 1964, an estimated 200 Soviet ICBMs against 834 American,
and 120 Soviet submarine-launched ballistic missiles against 416
American equivalents.[21] There is also abundant evidence[22] that by
October 1964 Khrushchev intended to increase the production of
consumer goods by cutting the defence budget, mainly at the expense of
conventional ground forces; the Ground Forces Command was suspended as a separate entity shortly before his fall.[23]

The fall of Khrushchev

Things did not go well for Khrushchev at home after the Cuban crisis.
True, in November 1962 he secured the Central Committee's approval
of a reform of the Party apparatus, which was then divided into agricultural and industrial specialists. But in 1963 the harvest was poor and the
rate of growth of Soviet national income was down. Khrushchev's
de-Stalinization policy ran into the sand (but not before Alexander
Solzhenitsyn's *A Day in the Life of Ivan Denisovich* was published, in
November 1962). Perhaps the last straw for his colleagues was the
knowledge that he was contemplating a sweeping reform of the agricultural system, which would have been submitted to the Central
Committee in November 1964. Khrushchev's handling of the Party
could have been sufficient reason in itself for his removal,[24] but the
evidence points to a combination of factors. Certainly one of them was
that Khrushchev was contemplating a fresh European initiative, this
time directly with the new Federal German Chancellor (Erhard, who
had succeeded Adenauer in October 1963), at a moment when the ink
was scarcely dry on the signature of a new treaty of friendship concluded between the Soviet Union and the German Democratic Republic
on 12 June 1964. The terms of this treaty cannot have satisfied Ulbricht
—in particular, it explicitly left unaffected rights conferred on the Four
Powers by their agreements on Germany, including the Potsdam
Agreement—and it coincided with a series of signs that something was
in the wind between Moscow and Bonn. These culminated in the visit

of a party of three Soviet journalists to the Federal German Republic in July and August. This visit looked innocent enough. But the fact that the Volga Germans[25] were rehabilitated in August can hardly have been a coincidence; and it seems virtually certain that the senior member of the trio, Alexei Adzubei, Khrushchev's son-in-law (whom he had made editor of *Izvestiya*), was sent by Khrushchev to pave the way for a visit that he himself would pay to Bonn, probably in December. Had the visit taken place, it would have been historic: the first time, nearly twenty years after the German surrender, that the ruler of the Soviet Union had visited the Federal Republic. That Khrushchev should have entrusted his son-in-law with such an important mission was resented; it seems likely that he laid himself open to the suspicion that he was planning some deal with the West Germans over the heads of the East Germans (now no longer living in a slum, but on the way to performing their own economic miracle) and of the Poles; and two of his own colleagues, Brezhnev and Suslov, made speeches on the eve of Khrushchev's fall reassuring the East Germans, on the occasion of the fifteenth anniversary of the German Democratic Republic in early October.

As has been suggested earlier, the Soviet Politburo may well have felt that however intractable the Chinese might be, a change of Soviet leadership might increase the chances of at least a marginal improvement. Relations between the two communist parties had reached their nadir. Khrushchev was committed to holding a preparatory meeting in Moscow in December of the twenty-six members of the 1960 conference drafting committee; but it is unlikely that they would have given the CPSU unqualified support against the Chinese Communist Party. In their letter to the CPSU of 28 July 1964, the Chinese warned that 'the day of your so-called meeting will be the day you step into the grave'. By a superb coincidence, the Chinese exploded their first nuclear device on the day that Khrushchev fell—14 October.

NOTES

1. The profession of faith mentioned in the second sentence of this book; the full text of Castro's speech was carried in *Hoy* (Havana), 2 December 1961. For the evolution of the Soviet-Cuban relationship during this period, see Stephen Clissold, *Soviet Relations with Latin America 1918–68*, Oxford University Press, London, 1970, pp. 47–50.
2. For example, some publicity had been given to a large-scale amphibious

exercise which was to take place off the south-east coast of Puerto Rico, with the object of liberating a mythical republic from a dictator named Ortsac: see Allison, op. cit., p. 47. But Allison strains the imagination when he suggests that the importance of the Cuban issue in American domestic politics could have escaped the attention of any observer, Soviet or otherwise, in 1962.

3. See ibid., p. 49, for a fuller discussion of this proposition.

4. Khrushchev's complicated domestic position at this time is described in Tatu, op. cit., Pt. Three, 'The Cuban Fiasco'. For Castro's evidence—that the purpose of the Soviet missiles in Cuba was 'strengthening the socialist camp on the world scale' and 'we considered that we could not decline'—see *Le Monde*, 22 March 1963 (subsequently confirmed in a speech carried by *Pravda*). The idea that at this late hour China could have been prevented from joining the strategic nuclear club may seem far-fetched today, but it may not have been a pipe-dream for Khrushchev early in 1962: for an exposition of this view, see Ulam, op. cit., pp. 661 ff.

5. He was replaced as Commander-in-Chief of the Strategic Missile Forces by Biryuzov, a Ukrainian who may perhaps have been a political client of Khrushchev; see Tatu, op. cit., pp. 236–7.

6. P. Salinger, *With Kennedy*, Cape, London, 1967, ch. XI; A. M. Schlesinger, *A Thousand Days*, Deutsch, London, 1966, pp. 324–40; T. C. Sorensen, *Kennedy*, Hodder and Stoughton, London, 1965, pp. 543–600.

7. Salinger, op. cit., p. 176.

8. Ibid., p. 182.

9. Sorensen, op. cit., p. 550. There is nothing in the account given by A. A. Gromyko in *1036 dniei prezidenta Kennedi*, Moscow, 1968, to support this legend either.

10. *The Military Balance 1969–70*, IISS, London, p. 55. It is, however, conceivable that Soviet intelligence was less well informed about the relative strategic nuclear power of the two countries than was American intelligence, which had the benefit not only of U-2 but also of satellite reconnaissance—not to mention Penkovsky.

11. Op. cit., pp. 106 ff. In fairness to the Russians, the same book also points out some remarkable American mistakes, for example, the fact that no U-2 flight was directed over western Cuba between 5 September and 4 October: see p. 120.

12. Statement by Chinese Government spokesman, 1 September 1963, (*Peking Review*, 6 September 1963): text in Gittings, op. cit., pp. 181–3. The Soviet-US agreement over Cuba was not even registered officially at the UN, as was the original intention. For a discussion of the question whether there was also an unofficial US commitment to withdraw the fifteen obsolete Jupiter missiles from Turkey, see Allison, op. cit., pp. 229–30.

13. Allison, op. cit., pp. 200 ff., is the best recent example.

14. Wellington's much misquoted description of Waterloo: 'It was a damned nice thing—the nearest run thing you ever saw in your life'; Thomas Creevey, *The Creevey Papers*, p. 142, ed. John Gore, London, 1934.

15. *Pravda*, 13 December 1962. The relevant passage in the History of Soviet Foreign Policy is op. cit., vol. 2, pp. 364–5, to which the chapter concerned in *Mezhdunarodnye konflikty*, Moscow, 1972, eds. V. V. Zhurin and E. M. Primakov, adds little, summing up the outcome of the crisis as being that 'the USA was compelled to agree to renounce its plans of aggression against ... Cuba' after a 'fairly intensive exchange of messages between the two governments'—pp. 84 and 95. Gromyko told the Supreme Soviet flatly that

'the leaders of the USA brought the world one step, perhaps only half a step, from the abyss'—*Pravda*, 14 December 1962.

16. Anatolyi A. Gromyko 'Karibskii Krizis', *Voprosy Istorii*, nos. 7 and 8, Moscow, 1971.

17. Robert Kennedy, *Thirteen Days*, *a Memoir of the Cuban Crisis*, Macmillan, New York, 1969.

18. This accusation is borne out by the text of Khrushchev's 'Friday' letter. The 'Trollope ploy', whereby Kennedy replied to the 'Friday' letter rather than to the 'Saturday' letter, is described in Allison, op. cit., pp. 227 ff.

19. In Khrushchev's letter to Kennedy of 27 October 1962, which was broadcast over Moscow radio on that day, he said that agreement over Cuba would 'make it easier to reach agreement on banning nuclear weapons tests' and in his letter of the following day, which was also broadcast, he said that the Soviet Government would 'like to continue the exchange of views on the prohibition of atomic and thermonuclear weapons'. In Kennedy's letter of 28 October, which was released to the press, he suggested that the two governments 'should give priority to questions relating to the proliferation of nuclear weapons, on earth and in outer space, and to the effort for a nuclear test ban'. Macmillan (whose greatest achievement in foreign policy was perhaps the conclusion of the Nuclear Test Ban Agreement) also regarded a ban on tests as a measure that would enable the three governments 'to proceed rapidly to specific and fruitful discussions about the non-dissemination of nuclear power leading to an agreement on this subject': see the joint Anglo-American letter to Khrushchev of 15 April 1963, quoted in his *At the End of the Day*, Macmillan, London, 1973, p. 467. Ibid., p. 480 gives Macmillan's own view about this during the actual negotiations three months later.

20. *Pravda*, 14 July 1963: Griffith, op. cit., pp. 289–325, contains a translation of this document, which covered seven out of *Pravda*'s eight pages.

21. *The Military Balance 1969/70*, loc. cit.

22. In particular, *Pravda* of 2 October 1964, 'On the main directions for drawing up the plan for the development of the national economy in the next period'. In three columns describing Khrushchev's intervention there is only a single sentence on the needs of defence, which must be 'maintained at the appropriate level', whereas the need to make consumer goods top priority is repeatedly mentioned. Khrushchev's clear implication was that heavy industry was now strong enough to sustain both these objectives. This intervention is all the more striking in that it coincided with the publication of an article in the current issue of *Kommunist Vooruzhennykh Sil* which emphasized the continuing role of heavy industry as the economic foundation of the Soviet Union's progress: see the article reporting this in the *Guardian* of 2 October 1964 by Victor Zorza, whose articles in the *Guardian* of 18 and 25 September also described the controversy between Khrushchev and the Soviet military about the value of conventional weapons, particularly tanks.

23. T. W. Wolfe, op. cit. p. 464; Khrushchev's decision to subordinate the Ground Forces directly to the Defence Ministry was not revealed until 1968 (by Marshal Zakharov, Chief of the General Staff).

24. As was argued by P. B. Reddaway in his article on 'The Fall of Khrushchev' published in *Survey*, July 1965.

25. Deported from their homes by Stalin's order, for alleged collaboration with the German forces.

PART TWO

The Foreign Policy of the Collective Leadership: The Years of Consolidation

4

DEFENCE POLICY

The triumvirate which succeeded Khrushchev hastened to make it clear that the decisions of the XXth Congress, taken under his leadership, held good so far as doctrine was concerned: their validity was re-affirmed both in the CPSU Central Committee's communiqué announcing Khrushchev's resignation and in Brezhnev's speech delivered at the celebrations of the October Revolution. True, whereas the concept of peaceful coexistence between states with different social systems had, under Khrushchev, been described as the general line of the foreign policy of the Soviet state, in the formulation approved at the two party congresses presided over by his successors it was demoted to fourth place. But so long as American forces were fighting in Vietnam, the new leadership could scarcely have avoided this change of emphasis. Their indictment of Khrushchev was indirect: *Pravda* of 17 October 1964 described the Leninist Party as the enemy of subjectivism and drifting in communist construction; and as foreign to hare-brained scheming, immature conclusions, hasty and unrealistic decisions and actions, boasting, and idle talk. At a pinch, this could be construed as the indictment of an old man in a hurry at home, rather than in his foreign policy; and indeed radical changes on the home front were soon effected. The new leaders also lost no time in reassuring the military that the Party had the interests of the armed forces at heart;[1] and it is significant that the epithet 'hare-brained' recurred in the military newspaper *Krasnaya Zvezda* four months later, when Zakharov, reappointed Chief of Staff, wrote: 'with the appearance of nuclear weapons, cybernetics, electronics, and computer technology, a subjective approach to military problems, hare-brained schemes, and superficiality can cost very dear and cause irreparable harm'.[2]

The broad aims of Soviet foreign policy remained a global role for the Soviet Union and an accommodation with the United States. Both were to be pursued with prudence; there were to be no more games of bluff. At the same time, a further attempt would be made to restore order in the world communist movement. Finally—and this affected foreign policy as much as it did policy at home—the new leadership was collective. It is inconceivable that the great issues which the triumvirate has had to face have not given rise to sharp differences of opinion; but so far as we know, these have never attained the dimensions of a true struggle for power, and have been kept within reasonable bounds. None of Khrushchev's colleagues was dismissed with him. Brezhnev soon[3] emerged as *primus inter pares*, in his capacity as General-Secretary of the CPSU. But it is extremely unlikely that a single member of the Soviet élite will ever be allowed to assume all the offices held by Khrushchev.* The Soviet system of government is now so complex that these offices are too much for one man to hold efficiently, quite apart from the dangers ensuing from concentration of personal power. In short, in 1964 what the Soviet Union needed was a period of consolidation. This process was to be presided over by three serious men—Leonid Brezhnev, General-Secretary of the CPSU, Alexei Kosygin, Prime Minister, and Nikolai Podgorny, who succeeded Mikoyan as Head of State in December 1965. Their intentions were harder to interpret at first, since they were not well known to Western observers, who were to miss the outbursts that had often illuminated the policies of Khrushchev.

The Khrushchevian concept of minimum nuclear deterrence was set aside. It is a matter of debate whether the new leadership deliberately decided to achieve strategic parity with the United States; or whether

---

* The importance that the new leadership attached to the principle of collective leadership, and their criticisms of Khrushchev's personal failings, emerge clearly from the leading article in *Pravda* of 17 October, which was intended as the keynote of the new regime. Khrushchev headed both Party and Government. Although in the Soviet system the former is, by definition, supreme, the latter's power resides in the fact that it is responsible for the day-to-day running of the Soviet economy, including the eight ministries relating to the military-industrial sector. In my view, Khrushchev also held the post of Supreme Commander-in-Chief: see the last paragraph of Grechko's article on Khrushchev's seventieth birthday in *Izvestiya* of 17 April 1964. In any case, Khrushchev—like Brezhnev—was *ex officio* chairman of a body variously referred to as the War (or Defence) Committee and the Higher Military Council.[4]

they aimed at strategic superiority; or whether they embarked on the defence build-up over the next five years without any single clearly defined aim.* The factor common to all three of these is that the missile gap, which had grown even wider—to the advantage of the United States—since 1962, should be closed as quickly as possible. The under-lying concept is summed up in a remark allegedly made after the Cuban missile crisis by a senior Soviet diplomat to an American interlocutor: 'you will never do that to us again!' At the same time the Soviet armed forces were now to be trained and equipped alike for general nuclear war, conventional operations, and operations in which nuclear weapons would be used on a limited scale. The management of defence industries, one of the victims of Khrushchev's policy of decentralization, was brought back to the centre. The subsequent investment in ICBMs and submarines carrying ballistic missiles was so enormous that by the end of the decade rough numerical parity had at last been achieved, enabling the Soviet Union to escape from its position of strategic hostage in Europe.

As between super-powers, what do the concepts of strategic nuclear parity, superiority, and inferiority mean?† This question can be evaded by taking refuge in the fact that today the governments of the Soviet Union, the United States, and China are all acting on the assumption that these concepts have a real meaning. Why otherwise would they be spending vast sums on their nuclear arsenals, and why are the first two of these governments currently engaged in negotiations the nub of which is to agree on a definition of what, in American terminology, is 'essential equivalence'?[5] But this is too simple. The argument that the concept of nuclear superiority and inferiority is, at any rate in a super-

* Each of these three views is examined in the final chapter of Wolfe, op. cit. Whichever is correct, it is also true that the Research and Development work on the weapons systems deployed by the end of the decade had already been begun under Khrushchev: the SS-9 ICBM did not spring out of the ground like the Theban warriors. In this sense it is arguable that Soviet defence policy devel-oped continuously throughout the sixties. But there is a vast financial and economic difference between allowing resources to be committed to the Research and Development of a major weapons system and taking the final decision to produce and deploy it on a large scale.

† According to our definition, a super-power is a state possessing two military characteristics that differentiate it from medium or regional powers: the full range of the strategic nuclear armoury and the capacity to deploy its forces, whether armed conventionally or with nuclear weapons, in any strategic theatre of the world. Although the adjective 'strategic' is used throughout this book, the comforting distinction drawn by some between the effects of tactical and those of strategic nuclear weapons is dubious. For arguments to support scepticism about this distinction, see Zuckerman, op. cit., pp. 66–70.

power context, meaningless, is twofold. Would any sane man ever press the button unleashing a first-strike nuclear attack, knowing what the consequences[6] would be, for the population of just one of his country's major cities, of even a single megaton explosion forming part of a second-strike, retaliatory attack launched by the other super-power, still less the full consequences of an all-out second strike? Secondly, looking back over the period of nearly thirty years that has elapsed since the only atomic attack in history, how much weight have the Soviet and US governments given to each other's strategic nuclear power in the conduct of their bilateral relations? For example, it is maintained by some that in 1962, although the Soviet strategic arsenal was much smaller than that of the United States (intercontinentally,[7] not much more than a powerful *force de frappe*), it was already large enough to have inflicted an unacceptable number of American casualties; and that the nuclear capacities of the two sides in effect cancelled each other out in the Cuban crisis, which was in the end resolved by the superiority, not of American strategic power, but of American conventionally armed forces in the Caribbean. And even if this explanation of the outcome of the Cuban crisis contains only an element of truth, it is incontestable that all major wars since 1945 (Korea, Indo-China, the Middle East) have been fought with conventional weapons which for the most part are a technological extension of those used in the European theatre of operations during the Second World War.

The answer to the 'no sane man' question is to pose a counter-question: what is sanity in international relations? Both deterrence and security are largely states of mind; governments are controlled not by precise machines, but by fallible[8] men; and the governments of super-powers are no exception. Thus it may be scientifically demonstrable that the destructive capacity of modern megaton warheads must reach a point of 'overkill' where it no longer makes sense for one super-power to seek to increase its own destructive capacity, either quantitatively or qualitatively, regardless of whether the other super-power does so. Yet no computer will ever be devised whose calculations the leaders of any government will trust enough for it to determine for them exactly where this point lies. Therefore, so long as nuclear weapons exist, the government of a super-power must be haunted by the fear that the counsels of sanity may not prevail in the mind of its potential adversary, and that he will somehow or other contrive to steal a nuclear march, unless they can reach agreement to open their minds to each other, at least to the extent necessary to enable both of them to keep their fears within bounds.

With states, as with individuals, to be aware of the truth is safer than to act on fantasies conjured up by fear of the unknown; *omne ignotum pro magnifico*.

The answer to the historical argument[9] (that the super-powers' nuclear capacities have so far largely cancelled each other out) is that, although no one has used nuclear weapons in war since 1945, it remains equally true that all governments, and especially those of the Soviet Union and the United States, have been obliged to deal with each other, and to frame their foreign policies in the knowledge that, if the worst came to the worst, those weapons might be used—and 'might' is quite enough for international discomfort. The Cuban example is debatable— a study of the text of Khrushchev's messages to Kennedy leaves little doubt that, as the crisis developed, he became acutely aware of the danger that it would lead to a nuclear world war. A clearer example is provided by the course of Stalin's and Khrushchev's attempts to settle the question of Berlin in the Soviet interest. That they failed to do so is surely best explained by the assumption that each of them realized in his turn that, although Soviet forces possessed the local conventional superiority required to take West Berlin, they could not afford to press their aims beyond the point where there was the slightest risk of nuclear escalation;[10] and it is significant that Khrushchev never attempted to use Soviet local strength in and around Berlin as a bargaining counter during the Cuban crisis.* In my view, the concepts of nuclear inferiority, parity, and superiority, however questionable they may be as scientific-technological propositions, do have a profound significance, although their significance may be greater in political than in strategic terms. This distinction is sometimes tenuous but is always important, above all for the super-powers, for whom (as the US Secretary of State reminded the Senate Foreign Relations Committee in October 1974) 'the prospect of a decisive military advantage, even if theoretically possible, is politically intolerable'.

It was against this background that after the Cuban crisis Khrushchev settled for minimum nuclear deterrence. His scale of deterrence was minimal only by Soviet standards: that is to say, a defence posture of strategic nuclear inferiority which would still have assured the Soviet Union posthumous revenge in a second-strike, retaliatory attack that would have inflicted immense damage on the United States.

---

* The point about Berlin, though in reverse, struck the then British Prime Minister when compiling his impressions of the Cuban crisis on 4 November 1962: see Macmillan, op. cit., p. 218, 'What Are the Strategic Lessons?'.

His successors were content neither with this, admittedly high, status of inferiority, nor with the single, nuclear option on which Khrushchevian defence policy was based. Profiting by the Research and Development programmes already in the pipeline, they embarked on a defence effort, which, coupled with their space programme, required the allocation of a proportion of Soviet resources whose exact size has been the subject of much debate. In 1965 the Soviet military budget was actually cut by 4 per cent. Thereafter, it rose annually, reaching a figure of 17·9 billion roubles in 1969, while the figure for scientific research doubled in the same period. In a series of papers presented to the Joint Economic Committee of the United States Congress in September 1970, it was even argued that by the end of the Soviet Five-Year Plan in that year the Soviet armed forces might be getting as much as 40 per cent more hardware than the United States armed forces, which would have meant that Soviet defence and space expenditure had increased more than five-fold between 1958 and 1968.[11]

Any calculation of the proportion of the Soviet budget devoted to defence depends on how much defence expenditure is concealed in other sections of the budget: in particular, the cost of nuclear warheads, Research and Development on advanced weapons systems, and the military elements of the space programme. *Military Balance 1969/70* suggested that, on a conservative estimate, Soviet declared defence appropriations of 17,700 million roubles for 1969, if calculated on the basis of the real resources mobilized by the Soviet Union in equivalent American prices, were the equivalent of 42 billion dollars, and that the total defence expenditure was the equivalent of 53 billion dollars. (Based on a GNP over twice the size of that of the Soviet Union, United States defence estimates for 1969/70 were 78,475,000,000 dollars, of which an estimated 25–30 billions were attributable to the Vietnam war.) Brezhnev's allusions to defence expenditure, made at the XXIVth Party Congress and in a speech in June 1971, suggest that this is a delicate subject even within the Soviet Union. Of one thing there can be little doubt: the size of the resources committed to the defence sector in the second half of the 1960s was a major cause of the Soviet economic dilemma at the end of the decade.[12]

As well as the massive deployment of offensive strategic nuclear weapons, a start was made with the deployment of an anti-ballistic missile system round Moscow in 1966. But the Strategic Missile Forces —the élite of the Soviet armed forces, numbering some 350,000 men— were not the only recipients of funds designed for expansion. The substantial Soviet Mediterranean Squadron, which made its first appearance in 1963, is now an accepted feature of the strategic naval scene. The Indian Ocean was first visited in 1968 by a cruiser and a destroyer from the Soviet Pacific Fleet, which now detaches ships to provide a permanent naval presence there. The Soviet naval infantry arm (disbanded after the Second World War) was revived shortly before Khrushchev's fall; its strength was doubled between 1966 and 1969; and from 1967 onwards there was increasing emphasis on amphibious operations. The new Soviet Navy's role was no longer confined to defence of the Soviet Union's coasts, but became long range, as was to be demonstrated in 1970 by the *Okean* manoeuvres, in which over 250 Soviet ships took part, in every ocean (and some rivers) of the world. The new navy's main weakness was its lack of air support, although in 1973 this gap was partly filled by the first Soviet aircraft carrier. Finally, the size of the Soviet fishing fleet, the largest and most modern in the world, is also a factor to be reckoned with, given the electronic intelligence duties of its vessels. At the same time the Soviet Air Force was expanded and modernized, with the aim of establishing air superiority over the battlefield, and its capacity to intervene was also greatly increased. Already well demonstrated in the Middle East, this capacity is today an important factor in assessing the Soviet Union's ability to reinforce its divisions in the vital sector of Central Europe.

The collective leadership broadly continued Khrushchev's policy of re-equipping and modernizing the forces of the Soviet Union's allies in the Warsaw Pact, with the main emphasis on conventional warfare, although tactical nuclear missile launchers were also supplied (the nuclear warheads remaining in Soviet hands). The lion's share of new equipment went to the northern tier countries—Poland, Czechoslovakia, and East Germany—in whose territory most of the joint Warsaw Pact manoeuvres were held, these becoming much more frequent than under Khrushchev. Because of this policy, these three countries provided a large addition to Soviet military strength in Central Europe. The value of the Czechoslovak contribution became doubtful after 1968. But neither this setback, nor quarrels with the Romanians about burden-sharing and nuclear planning (both familiar concepts in the West), deterred the Russians from making full use of the Pact for both political and military purposes. The frequent meetings of the Pact's Political Consultative Committee (consisting of Communist Party First Secretaries, Heads of Governments, and Foreign and Defence Ministers of the member countries) became an important means of coordinating policy, for example, on the question of the European Conference; and in 1969 the command structure of the Pact was reformed. Whereas before the Eastern Europeans had little or no say, the new structure bore at least some resemblance to an integrated command, even though Soviet influence remained paramount.[13]

Finally, the Soviet Government introduced a major reform in 1967, when conscripted military service was cut to two years. This was followed in 1968 by compensating regulations which made participation in pre-conscription training obligatory. The 1967 law also established sixty as the compulsory retiring age for all senior officers below the rank of marshal. The second half of the 1960s was the period in which the Soviet officer corps was reformed and rejuvenated. (This process had been begun by Khrushchev, as part of his successive reductions of Soviet military manpower from the peak of 5·7 millions reached in 1955; in 1958–60, 250,000 officers were demobilized, and in 1960, 454 new generals were appointed.) What was most striking about this reform was the priority given to engineer officers, who by 1969 accounted for 80 per cent of the officer corps of the Strategic Missile Forces.[14] The influence of these military technocrats in Soviet society must be considerable, though this does not imply a conflict of interest between the military and the Party. In 1966, 93 per cent of all officers were members either of the Party or of the *Komsomol*. And Brezhnev's attendance at the final parade of the *Dvina* manoeuvres in 1970 (a year in which fifty-eight marshals, generals, and admirals were elected to the Supreme Soviet) marked the close relationship between the military and the Party—and particularly himself.

To sum up, the political consequence of this relationship, underpinned by the Soviet leadership's vast allocation of national resources to the armed forces, both nuclear and conventional, was that in the next decade Brezhnev was able to embark, with full military backing, on a Soviet-American dialogue of a different kind from that which had been attempted by Khrushchev.

NOTES

1. *Pravda*, 17 October and 8 November 1964. See also Brezhnev, *Leninskim Kursom*, vol. 3, p. 30.
2. *Krasnaya Zvezda*, 4 February 1965. It is evident from the context that Khrushchev—not Stalin, who is mentioned elsewhere in the article—is the target of this criticism.

3. At the latest, by March 1966, when Brezhnev resumed the old title of General-Secretary at the XXIIIrd CPSU Congress. But the first occasion on which he was specifically described by *Pravda* as leading a delegation abroad (to Poland) was on 5 April 1965.
4. About this little is known, but it is presumed to bear ultimate responsibility for strategic nuclear decisions. For a discussion of the present functioning of these three bodies, and also of the important role of the General-Secretary's personal secretariat, see Alain Jacob's article in *Le Monde*, 12 February 1974, *L'URSS, société socialiste développée*. Finally, Khrushchev was chairman of the Central Committee Bureau of the RSFSR, an office which was abolished in 1966.
5. This American term of art has been defined as rough equality in numbers of weapons and deliverable 'throw-weight' by Maxwell D. Taylor in an article in *Foreign Affairs*, April 1974, p. 580.
6. What these consequences would be for Birmingham are assessed by Zuckerman, op. cit., pp. 55–8.
7. Intercontinentally needs under-lining, because within the European continent Soviet medium and intermediate range nuclear weapons targeted on NATO countries could have wrought havoc, had the Cuban crisis ended in a nuclear exchange: see the final paragraph of 'The temporary *détente*' in the preceding chapter.
8. Fallible, but with brains, values, and judgements still perhaps 'superior to the mechanics and processes of electronic computers or guidance systems': Zuckerman, op. cit., p. 26.
9. This argument is deployed in Taylor, op. cit., for example.
10. For a criticism of this term, see Zuckerman, op. cit., pp. 63–4; also Tom Lehrer's marching song of the Third World War in his record *That was the year, that was* (in particular, the line 'describing contrapuntally the cities we have lost').
11. This argument was put forward by Michael Boretsky, whose conclusions were called in question by Alec Nove in *Survival* of January 1971, particularly those relating to comparative prices. For a discussion, see *The Military Balance 1973/4*, IISS, London, 1973, pp. 8–9.
12. For Brezhnev's allusions, see ch. 9. John Erickson, in *Soviet Military Power*, Royal United Services Institute for Defence Studies, 1971, p. 100, suggests that in macro-economic terms the Soviet leadership is prepared to see military expenditure 'move ahead at the rate of 4 per cent per annum within an annual growth rate of about 5 or 6 per cent'. The section of the present chapter that follows is indebted to Erickson's book.
13. The Budapest reforms of the Warsaw Pact introduced in 1969 are described in *Survival*, May/June 1974, 'The Warsaw Pact Today' by Malcolm Mackintosh, pp. 123–4, IISS, London, 1974.
14. By 1973 more than half the officer corps of the Soviet Navy also had engineering degrees, according to *Krasnaya Zvezda*; see *The Times*, 30 July 1973.

5

ASIA

The Vietnam War

It is the official Soviet view that the two principal causes of the worsening of Soviet-American relations in the second half of the 1960s were the Vietnam War and United States support of Israel. To these an objective historian must add the invasion of Czechoslovakia, although East-West relations did not take long to absorb this shock. But if the Americans had not become engaged in Vietnam on the vast scale which followed the Tonkin Gulf incident of August 1964, would the Soviet leaders have been ready for a full dialogue with them sooner than they were, that is to say, before they could conduct it as equal partners? It seems doubtful.[1]

The American involvement in Vietnam was a windfall for the Soviet Union, for a number of reasons: whereas Soviet support for North Vietnam was not expensive, the war took up a large slice of the United States defence budget (over 100 billion dollars in the years 1965–72); it increasingly antagonized world opinion against the United States Government; as Vietnam absorbed American attention more and more, the Administration found it increasingly difficult to give the problems of the rest of the world all the attention that they deserved; and finally it split American society and brought down President Johnson. Even so, the war in Indo-China must have given the Soviet leadership some anxious moments, for they could not tell for certain—any more than any other government—how far the war would develop; it complicated their quarrel with the Chinese still further; and the Soviet military may have envied their American opposite numbers their ability to test modern weapons systems in battle conditions (the Soviet armed forces, though highly professional, have barely heard a shot fired in anger since the Japanese Armistice, whereas the American armed forces saw active service almost continuously from 1941 until their final withdrawal from the war in Indo-China).

Following Khrushchev's agreement with Kennedy on the neutralization of Laos at their meeting in Vienna, the Soviet Government proposed in July 1964 that the Geneva Conference on Laos should be reconvened (a proposal to which the United States was known to be hostile), and gave warning that the Soviet Government might be compelled to withdraw from its position as co-Chairman of the Conference. Khrushchev may well have wished to disengage from Indo-China altogether. Certainly, the first Soviet reaction to the incident of August 1964 and to the Joint Congressional Resolution* which followed it was to support the American proposal, rejected by the North Vietnamese, to take the matter to the Security Council. The Chinese protested both against the incident and the proposal. One of the first decisions of the new Soviet leadership was to reverse Khrushchev's decision. In November the Soviet Government pledged its support for the North Vietnamese Government if North Vietnam was attacked by the Americans. No doubt they had several motives for this: conceivably, the hope that the United States Government might think again; certainly, the hope of winning back the support of the North Vietnamese and the North Koreans from the Chinese; and probably, the belief that failure to come out in support of Hanoi would be used against them by the Chinese, who had sent a senior delegation to the celebrations of the October Revolution in Moscow, while both sides had suspended polemics. Even so, when Kosygin visited Hanoi the following February (and also North Korea, calling twice at Peking, where he talked with the Chinese leaders), he not only supported the convening of a new Geneva Conference on Indo-China, but also, according to the Chinese, conveyed to the North Vietnamese an American warning to stop supporting the National Liberation Front (NLF) in South Vietnam and to put an end to attacks on cities there. In the event, while the Soviet Prime Minister was in Hanoi, American bombers raided North Vietnamese targets, in retaliation for an attack by South Vietnamese NLF forces on their base at Pleiku in South Vietnam. The United States Government declined to consider negotiations. In April 1965 the First Secretary of the Central Committee of the North Vietnamese Communist Party

* This Resolution approved Johnson's 'determination to take all necessary measures' in Vietnam.

visited Moscow at the head of a delegation; agreement was reached on
the aid which the Soviet Union would give North Vietnam; and the
NLF was allowed to establish a mission in Moscow. For the rest of the
decade the Soviet role in Vietnam was no less important in the context
of the Sino-Soviet dispute than in that of Soviet-American relations.

The Sino-Soviet dispute

The lull in polemics between the CPSU and the CCP did not last long.
There was no meeting of minds between the new Soviet leadership and
the Chinese delegation when they talked in Moscow in November 1964,
and the year that followed exacerbated the dispute still further. The
meeting of the drafting committee, which Khrushchev had intended to
take place in December 1964, was held the following March. Only
eighteen out of the twenty-six communist parties were represented, and
the communiqué was equivocal, agreeing only that a new international
conference should be held at a suitable time, after thorough preparation
in which all fraternal parties should take part. But it did call for united
action in support of the Vietnamese people. Coming just before the
arrival of the Vietnamese delegation, this was a gain for the Russians,
who from now on used the Vietnamese issue as a stick for beating the
Chinese. Their accusations made at the time are repeated in the History
of Soviet Foreign Policy: over several years the Chinese 'created
obstacles to the transportation of arms and supplies across Chinese
territory' and held up deliveries for a long time. How serious these
obstacles were is hard to say; some could have been caused simply by
the chaos of the Chinese Cultural Revolution, which in 1968 was such
that in the border province of Kwangsi the Red Guards stormed the
North Vietnamese consulate at Nanning and assaulted its staff, on 2
June.[2] But the Chinese were on weak ground in rebutting Soviet
charges on this score, although they accused the new Soviet leadership
as hotly as they had Khrushchev, not only of revisionism, but also of
Soviet-American collaboration for the domination of the world, which
in Chinese eyes made the Soviet call for united action over Vietnam
fraudulent. (Not that the Chinese did not give the North Vietnamese
military aid themselves—they did, although Soviet military aid,
estimated at 1,660 million dollars in 1965–71, was nearly three times as
great as the Chinese during the same period.)[3]

During the Indo-Pakistan war of August/September 1965, the
Chinese accused the Russians of supporting the Indian reactionaries.

The success of the Tashkent meeting in January 1966, when the Indian and Pakistani leaders met the Soviet Prime Minister in the role of mediator, must have been galling to the Chinese, since it showed the Soviet Union as an Asian Great Power exercising its influence for peace. The Russians also scored over the Chinese in the affair of the Second Afro-Asian Conference, from which the Chinese sought to exclude them. It should have been held in Algiers in June 1965, but in the end it never took place. By that time the opening shots of the Cultural Revolution were being fired. This movement, literally translated 'a full-scale revolution to establish a working class culture', was to put the Chinese Government in baulk internationally in 1966. Not surprisingly, the Chinese sent no delegation to the XXIIIrd CPSU Congress in March of that year. But the eighty-odd parties who were represented included those of North Vietnam and North Korea. At the Congress Brezhnev spoke moderately about the CCP. In January 1967 Red Guards block-aded the Soviet Embassy in Peking; in February, the families of Soviet Staff were evacuated; and the Chinese withdrew their students from the Soviet Union after riots in the Red Square.

Whereas the Soviet Government gave full support to the North Vietnamese proposal of January 1967—that talks with the Americans could begin if the latter unconditionally stopped bombing and other acts of war against North Vietnam—the Chinese eventually condemned it as a Soviet-American conspiracy to compel the Vietnamese to give in, and accused the Russians of seeking to put the North Vietnamese and themselves at loggerheads. By now the Soviet leaders were 'the biggest group of renegades and scabs in history' for the Chinese, for whom Mao Tse-tung was Lenin's genuine successor. The Russians, as well as ridiculing the Cultural Revolution and the adulation of Mao, drew a distinction between the Maoist clique on the one hand and the CCP and the Chinese people on the other. Moreover they accused the Chinese of a tacit agreement with the Americans over Vietnam. This was partly based on Chinese statements that they would not intervene militarily in Vietnam unless themselves attacked by the United States, but may also have been connected with the Chinese formula for a North Vietnamese victory: a protracted people's war (such as they themselves had success-fully fought for so many years), to be won primarily through self-reliant effort, rather than with the aid of sophisticated Soviet military equipment—a formula which, in Soviet eyes, could be interpreted as meaning that the Chinese would be content for the war to last in-definitely.

Thus there was too much at stake for a Sino-Soviet rapprochement to be possible: the leadership of the world communist movement and competition for influence throughout the Third World, to which the Chinese offered the Maoist slogan that the 'world city' must fall to the assault of the 'world village'. In Asia the only major communist parties to remain pro-Soviet, other than the Mongolian Party, were those of India and Ceylon. Elsewhere the Chinese had only modest success. Rival communist parties were set up in the 1960s in several countries with Chinese support; pro-Chinese groups appeared in Europe, where both ruling (Romania partially excepted) and non-ruling parties were broadly pro-Soviet; but in Latin America, where the existence of guerrilla movements and the Che Guevara mystique might have been expected to offer exploitable opportunities, such pro-Chinese groups as were formed remained minuscule. (Castro, who by the middle of the decade[4] had adopted a position somewhere between the Chinese and the Russians, was a complicating factor.) In the Middle East the Chinese continued to accuse the Russians of cooperation with the Americans. They officially recognized the Palestinian *fedayeen* (towards whom the Soviet attitude was ambivalent until 1974*), by signing an agreement with them in 1965, promising diplomatic, military, and economic support. And they worked hard further south: in Africa their most spectacular achievement was the offer, which was accepted by the governments of Tanzania and Zambia, of 400 million dollars for the construction of the Tanzania–Zambia railway—more than the Russians had given for the Aswan Dam.

Behind all this lay the Soviet Government's conclusion, reached towards the end of 1965, that it was to its advantage to sign a Nuclear Non-Proliferation Treaty, which the Chinese regarded just as they had the Test Ban Treaty: an obstacle deliberately set in the way of the nuclear capability that they were slowly developing. Given the state of Sino-Soviet relations in the 1960s, it would have been surprising if there had been no incidents along the 4,000 mile frontier. 60,000 Chinese Moslem inhabitants of Sinkiang are believed to have been given asylum by the Soviet Union in 1962, for example; and the climax was reached in March 1969, when a major engagement was fought on Damansky Island,[5] the first among a series of incidents between March and August of that year. More Soviet troops were moved eastwards (they had been stationed in Mongolia since 1967); a

* When the Soviet Government finally gave official recognition to the Palestine Liberation Organization: see *The Times*, 19 October 1974.

new Central Asian Military District was established, with responsibility for the Sinkiang border; and a missile specialist, General V. F. Tolubko, was appointed in August to command the Far East Military District. On 16 September Victor Louis, the Soviet journalist who had scooped the fall of Khrushchev, wrote an article in the *Evening News* about the danger of war, which included the following passage:

The Soviet Union is adhering to the doctrine that socialist countries have the right to interfere in each other's affairs in their own interests or those of others who are threatened. The fact that China is many times larger than Czechoslovakia and might offer active resistance is, according to Marxist theoreticians, no reason for not applying this doctrine.

In that month two Chinese nuclear tests took place in Sinkiang. Although the Chinese had not yet developed modern delivery systems for nuclear weapons, they were within sight of launching their first earth satellite (in April 1970). China was just reaching the most vulnerable point in the development of strategic nuclear power: the moment when its nuclear force was beginning to pose a threat but was not yet certain of being able to survive a first-strike attack. By the autumn there were rumours of a Soviet pre-emptive strike against China. They were no more than rumours; for if such an extreme course was ever considered in Moscow, by that time the strike would have had not merely to destroy the Chinese nuclear installations, both in Sinkiang and in eastern China, but also several thousand Chinese nuclear scientists as well. Undeterred, or perhaps even spurred on, by Soviet psychological warfare, the Chinese Government warned the population of the danger of a Soviet attack, and shelters were dug in the cities.

As had happened a decade earlier, this conflict coincided with ideological dissension. At the IXth CCP Congress, held in April 1969, the Chinese leadership formally elevated Maoism to a position of equality with Marxism-Leninism, denouncing the revisionism of the Soviet leadership, who became in Chinese terms 'social imperialists'. Yet in September the Soviet and Chinese Prime Ministers met in Peking, as Kosygin was on his way back from a visit to Hanoi. They agreed that, however acute their ideological rivalry, a working relationship between the two governments should be restored (both missions had been reduced to the level of Chargés d'Affaires, and the Chinese Embassy in Moscow had left its broken windows unrepaired as a reminder of the past). Ambassadors were exchanged in 1970, the year in which Chinese diplomacy[6] was released from the self-denying ordinance imposed by the Cultural Revolution. But talks on the frontier question, which have continued to this day, achieved no perceptible results. Even though the Soviet and Chinese governments were again on speaking terms, they remained as far apart as ever on questions of substance.

Conference of the world communist parties

In June 1969 the Soviet leadership did succeed in holding this long deferred conference. As it turned out, the delegates met with the invasion of Czechoslovakia as much in mind as the Sino-Soviet dispute (but for the invasion, the conference would have been held six months earlier). Seventy-five parties took part. Of the fourteen ruling parties, five boycotted the conference—China, Albania, North Korea, North Vietnam, and Yugoslavia—and Cuba sent only an observer. There were no representatives from Japan, Indonesia, or any East Asian or South-East Asian party. Exceptionally, *Pravda* published summaries of speeches even when critical of Soviet policies. These included a statement by Enrico Berlinguer, Secretary-General of the Italian Communist Party, sympathizing with the Czechoslovak experiment and condemning the invasion of 1968, and one by Nicolae Ceausescu describing China as the great socialist state and declaring that no force in the world could conquer a nation which was fully determined to defend courageously its freedom and national independence.[7] A group of parties submitted a draft declaration, which was chiefly the work of the Russians, the Hungarians, and the French. Over 400 amendments were submitted, of which a hundred found their way in one form or another into the compromise text, an anodyne document which some parties refused to sign (the Romanians did sign it). Even though the conference achieved little, the fact that it was held at all was a Soviet achievement.[8] Nevertheless, by the end of the decade, the Soviet leadership had proved no more successful than Khrushchev in restoring the unity of the world communist movement.

NOTES

1. Adam Ulam in *The Rivals*, Viking Press, New York, 1971, has argued that American diplomacy missed the opportunity for such a dialogue after the Cuban crisis had revealed the weakness of the Soviet position. But Khrushchev's personal position had also been weakened at home. Would he have had the authority to go further towards Kennedy than he did during his remaining two years of office?

2. Op. cit., vol. 2, p. 422, gives the Soviet view. For the Nanning incident, see Stanley Karnow, *Mao and China*, Macmillan, London, 1973, p. 439.

3. *Strategic Survey 1972*, IISS, London, 1973, p. 50, which describes the estimated figures given as rough. For the Chinese view of the North Vietnam War in the sixties, see Karnow's analysis in op. cit., pp. 479 ff.

4. In 1966, Carlos Rafael Rodriguez, when asked by the author to which Communist Party Cuban Communists felt closest, replied without hesitation 'the North Korean'.

5. Chenpao Island for the Chinese, whose account of what they have claimed as a Soviet defeat was given in the *Observer* of 23 September 1973. For Sinkiang, see Karnow, op. cit., p. 135.

6. Chinese ambassadors who had been withdrawn from their posts returned, after years of absence; diplomatic relations were even restored with the capital of arch-revisionists, Belgrade; and Yugoslavia itself resumed relations with the arch-dogmatist Albania.

7. *Pravda*, 14 and 11 June 1969.

8. For details, see *Novosti*, Moscow, and the *World Marxist Review*, Prague, 1969.

6

THE THIRD WORLD

Policy towards the underdeveloped countries

Under Khrushchev, the stilted jargon of the third of the basic tasks of
Soviet foreign policy (to support national liberation movements and to
cooperate in every way with underdeveloped countries) expressed an
ambitious new approach towards former colonies comparable in scope
with Canning's calling in the New World to redress the balance of the
Old.

Khrushchev's new policy complicated relations between the CPSU
and the local communist parties, even in Cuba.[1] In the Middle East, the
communist parties of one country after another split under the strain of
Soviet support for the government that was suppressing them (a strain
that was aggravated by the Sino-Soviet dispute). True, this dichotomy
between Soviet national interests and those of a local communist party
was not a new phenomenon: one of the earliest examples was the sup-
pression of the Turkish Communist Party by Atatürk, who was cultiv-
ated by the Soviet Government soon after the Revolution. But it was
sharpened under Khrushchev. Moreover, his policy towards the Third
World met with some grievous disappointments, such as the fall of
Lumumba, Nkrumah, Kassem, Ben Bella, and Sukarno. Of these, by
far the worst blow to the international communist cause was the last.
Although Sukarno was not formally deposed as President until two and
a half years after the fall of Khrushchev, in the fighting that followed
the abortive *coup d'état* of September 1965 at least 100,000 members of
the Indonesian Communist Party were slaughtered, and an equal
number of the Party's sympathizers. Politically, this blow was as hard to
bear in Peking as it was in Moscow. But financially, it was the Soviet

Government that suffered. Not only was the new Indonesian regime left a handsome legacy of Soviet military hardware, including tanks and warships, but the Soviet Union was left with an unpaid Indonesian debt of over $1,000 million, 791 million of which was for military equipment; and in 1970 the debt rescheduling agreement finally reached between the Soviet and Indonesian governments provided for the period of repayment to be extended until the end of the century.[2]

In the early 1960s the approved model for a developing country was defined as an independent state of national democracy, which, based on a strong peasant-proletarian alliance with *petit bourgeois* support, could prepare the way for 'non-capitalist' development. Such a regime must be anti-imperialist, friendly towards the Soviet Union, and ready both to execute radical social and economic reforms and to give local communist parties full freedom of political action. But by 1964 Nasser, who did not treat Egyptian communists kindly, had been made a Hero of the Soviet Union. The role of local communist parties was now defined as that of friend and assistant of the national democrats: cold comfort for the parties concerned and grist to the Chinese mill. By the end of the decade, developing countries were broadly divided into three categories: those which had adopted the path of 'non-capitalist', or 'progressive social', development; those trying to strengthen their national independence and to create a modern economy with the broad participation of the national bourgeoisie; and those accepting a semi-colonial way of life and acting as the accomplices of imperialist exploiters. And in 1971 it was recognized by a Soviet theorist that in many, if not in most, of the developing Asian and African countries, no forces except the national democrats were capable of 'a nation-wide struggle for the attainment of the aims of the present stage of revolution'.[3] National democrats might well be army officers, as in Peru, whose military regime received Soviet support after the *coup* of October 1968. In short, the Khrushchevian belief that 'within the briefest period of time the overwhelming majority of former colonies would allegedly take, if not the socialist, then at least the non-capitalist, road of development' was acknowledged as an 'illusion'.[4]

Under the present Soviet leadership policy towards the Third World has become selective and pragmatic. The terms of Soviet aid are less generous than those of either the Chinese or the International Development Association: a Soviet loan, granted in inconvertible roubles, is usually repayable over 10–15 years, with interest at $2\frac{1}{2}$–3 per cent. Any comparison of the Soviet aid programme with that of the United States or of any major Western country is difficult, because Soviet aid figures are not published; according to the OECD's 1972 *Review of Development Cooperation*, three-quarters of the Soviet aid flow went to communist countries; and confusion frequently arises between amounts of Soviet aid offered and Soviet aid actually delivered. On a rough estimate, Soviet bloc and Chinese aid delivered to non-communist developing countries totalled about 600 million dollars in 1972, half of which came from the Soviet Union. But the rising flow of debt repayments from the developing countries to the latter probably reduced the net Soviet aid flow to the Third World from a high point of 300 million dollars, at the time of Khrushchev's fall, to less than 100 million dollars in 1972—a year in which one of the four major recipients of Soviet aid, economic and military, India, paid to the Soviet Union 35 million dollars more than the value of Soviet deliveries, even though India had been provided by the Soviet Union with a multi-million dollar turn-key project—the Bhilai steelworks, which was on a scale comparable to that of the Aswan High Dam in Egypt. It is significant that at the Second United Nations Conference on Trade and Development, held in Delhi in 1968, the representatives of the Soviet Union and its allies abstained from voting on the resolution committing developed countries to adopt one per cent of gross national product as the target for their annual transfer of resources to the developing countries.

American intervention in Vietnam made this country a special case for the Soviet Union, justifying almost any level of expenditure. Of all the aid programmes ever undertaken by the Soviet Government, the one that must have troubled the cost-effectiveness experts in the Kremlin most is the aid, direct and indirect, extended to Cuba. Whichever government originally suggested the installing of Soviet missiles in Cuba in 1962, it is certain that the negotiations for their removal were carried on over Castro's head; it is therefore not surprising that for the rest of the decade he remained a difficult ally for the Soviet Union. The difficulties were both economic and political. In the early years after the Cuban Revolution, its leaders looked to a combination of rapid industrialization and the establishment of giant state farms, run by officials responsible to highly centralized direction from Havana, as the key to economic progress, with unfortunate results,[5] which were accentuated by Che Guevara's belief that Cuba had already entered the final Marxist phase of pure communism. Under the terms of the original trade agreement negotiated by Mikoyan during his visit to Havana in February 1960, the Soviet Government had agreed to buy nearly 5 million tons of Cuban sugar over the next five years, and offered a credit of 100 million dollars in aid. At the end of 1963, in conditions bordering on economic chaos, Castro decided to abandon his original plan of economic autarky and to make agriculture the basis of Cuban economic development for the rest of the decade, sugar being given top priority. The Soviet Government was therefore obliged increasingly to underwrite the Cuban economy, mainly by taking annually rising quantities of Cuban sugar at prices higher than those on the world market. By 1973 it was estimated that in all, Cuba was costing the Soviet Union $1,500,000 a day and that repayment of the Cuban debt would last into the twenty-first century.

During the 1960s the basic political[6] difference between the Soviet Union and Cuba centred on the fact that Castro—who had come to power in Havana straight from his guerrilla base in the Sierra Maestra—continued to advocate the *via armada* (as opposed to the *via pacifica*) as the model for Latin American communist parties. At its XXIIIrd Congress the CPSU even found itself under Cuban fire for not doing more to help North Vietnam. For the Soviet Union, the Cuban alliance was an irritant in cultivating relationships with other Latin American countries. But Castro's qualified support of the invasion of Czechoslovakia (which, in a speech on 28 August 1968, he described as a bitter necessity)[7] marked the beginning of the closer alignment between the policies of the two countries that has followed in the present decade.

After what happened in October 1962, and with the Chinese as watchful rivals in Havana, Soviet historians would no doubt argue that no Soviet Government could have acted towards Cuba in any other way during the rest of the decade. Yet, if at some future conference Soviet and American historians were invited to re-write, with the advantage of hindsight, a fresh scenario for US-Cuban and Soviet-Cuban relations during the 1960s, it is hard to believe that they could not devise better policies than those actually pursued by their governments towards Cuba, and that they could not suggest ways in which both could have contributed to the development of a small island inhabited by a gifted people, with great natural resources.

The Middle East

If the Cuban aid programme was in financial terms the most costly legacy of Khrushchev's policy towards the Third World, in political and strategic terms by far the most important was the Soviet commitment to the Middle East, which in the 1970s was to replace South-East

Asia as the most explosive source of conflict in the world. Today this commitment has two aspects: one strategic and the other politico-economic. The former antedates Khrushchev, and for that matter the Russian Revolution itself. The traditional thrust of Tsarist diplomacy towards the Straits and southward from Central Asia was resumed by Stalin immediately after the Second World War (Stalin's request for a base in the Straits, the territorial claims made against Turkey, formally dropped only after Stalin's death in 1953, and the Azerbaijan episode of 1945-6). A glance at the map is enough to show that strategically the Middle East is for Russia—whether Tsarist or Soviet—what the Caribbean is for the United States: its backyard. After the failure of this forward policy towards Turkey and Iran in 1946, Stalin withdrew to his European fortress. Under Khrushchev, the strategic aspect of Soviet policy towards the Middle East received a fresh emphasis, beginning with the Egyptian arms deal. (Formally the arms then supplied to Egypt were Czechoslovak, but the deal must have received the approval of the Soviet Government, which by 1958 had assumed the main responsibility for equipping the Egyptian armed forces.) Soviet financing of the Aswan Dam and Soviet purchase of Egyptian cotton at premium prices in the mid-1950s added a new dimension to Soviet foreign policy: politico-economic rivalry in the Middle East with the Western countries whose exclusive preserve it had been ever since the break-up of the Ottoman Empire nearly forty years earlier. Among these countries Britain remained the predominant power in the Middle East until the collapse of the Anglo-French Suez expedition in 1956. The steady erosion of British power in the area left a vacuum which the United States found it hard to fill, because of its commitment to Israel, and which it would have been hard for the Soviet Union not to fill, even though it had been one of the State of Israel's original sponsors in 1948. As the Soviet Union gradually filled this vacuum, so too it assumed the role of the champion of the Arab cause against Israel, in the process acquiring a position in the Middle East which recalls that of Tsarist Russia in the Balkans.

The Middle East may indeed be described, in politico-strategic terms, as the Balkans of the late twentieth century. Thus, in pursuing its new policy in the Middle East, the Soviet Union has had to contend with the volatility of Arab politics, as well as with the problem of underpinning this policy with respectable ideological justification. In the northern tier, Soviet national interests—in particular mistrust of the CENTO[8] Alliance—obliged the Soviet Union to mend its fences with Turkey and

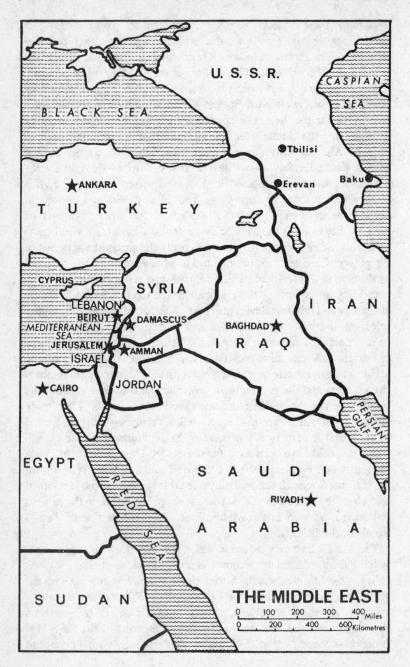

THE MIDDLE EAST

| 0 | 100 | 200 | 300 | 400 | Miles |
| 0 | 200 | 400 | 600 | Kilometres |

Iran. This rapprochement was cemented under the collective leadership by official visits paid by Kosygin to Teheran in 1968 and to Ankara in 1966. (The Soviet-Iranian agreement of January 1966, whereby Iran undertook to deliver natural gas to the Soviet Union for twelve years, in return for industrial projects in Iran carried out by the latter, also marked a turning point in Soviet oil policy.) Although all Arabs are anti-imperialist in the sense that they are anti-Israeli, the political spectrum of Arab regimes is extremely broad. The Soviet leadership began by attempting to define some of the Arab states as 'progressive social'—for example, the Ba'ath regimes in Iraq and Syria. But in the Middle East, as elsewhere, this attempt has ended with the acknowledgement of reality quoted in the previous section of this chapter; and the touchstone of Soviet policy in Arab eyes has become more and more the Soviet leadership's handling of the dispute between the Arab states and Israel.

The Arab-Israeli dispute

This dispute erupted again in June 1967. Soviet motives for stoking the fire that led to the Six Day War are obscure. On 21 April 1967, presumably under Arab pressure, the Soviet Government addressed a note of protest to Israel against the air raid which—as a reprisal—the Israeli Air Force had carried out on Damascus a fortnight earlier (previously the Soviet press had spoken only of border clashes). At the end of April Kosygin had talks in Moscow with a visiting Egyptian delegation, led by Anwar Sadat. According to a speech made by Nasser after his defeat, the delegation was told, presumably by the Soviet Prime Minister, that Israel was concentrating troops with the premeditated intent of attacking Syria. When Nasser closed the Straits of Tiran in May, the Soviet Government did not condone his action; but the Soviet press gave no hint of disapproval; on the contrary, *Pravda* of 26 May stated that the gulf waters could not be regarded as Israeli waters under any United Nations decision, three days after the Soviet Government had declared that aggressors in the Middle East would face not only the united strength of the Arab countries, but also a firm riposte from the Soviet Union. On this evidence, either the Soviet leadership completely miscalculated the military situation on the ground, or 'no one calculated at all'; in any event, having urged restraint on both sides, Brezhnev, Kosygin, and the Defence Minister left Moscow, to spend the critical days from 31 May to 4 June inspecting the Soviet fleet at Murmansk and Archangel.[9]

Whatever the explanation for Soviet behaviour before the Six Day War, there is no doubt about the energy with which the Soviet Government reacted to it. The Soviet Prime Minister used the hot line to the US President more than once. After the cease-fire, a summit meeting of communist states was held in Europe. Soviet leaders visited their Middle Eastern friends; Soviet warships were sent to Alexandria and Port Said; the vast Egyptian losses of equipment were swiftly made good; and although the Algerian President publicly blamed the Russians* for the humiliating Arab defeat—which left Israeli forces occupying the Sinai peninsula, the west bank of Jordan, and the Golan heights in Syria—the Soviet position in the Arab world and the eastern Mediterranean was soon restored. In November 1967 the Soviet Union intervened militarily in the Yemeni civil war, from which Egyptian troops were at last pulling out, and in the following year an agreement on military and technical assistance was signed with the new South Yemen Government, which was established after the British withdrawal from Aden. In the Cyprus crisis of November 1967, the Soviet Government succeeded in maintaining an even-handed posture towards both the Turkish and the Cyprus governments, while blaming the West for allegedly pursuing policies in Cyprus which brought two NATO allies—Turkey and Greece—to the brink of war.

Meanwhile, in the aftermath of the Six Day War, Kosygin led the Soviet delegation to the United Nations. (While he was in the United States he met President Johnson at Glasboro, without result.) On the Arab-Israeli dispute the Security Council finally adopted a compromise resolution on 22 November, for which the British delegation was entitled to the credit. This resolution was an ingenious attempt to square the circle. The preamble to the resolution having emphasized, among other things 'the inadmissibility of the acquisition of territory by war and the need to work for a just and lasting peace, in which every state in the area can live in security.' the resolution itself consisted of three points. The first of these was:

the establishment of a just and lasting peace in the Middle East, which should include the application of both the following principles:

(i) Withdrawal of Israel armed forces from territories occupied in the recent conflict;

(ii) Termination of claims or states of belligerency, and respect for and acknowledgement of the sovereignty, territorial integrity and political

* The Russians themselves blamed both the superiority of Israeli equipment and Nasser's betrayal by the military bourgeoisie.

independence of every state in the area and their right to live in peace within secure and recognized boundaries free from acts or threats of force.

The resolution's second point affirmed the necessity for:

(a) guaranteeing freedom of navigation through international waterways in the area;

(b) achieving a just settlement of the refugee problem;

(c) guaranteeing the territorial inviolability and political independence of every state in the area, through measures including the establishment of demilitarized zones.

Thirdly, the Security Council requested the Secretary-General of the United Nations to designate a Special Representative to go to the Middle East, in order to help to achieve a peaceful and accepted settlement in accordance with the provisions and principles of the resolution.

This resolution, which the Security Council was to re-affirm in 1969 and in 1973, remains at the centre of the dispute. Whether it would have been passed unanimously if there were a definite article in the Russian language is an interesting speculation: the Soviet Union has supported its Arab clients in interpreting the word 'territories' in 1(i) of the resolution as meaning all 'the territories',[10] whereas it has been a cardinal point of the Israeli case that there are certain territories which they could never reasonably be expected to return to Arab hands, such as the Golan Heights, Sharm-el-Sheikh, and Jerusalem itself. U Thant's Special Representative, Gunnar Jarring, then Swedish Ambassador in Moscow, made repeated efforts over the years that followed to fulfil the mission entrusted to him. The main rocks that he hit were: on the Israeli side, their unwillingness not only to return all that they had conquered but also to negotiate other than directly with the Arab governments concerned; and on the Arab side, a matching reluctance to negotiate before a complete Israeli withdrawal—not to mention the special problem of Jerusalem and the future of the Arab refugees, their numbers swollen by the outcome of the 1967 war.[11]

The year 1969 opened with a Soviet initiative: on 2 January the Soviet Government suggested the outline of a settlement to the British, French, and United States governments. This led in the course of the year to discussions between the Representatives of the Four Powers in New York and to a Soviet-American bilateral dialogue, in which the two governments, as well as negotiating with each other, were also acting as lawyers for their respective clients in the Middle East. On the ground matters grew steadily worse. By April the United Nations

Secretary-General reported that open warfare was being waged: the War of Attrition, as it came to be called. Against a background of Arab guerrilla operations conducted in the territories occupied by Israel, in Israel itself, and in many other countries, the Egyptian Army used its superiority in artillery to conduct a shelling duel across the Suez Canal, while the Israeli Air Force, using the Phantom aircraft supplied by the United States, attacked targets nearer and nearer Cairo. These attacks were to lead the Soviet Union, early in 1970, to embark on a massive, direct intervention in Egypt. This will be described in later chapters; for present purposes, it must be recorded as marking a watershed in Soviet policy towards the Middle East and the Third World, and in the Soviet relationship with the United States.

NOTES

1. For example, the affair of Aníbal Escalante: see Stephen Clissold, op. cit., pp. 294 ff.
2. By 1970 the joint total of military and commercial Indonesian debt to the Soviet Union was still $750 million. The $400 million owed by Indonesia to Eastern European Governments was not rescheduled until 1971–2.
3. The evolution of Soviet aid policy is traced in ch. 6 of W. W. Kulski, *The Soviet Union in World Affairs 1964–1972*, Syracuse University Press, New York, 1973. For the threefold classification, see p. 161. The Soviet theorist is Ulyanovsky whose article in *International Affairs* is quoted in *The Conduct of Soviet Foreign Policy*, eds. Erik Hoffman and F. Fleron, Aldine and Atherton, Chicago, 1971, pp. 410 ff.
4. This 'illusion' is specifically attributed to the 'late fifties and in particular the early sixties' by V. Tiagunenko in *Nekotorye problemy natsional'no—osvoboditel'nykh revoliutsii v svete Leninizma*, 1970, quoted by Kulski, op. cit. pp. 188–9.
5. These were described soon afterwards by René Dumont, a left-wing writer sympathetic towards the Cuban Revolution, in his book *Cuba: socialisme et développement*, Editions du Seuil, Paris, 1964. In 1961/2, for example, only half the fruit and vegetables available in Cuba were collected by the Land Reform Agency, which was headed by a geographer, Professor Nuñez Jimenez; and in 1963 agricultural productivity on the state farms was less than half that in what remained of the private sector.
6. The Soviet-Cuban political balance sheet has been drawn up by Clissold, op. cit., pp. 42–59, although given the date of publication (1970), he had to end this chapter of his book with a question mark.
7. Ibid., pp. 304–6, which gives the full text. By the time of the Non-Aligned Conference held in Algiers in 1973, Castro had become an out-and-out defender of the Soviet Union against all comers: see *Pravda* of 9 September 1973, reporting his speech of the previous day.
8. The Central Treaty Organization, consisting of Turkey, Iran, Pakistan, and Great Britain. This succeeded the Baghdad Pact, from which Iraq withdrew after the *coup d'état* in 1958, in which both the King and the Prime Minister

were assassinated. Its headquarters was moved from Baghdad to Ankara in 1959.

9. Tatu, op. cit., 'Postscript', pp. 532 ff., gives the Soviet aspect of the chronology of the crisis. This particular incident is refered to on p. 536, from which the quotation is also taken.

10. Which is what the French text of the resolution said.

11. Of an estimated Palestinian Arab population of about three million, roughly half are now outside the 1948 frontiers of Palestine, and a further 600,000 are living in the West Bank area and the Gaza Strip under Israeli rule. 1,300,000 Palestinians are registered as refugees qualifying for United Nations assistance.

7

EUROPE

New ideas

Under Stalin, Europe was central to Soviet foreign policy. Under Khrushchev, in spite of his adventures in the Third World, it remained so. The heart of the matter was Germany. In 1958 the Soviet Government put forward a draft Treaty of Friendship and Cooperation of European States; and in 1960 the Warsaw Pact governments made, not for the first time, a proposal for a non-aggression pact between the NATO and the Warsaw Pact groups of states. Both these proposals would have involved recognition of the German Democratic Republic by the West, and hence the jettisoning of the Hallstein doctrine, which ostracized the GDR. In the 1960s new ideas were beginning to be discussed, both in Western and in Eastern Europe.

In Eastern Europe, the new look began in Romania, from which Soviet troops had been withdrawn in 1958, in the aftermath of the convulsions that had wracked Eastern Europe after the XXth Congress of the CPSU two years before. The Romanian attempt to mediate between the Russians and the Chinese in 1964 was part of a broad decision to pursue an independent foreign policy, based on what the Romanian leadership perceived as their country's national interests, while at the same time allowing no relaxation of party-imposed discipline at home. They began in the field of foreign trade, claiming the right to trade with whom they pleased, and rejected the Soviet proposal put forward in COMECON in 1962, for the division of labour between members of that organization in accordance with the directives of a central planning organ.[1] The new Romanian constitution of 1965 included a provision intended to prevent Romania from becoming involved in war except by its own decision. In May 1966 Ceausescu, who had become leader of the Romanian Communist Party the year before, delivered a speech[2] in which he publicly attacked the concept of military blocs and touched a raw Soviet nerve by referring to the lost provinces of Bessarabia and Northern Bukovina (acquired by the Soviet Union as a fruit of the Nazi-Soviet Pact of 1939). Romania was the first Eastern European country, other than the Soviet Union itself, to enter into diplomatic relations with the Federal Republic of Germany; and the Soviet Union had to acquiesce in Romania's maintaining relations with Israel after the 1967 war—and ultimately in her resumption of relations with China, where Ceausescu was to receive a lavish welcome in 1971.

'Polycentrism' (as it was described in the Italian Communist leader Togliatti's memorandum, published in *Pravda* after his death in September 1964) was matched in the West by de Gaulle's concept of Europe from the Atlantic to the Urals. According to Soviet theory, relations between communist countries are unique, because they involve not only their governments but also their whole peoples, led by their respective Communist parties.[3] The international obligations of the working class do not permit of any divergence of interest between one communist country and another. Nevertheless, the Soviet leadership decided to put up with the Romanians, and to foster a special Franco-Soviet relationship, because with it went the idea of Europe for the Europeans—not to mention the gap in the NATO order of battle left by the French forces, which de Gaulle withdrew from integrated international command before his visit to Moscow in 1966.

Most important of all, *Ostpolitik* was being re-thought in West Germany itself. On 26 January 1965, the *Frankfurter Allegemeine Zeitung* published a memorandum on this subject written by Willy Brandt the previous August. This memorandum took as its premise that it was a Western interest to support the independence of East European nations and their efforts to use their field of manoeuvre. Such a policy should concentrate on economic and cultural measures (linked with 'humanitarian regulations'), respecting each East European state as an equal partner, and taking into account its military and ideological links. Brandt foresaw, though he described the time as not yet ripe for it, a major increase in East-West trade, for which the Western countries would have to be prepared to grant substantial economic and financial support, and the development of joint projects on a European scale. The memorandum stopped short of recommending any change in the policy of refusing to recognize the Soviet Zone of Germany as an independent state, but contemplated greater economic and cultural contact between it and the Federal Republic, and expressed the hope that increased contact between the West and other Eastern European countries would affect the Soviet Zone as well. And towards the end, the memorandum recalled Brandt's remark in a speech made in New York in May 1964, that it was time to acknowledge the fact that Europe does not end at the Iron Curtain.

Six weeks before Brandt's article was published, the Polish Foreign Minister briefly remarked, at the United Nations General Assembly, that the time was ripe for convening a conference of all European states, to examine the problem of European security as a whole. (Rapacki expressly added that both the Soviet Union and the United States should take part.) On 20 January 1965 the political Consultative Committee of the Warsaw Pact countries endorsed the Polish initiative, proposing a conference of European states (with no mention of the United States or Canada) to discuss measures for collective security in Europe,[4] and followed this up at Bucharest, in July 1966, with a long 'Declaration on Strengthening Peace and Security in Europe'.[5] This foresaw an all-European declaration providing for pledges on the part of signatory states to be guided in their relations with one another by the interests of peace, to settle disputed questions only by peaceful means, to hold consultations and exchange information on questions of mutual interest, and to assist in the comprehensive development of economic, scientific-technical, and cultural ties with one another: a proposal repeated in the Karlovy Vary statement of European communist parties of 26 April 1967, according to which European security[6] depended on:

respecting the realities of post-war Europe ... the inviolability of the existing frontiers in Europe, especially the Oder-Neisse frontier and the frontier between the two German states ... the existence of two sovereign German states with equal rights ... denying the Federal German Republic access to nuclear weapons in any form either European or Atlantic[7] ... recognizing the Munich Pact as invalid from the very moment of its conclusion.

The Karlovy Vary statement was important not only because it made it clear that the idea of a European conference was already linked in the minds of its proposers with the German question, but also because it followed the announcement in the Bundestag, in December 1966, of the new *Ostpolitik* proposals of the Grand Coalition Government of Christian Democrats and Social Democrats, in which Brandt held the post of Foreign Minister. Although these proposals stopped well short of recognizing the German Democratic Republic, with whom a policy of 'regulated coexistence' was envisaged, they marked the beginning of the end of the Hallstein doctrine of 1955, whereby the Federal German Government had refused to recognize any government—with the single exception of the Soviet Union—which recognized the German Democratic Republic. Romania, which boycotted the Karlovy Vary conference, established diplomatic relations with the Federal Republic on this basis without delay. The East Germans and the Poles denounced the new policy as German revanchism in a new guise. After a period of apparent hesitation, the Soviet Union joined the Germans and the Poles. As though to emphasize the unity of the Eastern European bloc, in the course of 1967 all its members, except Romania, signed bilateral treaties of mutual assistance with the German Democratic Republic, and the Soviet Union began to bring its bilateral treaties with each member country up to date. But in the second half of 1967 and the first half of 1968 the Soviet Government did not feel inhibited from engaging in bilateral talks with the Federal German Government on the possibility of an agreement renouncing the use of force—with no result, although the talks proved to be the forerunner of the Soviet–German negotiations of 1970.

No direct response was made by the Western Alliance until the very end of 1969. But after the ministerial meeting held in Brussels in December 1967 the communiqué had annexed to it the Harmel Report on the future tasks of the Alliance.[8] The essence of this report was the concept that military security and a policy of *détente* were not contradictory, but complementary. The report spoke of 'realistic measures designed to further a *détente* in East-West relations', not as the final goal, but as 'part of a long-term process to promote better relations and to foster a European settlement'. Its final pragraph contained the first mention of balanced force reductions. Six months later—the French abstaining—NATO Ministers meeting at Reykjavik formally put forward a proposal for such reductions in Europe, and invited the Warsaw Pact countries to 'join in this search for progress towards peace'. But in August 1968 the dialogue was brusquely interrupted, when the forces of the Soviet Union, together with some units supplied by its Warsaw Pact allies (excluding Romania), invaded Czechoslovakia—some half million men in all.

Czechoslovakia

Ironically, it was Czechoslovakia, where Stalin's gigantic statue had been left standing in Prague long after Khrushchev had denounced him at the XXth CPSU Congress, that produced the most serious threat to Soviet authority in Eastern Europe since the Hungarian Revolution, and, in the process, retarded the Soviet grand design for Europe by one year. The origins of the Czechoslovak upheaval were complex: political (general dissatisfaction with fifteen years of rule by Antonin Novotny, who during most of this period combined the offices of President and First Secretary of the Czechoslovak Communist Party); regional (the Slovaks demanded the same rights as the Czechs); and economic. E. G. Liberman's thesis on profitability had been published in *Pravda* in September 1962; it was not followed up until three years later, when the Soviet leadership introduced a limited measure of economic reform, which was attacked by the Chinese as a big step towards the restoration of capitalism and 'a new *kulak* economy'. The success of the German economic reforms has already been mentioned; the Hungarian reform began in 1968; the Czechoslovak reform, approved in 1965, began on 1 January 1967, but was diluted by the conservatism of party officials. On all these grounds Brezhnev, who visited Prague in December 1967, cannot have been greatly surprised when Novotny was obliged to resign as First Secretary of the Czechoslovak Communist Party in January 1968 (three months later he was succeeded as President by General Svoboda). His successor as First Secretary, Alexander Dubcek, the Moscow-trained First Secretary of the Slovak Communist Party, may well have seemed reliable enough at first. From start to finish he was at pains to stress his commitment to the communist cause; and hence to keep Czechoslovakia in COMECON and in the Warsaw Pact. Indeed he reversed the Romanian experiment: his 'socialism with a human face' was loyal to Moscow abroad and became increasingly heterodox at home.

There is no evidence that when Dubcek, who combined diffidence with obstinacy in a remarkable way, took over in Prague in January 1968, he had any intention of liberalizing the Czechoslovak political system as he did during the next seven months, although he must have approved of Ota Sik's economic reforms. He was borne along by the wave of popular expectations, rather like Wladyslaw Gomulka in Poland twelve years earlier, but—unlike Gomulka—he did not drive it back again. Events moved so rapidly that on 2 May *Rude Pravo* was able to

EASTERN EUROPE

write of the springlike blossoming of a new public life and of the breath of fresh air brought by democratic freedoms. It might have been nearer the truth at that moment to describe Dubcek as unwilling to rule the country by force and unqualified to rule it by democratic means. He therefore fell between two stools. For example, having discontinued press censorship in March, at the end of May the Ministry of Interior announced that the formation of new political parties—in particular, this applied to the resuscitation of the Social Democratic Party—would be considered illegal. Yet the Ministry allowed a preparatory committee of the 'club of engaged non-party members' to operate, recognized the statute of the society for human rights, and permitted the Communist Party-sponsored youth organization to divide into a number of independent groups. Soviet influence in the Ministry of Interior and in the Czechoslovak Army was curbed. Worst of all perhaps in Soviet eyes was the Czechoslovak Party's decision, taken in May, to hold a Congress on 9 September, which was expected to consist of delegates holding reformist views.

Soviet concern at this trend of events was expressed to Dubcek and his colleagues at their first confrontation with representatives of five Warsaw Pact powers (Romania alone being absent) at Dresden on 23 March. This concern was heightened by the Czechoslovak Central Committee's approval, on 5 April, of the liberal Action Programme. On 27 June seventy prominent Czechoslovaks published a manifesto calling for even more radical reform, *The Two Thousand Words*, which led *Pravda* on 11 July to draw an ominous comparison between Czechoslovakia in 1968 and Hungary in 1956.[9] The Warsaw Letter of 15 July,[10] addressed to the Czechoslovaks by their five Warsaw Pact allies (they themselves had refused to attend the meeting), laid particular emphasis on the Czechoslovak Party's loss of control of the mass media. Of their allies' chief anxieties, the first was political: the fear that the Czechoslovak Communist Party would sooner or later lose control of the levers of power. ('Undermining the leading role of the Communist Party leads to the liquidation of socialist democracy and of the socialist system . . .') The second was military. ('The frontiers of the socialist world have moved to the centre of Europe, to the Elbe and the Sumav mountains.') The third was a bit of both: fear of West Germany, and the response among the ruling circles in Czechoslovakia which the Federal Republic's overtures were allegedly meeting. The Warsaw Letter was followed by a Soviet demand that the Czechoslovak Presidium should meet the Soviet Politburo, either in Moscow or in the

Ukraine. The Czechoslovaks agreed to the meeting, but succeeded in persuading the Soviet Politburo, all but two of whose members attended, to hold the meeting in Czechoslovakia.

Czechoslovakia was invaded on the night of 20/21 August, in spite of the apparent agreement reached between the Soviet and Czechoslovak party leaderships at Cierna[11] and between the leaders of all six parties at Bratislava,[12] at the end of July and the beginning of August respectively. The Czechoslovaks seem to have left the former meeting convinced that the Soviet troops who were conducting manoeuvres in Czechoslovakia would leave their country; that the Warsaw Letter was abrogated; and that Czechoslovak sovereignty was assured. Equally the Soviet leadership appear to have believed that the Czechoslovak leaders were now committed to regaining control over the mass media. The wording of the Bratislava Declaration was woolly. In any event, the political factor must have loomed larger in Soviet eyes after 10 August, when proposals for revising the statutes of the Czechoslovak Communist Party were published, condoning what in orthodox eyes was the crime of fractionalism: the right of the minority to state its views in public after a majority decision had been passed. Other visitors to Czechoslovakia during August included Presidents Tito and Ceausescu, Janos Kadar, and Ulbricht. The popular welcome given to the two presidents must have infuriated the Russians; Kadar, anxious for the future of his own economic reform, may well have advised Dubcek to slacken the pace; Ulbricht can only have reported in black. Throughout the summer the Soviet leaders were under pressure from Ulbricht and Gomulka, the second of whom feared the effect on his own regime (weakened by disorders that had taken place in Poland in March) if the Dubcek experiment succeeded. It was also widely believed that the Soviet leaders, particularly Piotr Shelest, then First Secretary of the Ukrainian Communist Party, were anxious lest the Czechoslovak liberal infection should cross the border into the Ukraine. Thus, the Russians were influenced by a domino theory in Eastern Europe similar to the one that obsessed American thinking on South-East Asia.

Was it the political or the military factor that in the end prevailed within the Soviet Politburo? Bismarck is reputed to have said that the master of Bohemia is the master of Europe. At the time of Dubcek's visit to Moscow in May, *Le Monde* published a report (later denied), according to which the Soviet Army was ready to answer appeals from faithful Czechoslovak communists for help in safeguarding socialism;[13] and Kovalev's article published in *Pravda* of 26 September alluded to the possibility that NATO troops might approach Soviet borders and that 'the commonwealth of European socialist countries might be dismembered'. (The same article included a warning shot against Yugoslavia, pointing out that non-aligned socialist states owed their national independence to the power of the socialist commonwealth and primarily to that of the Soviet Union.)

In my view, the political factor carried the greater weight. But the question remains why the members of the Soviet Politburo, beset by both political and military anxieties, took so long to make up their minds to take what the official History of Soviet Foreign Policy describes as an extraordinary but essential measure. (The role of the Central Committee seems to have been purely formal: it met on 20 August a few hours before the invasion began.) The delay in deciding on the invasion strongly suggests that there was a division of opinion within the Soviet leadership. No doubt all members of the Politburo must have hoped in the early months of the Dubcek regime that the combined pressure of five of Czechoslovakia's allies would eventually prevail without the need to resort to arms; and some of them may have gone on hoping against hope, as late as August. Those who believed in the *Westpolitik* of the Karlovy Vary meeting must have been prepared to go to considerable lengths to maintain the image of a Soviet Union dedicated to a peaceful Europe. On the other hand, with the Americans embroiled in a presidential electoral campaign as well as in Vietnam, and remembering the Western reaction to events in East Berlin in 1953 and Budapest in 1956, they can hardly have feared a Western response strong enough to outweigh the disadvantages of a Czechoslovakia ruled by reformists. As the summer went by, they could not have failed to note Western signals that any response would in no circumstances be military, but purely political. And politically, they had more reason to be concerned at the effect on the world communist movement, above all on China. It is also conceivable that the Soviet military, whose doctrine 'directs its primary attention towards the preparing of the nation and the armed forces for a world-wide thermonuclear war',[14] did not relish the prospect of the Soviet Army being employed in this uncongenial police role, more especially since the operation turned out to be based on the false premise that pro-Soviet members of the Presidium of the Czechoslovak Communist Party would at once come forward to take over from the leaders whom the invaders had imprisoned. It remains an interesting sidelight on the composition of the invasion force that it included units equipped with tactical nuclear weapons.[15]

The answer to the question why the Soviet leadership hesitated would throw a great deal of light not only on the whole Czechoslovak affair, but on the decision-making process in the Soviet Union and the relationship between the CPSU and the Soviet military. Once the decision to invade Czechoslovakia was taken, what it did demonstrate was both the paramount importance to the Soviet Union of maintaining its glacis in Eastern Europe and the frailty of the Eastern European communist regimes (Bulgaria being perhaps the only exception). As a military operation, the massive invasion of Czechoslovakia was effectively conducted. It is no reflection on the competence of the Soviet military planners to add that it could hardly have been otherwise, given that Warsaw Pact manoeuvres had been continuously in progress either in Czechoslovakia or on its borders since the beginning of June. But it was met with equally massive—though largely non-violent—opposition; Ludvik Svoboda refused to negotiate on the formation of a new government; and it became apparent that the invaders had no plan to cope with this contingency. Worse than that, they failed to gain control of either the mass media (which continued to operate, clandestinely) or the telecommunications network. The Soviet Union was therefore obliged to achieve its aims in Czechoslovakia according to a time-scale of months, instead of hours. This involved first releasing Dubcek, who had been abducted to the Soviet Union, together with other members of the Presidium, and then tolerating his remaining in office as First Secretary until the following April, when he was succeeded by Gustav Husak. But Dubcek had to accept, in October, a treaty sanctioning the stationing of Soviet troops on Czechoslovak territory (which not even Novotny had done), and he had to invalidate the XIVth Congress of the Czechoslovak Communist Party, which had met in a factory soon after the invasion. Slowly under Dubcek, and more effectively under Husak, Czechoslovak political life returned to normal. For his part, Dubcek refused to pronounce a self-criticism, and was stripped successively of his offices, including his short-lived mission to Turkey, and finally of his party membership.

Having done what was required of him (among other things, on 9 September 1969 the Czechoslovak Presidium rescinded its condemnation of the invasion a year before), Husak received the formal Soviet blessing during a visit to Moscow in October. That the Soviet leadership continued to feel uneasy about the intervention and the continuing presence of large Soviet forces in Czechoslovakia—eventually reduced to five divisions—is suggested by the fact that they sought to justify

both by what has come to be known in the West as the Brezhnev
doctrine. This was already implicit in the concluding paragraphs of the
statement published in *Pravda* of 22 August, which declared flatly that
counter-revolution could not be allowed 'to wrest Czechoslovakia from
the family of socialist states', and described the defence of Czechoslovakia as an international socialist duty. It was also anticipated in the
Pravda article of 26 September, which described socialism as indivisible
and declared its defence to be the common cause of all communists.
And although three years later—speaking at a banquet given in his
honour by Tito in Belgrade on 22 September 1971—Brezhnev himself
denied the existence of the 'so-called new doctrine of limited sovereignty',[16] he remains on the record as having told the Vth Polish Party
Congress on 12 November 1968:

> when internal and external forces, hostile to socialism, seek to reverse the
> development of any socialist country whatsoever in the direction of the
> restoration of the capitalist order, when a threat to the cause of socialism
> arises in that country, a threat to the security of the socialist common-
> wealth as a whole—this already becomes not only a problem of the people
> of the country concerned, but also a common problem and the concern of
> all socialist countries.[17]

The long term results of the Czechoslovak people's passive defiance
of the Soviet Union, which threw a glaring light on the poverty of the
Soviet concept of the socialist commonwealth, twenty years after the
Prague *coup d'état*, will be considered later. The immediate effect of the
Soviet intervention was a general outcry of horror. Not all the Soviet
Union's non-communist friends joined in, however. (Cairo radio took
the Soviet side in its broadcasts; so did the Iraqi Government; and Mrs.
Gandhi, though expressing profound concern, blocked a parliamentary
resolution condemning the invasion.) Perhaps the European non-ruling
communist parties suffered most damage: only the Luxembourg and
the Greek Cypriot communist parties supported the Soviet Union.
Both the Romanians and the Yugoslavs publicly condemned the invasion of Czechoslovakia; the following February, when Tito met Ceausescu in Romania, their communiqué emphasized the importance of
respect for the principles of the United Nations charter (an indirect
attack on the Brezhnev doctrine). In March the Romanian Government
adopted regulations making it impermissible for the troops of other
Warsaw Pact countries to enter Romania (a country surrounded on all
sides by Warsaw Pact countries, except for its common frontier with
Yugoslavia) without Romanian consent, no doubt recalling the Warsaw

Pact manoeuvres of the previous June in Czechoslovakia. The Yugoslav leadership, for whom the years 1962–8 had been a period of
rapprochement with the Soviet Union, took the Czechoslovak lesson to
heart. The concept of total national defence was now adopted, whereby
in the event of war units of the regular army would fight in depth along-
side the newly created territorial defence force, transforming the whole
country into a military 'hedgehog' and thus compelling the invader to
fight all the way.[18] For the Chinese the invasion of Czechoslovakia (like
the talks on the Arab-Israeli dispute) was an example of Soviet-American collusion. Much more important, seen from Peking, the Brezhnev
doctrine offered a potential precedent for a Soviet attack on China.

East-West relations were frozen. In the communiqué[19] issued after
their meeting in Brussels four months after the invasion, NATO
foreign ministers continued to denounce both the invasion and the
Brezhnev doctrine. Yet in May 1969 they announced their intention to
explore possibilities for negotiation with the Soviet Union and the other
countries of Eastern Europe.[20] The reason for this, at first sight remarkable, switch was neither Western cynicism nor Eastern cunning.
Rather, both sides were led by a complex of reasons into a new era of
multilateral diplomacy.[21]

NOTES

1. The Council of Mutual Economic Assistance was established in January
   1949, as the Soviet response to the European Recovery Programme. The
   Soviet proposal of 1962 was abandoned and replaced by the concept of
   coordination of long-term planning. Some progress was achieved. In the
   following year *Intermetall*, which began as a programming centre for iron
   and steel planning, was set up in Budapest; the *Druzhba* pipeline began to
   bring Soviet oil to Eastern Europe; and in 1965 COMECON established an
   International Bank of Economic Cooperation and a joint Institute for
   Nuclear Research.
2. *New York Times*, 13 May 1966.
3. See, for example, *Istoriya Vneshnei Politiki SSSR*, vol. 2, pp. 61 ff.
4. Text in *Keesing's Contemporary Archives 1967/8*, p. 21981.
5. Text of communiqué in *Pravda*, 8 July 1966.
6. Compare *Istoriya Vneshnei Politiki SSSR*, vol. 2, p. 352.
7. The Soviet Government continued to be concerned at this prospect long
   after the American proposal for a NATO multilateral nuclear force (MLF),
   first launched in 1963, had been abandoned. Instead, in 1966 the NATO
   nuclear planning and consultative committee was established, which *Pravda*
   of 20 July 1965 described as 'perhaps even more dangerous than the MLF'.
   The NATO MLF nuclear planning proposals may have influenced the Soviet
   reversal of policy over the Non-Proliferation Treaty.

8. Text in *Keesing's Contemporary Archives 1967/8*, p. 22425. The original reason for the French abstention from the MBFR proposal was partly that French forces no longer formed part of the integrated NATO command and partly that the idea of negotiations conducted *de bloc à bloc* was contrary to French policy. As time went by the French Government also became increasingly opposed to any withdrawal of US forces from Europe in principle.

9. The name of the author, I. Aleksandrov, is a pseudonym used for articles cleared at the highest level of the CPSU. The text of *The 2,000 Words* was published in *East Europe*, August 1968, pp. 25–8. Aleksandrov described its authors as both counter-revolutionary and linked with reaction.

10. For the full text, see *Pravda*, 18 July 1968.

11. For the text of the Cierna communiqué, see *Washington Post*, 2 August 1968.

12. For the text of the Bratislava communiqué, see *Pravda*, 4 August 1968.

13. William Hayter, *Russia and the World: a Study of Soviet Foreign Policy*, Secker and Warburg, London, 1970, p. 37.

14. An excerpt from an article entitled 'The political side to Soviet military doctrine' and published in *Kommunist Vooruzhennykh Sil*, no. 22, November 1968: quoted by C. G. Jacobsen in *Soviet Strategy—Soviet Foreign Policy*, Glasgow University Press, 1972, pp. 191 ff.

15. Presumably, as Wolfe suggests (op. cit., p. 474), to serve notice on NATO that the Soviet Army meant business. But if so, on what possible sources of information did the planning staff base their supposition that any such notice was necessary? Perhaps the units formed part of the forces' establishment and it was simplest not to leave them behind.

16. *Keesing's Contemporary Archives 1971/2*, p. 24935.

17. *Pravda*, 13 November 1968.

18. The Soviet-Yugoslav rapprochement, coming after the stresses and strains imposed on Yugoslavia as an ideological pig in the middle during the early years of the Sino-Soviet dispute, was effected at the time of Tito's visit to Moscow in December 1962. For an account of 'hedgehog' defence, see *Survival*, March/April 1973, 'Yugoslav Total National Defence' by A. Ross Johnson, IISS, London, 1973, pp. 54 ff. A further rapprochement began with a visit by Gromyko to Belgrade in September 1969, although relations between the two countries have had their ups and downs since then.

19. *Keesing's Contemporary Archives 1969/70*, p. 23750. It stated that 'the use of force and the stationing in Czechoslovakia of Soviet forces not hitherto deployed there have aroused grave uncertainty about the situation and about the calculations and intentions of the USSR'; this uncertainty demanded 'great vigilance' on the part of the Allies.

20. Ibid., p. 23403.

21. As Nixon described it, in his report to the US Congress of 25 February 1971 on 'US foreign policy for the 1970s'.

PART THREE

The Brezhnev Foreign Policy:
The Years of Negotiation

8

THE TURNING POINT

By the middle of 1968 the momentum of nuclear logic carrying the Soviet Union and the United States towards each other had become so powerful that even the Czechoslovak tragedy could not arrest it for more than a brief interlude. The year 1969 was, both abroad and at home, a turning point for the Soviet Union.

On the eve of the invasion of Czechoslovakia—on 1 July 1968, five years after the signature of the Nuclear Test Ban Treaty—the three signatories of the earlier agreement, banning nuclear tests in the atmosphere, outer space, and under water, finally signed one of the most significant documents of international history since the Second World War: the Treaty on the Non-Proliferation of Nuclear Weapons. Under the terms of this treaty, each signatory possessing nuclear weapons undertook 'not to transfer to any recipient whatsoever nuclear weapons or other nuclear explosive devices or control over such weapons or explosive devices directly, or indirectly; and not in any way to assist, encourage, or induce any non-nuclear-weapon State to manufacture or otherwise acquire nuclear weapons or other nuclear explosive devices, or control over such weapons or explosive devices'. Each signatory not possessing nuclear weapons gave an undertaking complementary to that given by those possessing such weapons; and also undertook to accept certain safeguards designed to prevent diversion of nuclear energy from peaceful uses to nuclear weapons or other nuclear explosive devices. The treaty committed all parties to it 'to pursue negotiations in good faith on effective measures relating to cessation of the nuclear arms race at an early date and to nuclear disarmament, and on a treaty on general and complete disarmament, under strict and effective

international control'. The treaty included a clause whereby it would not
enter into force until forty-three signatories, including Great Britain,
the Soviet Union, and the United States, had desposited their instruments of ratification (a point which was not reached until nearly two
years later). A further clause laid down that five years after the treaty's
entry into force the parties to the treaty would hold a conference in
Geneva, in order to review its operation and to ensure that its purposes
were being realized.[1]

Like its forerunner, this treaty was initially trilateral, in the sense that
all three capitals—London, Moscow, and Washington—were designated
for the depositing of instruments of ratification. But the second agreement was far more Soviet-American* than the first, because the protracted negotiations that led up to its signature were conducted in the
forum of the Geneva Disarmament Conference, whose co-Chairmen
were the Soviet Union and the United States, and because one of the
conditions enabling other, non-nuclear, governments to accede to the
non-proliferation treaty was in effect a joint guarantee offered them by
the Soviet and the US governments. This guarantee took the form of
Security Council Resolution No. 255, under the terms of which the
Governments of Britain, the United States, and the USSR declared on
17 June 1968 that aggression with nuclear weapons, or the threat of
such aggression, against a non-nuclear-weapon state 'would create a
qualitatively new situation in which the nuclear-weapon states which
are Permanent Members of the United Nations Security Council would
have to act immediately through the Security Council to take the
measures necessary to counter such aggression or to remove the threat
of aggression. . . .' They also affirmed their intention, in such a contingency, to 'seek immediate Security Council action' to assist any non-
nuclear-weapon signatory 'that is a victim of an act of aggression or an
object of a threat of aggression in which nuclear weapons are used.'

Eighteen months before this second major nuclear treaty was signed,
President Johnson had proposed that the governments of the United
States and the Soviet Union should engage in what became known as

---

* The agreement was trilateral because France and China remained aloof, for
the same reasons as in 1963. For the extent to which it was seen as bilateral in
Washington as early as 1965, see William C. Foster (then Head of the State
Department Disarmament Agency), 'New Directions in Arms Control and Disarmament', *Foreign Affairs*, 43, 1965, in which he suggested that a non-proliferation treaty would be worthwhile even if it meant some 'erosion of alliances
resulting from the high degree of US-Soviet cooperation which will be required
if a non-proliferation programme is to be successful'.

SALT—Strategic Arms Limitation Treaty—talks. There must have been divisions of opinion in Moscow about the wisdom of accepting this potentially far-reaching proposal, for it was not until June 1968 that the Soviet Foreign Minister formally did so, shortly before signing the Nuclear Non-Proliferation Treaty. One of the factors that no doubt weighed heavily in the Kremlin scales was the need to have rough numerical strategic parity at least in sight before accepting even the principle of such a negotiation. By 1969 the Soviet Union had at last achieved this goal. Although the United States remained well ahead in numbers of ballistic missile-launching submarines and strategic bombers, the Soviet Union had overtaken the United States in inter-continental ballistic missiles. The estimates of Soviet strengths for the end of the year were: 1,200 land-based ICBMs (including 270 massive SS-9s, with a yield of 20–25 megatons) against the United States' 1,054; 230 submarine-launched ballistic missiles against the United States' 656; and 150 strategic bombers against the United States' 540. The Soviet Union also had 67 anti-ballistic missile launchers round Moscow, while the United States had not so far deployed any.[2] On 20 January 1969—the day of Richard Nixon's inauguration as President of the United States—the Soviet Ministry of Foreign Affairs convened a special press conference in order to declare Soviet readiness to begin a serious exchange of views with the United States on the 'mutual limitation and subsequent reduction of strategic nuclear delivery vehicles, including defensive systems'. A week later Nixon referred in his first press conference to the doctrine of strategic sufficiency, thus in effect renouncing the American claim to strategic superiority over the Soviet Union; and he said that he was in favour of SALT.

By the time the delegations of the two super-powers finally began the SALT talks in Helsinki in November 1969, it was no longer simply a question of recognizing the fact that both sides now possessed a vast capacity of overkill. (In the course of his evidence given to the United States Senate Foreign Affairs Committee in 1969,[3] Melvin Laird, then Defence Secretary, estimated that 200 nuclear warheads of one megaton each would be enough to destroy 55 per cent of the American population and that it would take 1,200 equivalent American warheads to destroy 45 per cent of the more scattered Soviet population.) 'Lead-time' made it essential to plan as much as ten years ahead. Looking towards the end of the 1970s, both super-powers were aware that three technological developments in the strategic nuclear field threatened to make it just conceivable that a first-strike attack by one of the two powers might be successful—a perilously destabilizing factor—and to involve them in a further spiral of expenditure on strategic weapons. These developments were: first, new and more precise guidance systems, capable of increasing missile accuracy (down to a distance of 30 metres from the target), which is more important than yield in destroying land-based ICBMs; second, multiple re-entry warhead systems and—more important still—multiple, independently targetable re-entry vehicles (MIRV), each warhead being programmed for its specific target; and finally, anti-ballistic missile systems. On 14 March Nixon announced his decision to go ahead with the *Safeguard* anti-ballistic missile system, a decision which was confirmed in the Senate by a narrow vote in August. The SALT talks, which lasted until 23 December, were only preparatory. Nevertheless, they marked the opening of the first formally bilateral strategic negotiation between the two super-powers, each of whom had China's future potential in mind. As the Soviet Foreign Minister put it, in his report to the Supreme Soviet in July 1969, 'in questions of the maintenance of peace, the USSR and the USA can find a common language'.[4] Of a different order of importance, but none the less a sign of the times, was the Soviet-American agreement, in October, on a draft treaty banning the emplacement on the sea-bed of nuclear weapons, other weapons of mass destruction, or installations for the storing, testing, or using of such weapons.

By the end of this year the Soviet leadership must have had a further consideration in mind: in July the first American troops were withdrawn from Vietnam.* In November Nixon's broadcast about 'Vietnamization' made it clear that sooner or later, and if possible before the next presidential elections, he intended to pull out of Vietnam altogether. This was in line with the so-called Guam doctrine of stimulated self-help.[5] With the end of the United States' involvement in Indo-China at last in sight, and with no foreseeable conclusion to the Sino-Soviet dispute (which had erupted into armed conflict in March), it had become a major Soviet interest not only to engage the Americans in a direct dialogue but also to seek to bring about a European settlement. Here fate intervened: after the West German elections in October the Christian Democrats found themselves in opposition for the first time. Brandt became Federal Chancellor, depending for his majority in the Bundestag on his party's new alliance with the Free Democratic Party Liberals, whose leader, Walter Scheel, became Foreign Minister. On 28 October, in his inaugural speech, the Chancellor announced his

* Twelve days before the first American astronauts landed on the moon.

concept of two German states within one nation; a month later the Federal German Republic signed the Non-Proliferation Treaty; and on 8 December Soviet-German talks began in Moscow. In parallel, on 16 December the three Allied Powers renewed their proposal, first made to the Soviet Government in August, for talks on Berlin.

Meanwhile, the Warsaw Pact Political Consultative Committee had relaunched their proposal for an all-European conference at its meeting in Budapest in March, and seven months later in Prague they put forward two questions for the agenda: 'European security and the renunciation of the use of force or threats of force in relations between European states', and the expansion of 'trade, economic and scientific and technical ties'.[6] In May the Finnish Government had suggested Helsinki as the site of the conference, an offer which all the Warsaw Pact countries accepted. Finally, at Brussels in December 1969, NATO ministers made their first positive response to the prolonged barrage from Eastern Europe. It was guarded, mentioning careful advance preparation, prospects of concrete results, and the need for an assurance that such a meeting would not serve to ratify the existing division of Europe, and making it clear that progress in Soviet-German negotiations and in the Berlin negotiations would influence their future attitude to the proposal for a European Conference, 'in which, of course, the North American members of the alliance would participate'.[7]

These, then, were the beginnings—between the two super-powers, between the Soviet Union and West Germany, and between the two alliances—of the years of negotiation. Paradoxically, although the Soviet leadership entered this new era basking in American acknowledgement that their country had become a co-equal super-power, and confident that, at least for the time being, the Soviet presence in Eastern Europe had been made secure, they simultaneously faced a dilemma at home.

The change in the Soviet Union's international status was evident to any visitor to Moscow at the time. It was a city that had visibly arrived. In the year of Stalin's death, if the visitor could for a moment blot out from his mind both the dazzling cluster of monuments that form the Kremlin and the grotesque Stalinist skyscrapers, the greater part of Moscow looked like a provincial town, resembling a capital city far less than Leningrad, which still retained its elegance half a century after the transfer of the seat of government to Moscow. The boulevards were by Western standards almost empty of traffic; and what perhaps struck the visitor most of all was the queues of poorly-dressed Muscovites patiently waiting outside the shops. By contrast, the Moscow of 1970 was a bustling city. Still shabby and ill-lit at night—this, together with the large number of men walking about in uniform, recalled London towards the end of the Second World War—but none the less a great capital, it now accommodated the diplomatic missions of close on a hundred countries, compared with the handful represented in Moscow seventeen years earlier. (Most of the staff of these embassies lived in a diplomatic ghetto, their working hours spent in seeking Soviet attention and Soviet information, and their leisure in fulfilling the obligations of a social round whose formal character seemed to be accentuated, as through osmosis, by the hierarchical structure of the society by which they were surrounded.) An occasion which typified Moscow's transformation was the reopening of the magnificent Hall of St. George, the largest room in the Kremlin, its white walls decorated in gold with the names of Tsarist regiments and knights of the Order of St. George, the highest military distinction in Tsarist Russia. This gleaming chamber provided the setting for the first lavish evening reception offered by the Soviet leadership for several years, to which all ambassadors were invited, in honour of the visit paid to Moscow by Svoboda and Husak in October 1969.

By 1970 the Khrushchevian concept of the taxi had yielded to that of the private car; there were now a million on Soviet roads, with the factory built by Fiat[8] due to produce 660,000 private cars annually after its completion. The suburbs of the city now consisted of mile after mile of new blocks of flats, housing a population that had almost doubled in two decades. In the Arbat, the old quarter in the centre of the city, there were new buildings which would not look out of place in a Western capital. This new construction had already alarmed Soviet conservationists; still more dignified old buildings were threatened by future plans. Nevertheless, large sums were being spent on restoring old monuments, both secular and religious, in Moscow, as elsewhere in the Soviet Union. The city teemed with tourists, Soviet and foreign. True, there were still queues to be seen, but the woollen shawls, quilted jackets and felt boots of earlier years had almost disappeared. In short, the people of Moscow had 'never had it so good'. This was the centenary of Lenin's birth; and Moscow, even if no longer acknowledged by all Marxists as the Third Rome, had by universal consent become the centre of one of the world's two super-powers.

If this had been all that five years of power had given the Soviet leaders who succeeded Khrushchev, they would have had reason to congratulate themselves. The very fact that they felt able to enter into major negotiations proved the new confidence that they felt in themselves and in the immense military power that they had built up since October 1964. But this was not the whole story.

NOTES

1. Text in Command Paper 3683, HMSO, London, June 1968, reprinted 1969, which also contains the text of the security assurances given by the three nuclear powers which signed the treaty.
2. *Strategic Survey 1969*, IISS, London, 1969. One megaton = 1,000,000 tons of TNT, in terms of the yield of a nuclear explosion. For the fortuitous origin of the megaton, see York, op. cit., pp. 89–90.
3. *Keesing's Contemporary Archives, 1969/70*, p. 23291.
4. Quoted in *Istoriya Vneshnei Politiki SSSR*, vol. 2, p. 452.
5. This was more of an off-the-cuff statement than the exposition of a new doctrine, but none the less important for that. The difference between American global policy at the beginning and end of the decade can be seen by comparing the statement, in Kennedy's inaugural message, that the United States would help anyone, with Nixon's reformulation, that the United States would help anyone who would help themselves.
6. *Pravda*, 18 March and 1 November 1969.
7. *Keesing's Contemporary Archives 1969/70*, p. 23750.
8. This major contract was concluded by Fiat after Gromyko's visit to Italy in 1966, when he also became the first Soviet Foreign Minister to be received in audience by the Pope.

9

THE STATE OF THE UNION

The dilemma faced by the Soviet leadership, at the very moment when they should have been able to enjoy the fruit of their labours in the field of foreign relations, was both economic and political. It has been analysed in depth in *Kniga o sotsialisticheskoi democratii* by Roy Medvedev.[1] For him, as for Andrei Sakharov, the two sets of problems, in the economic and in the political field, are interdependent. Sakharov's book *Progress, Coexistence and Intellectual Freedom* includes this passage:

We are now catching up with the United States only in some of the old, traditional industries, which are no longer as important as they used to be for the United States (for example, coal and steel). In some of the newer fields, for example, automation, computers, petro-chemicals, and especially in industrial research and development, we are not only lagging behind, but are also growing more slowly. . . .[2]

Coming half a century after the October Revolution and seven years after Khrushchev's boast at the XXIInd Party Congress, this was a devastating indictment, even though what its author dared to write in 1968 was on the same lines as an article published in the Moscow *Journal of World Economics and International Relations* in January 1973, which listed the chemical industry, automobile construction, several branches of mechanical engineering, computer technology, gas processing, pulp and paper, and a range of branches of light industries among those sectors of modern industry in which Western development had reached a higher technical level. What had gone wrong with the Soviet economy? A great deal, as was reported to the CPSU Central Committee on 15 December 1969, and—in guarded terms—to the Soviet public by *Pravda*[3] a month later; so much so that the XXIVth Party Congress, which should have been held in 1970, and the publication of the new Five-Year Plan were both postponed.

In order to understand why it was that Soviet economic problems came to a head at the end of the 1960s, we must go back to Stalin's decision, forty years earlier, to abandon Lenin's moderate New Economic Policy and to launch the Soviet Union on its race to become a great industrial power, a ruthless transformation largely financed by the Soviet peasantry, whose land was forcibly collectivized in order to provide cheap food for the workers in the swiftly growing cities. This extraordinary feat, directed entirely from Moscow, from which every decision was handed down (*spuskat'*), lasted under Stalin's rule for a quarter of a century, through the purges, the Second World War, and the reconstruction of the country that followed, to be summed up afterwards by a distinguished Polish economist[4] as a *sui generis* war economy —surely one of the greatest understatements in history.

A year after the XXth CPSU Congress, Khrushchev attempted to put new life into the Soviet economy by decentralizing it. In consequence, all but two of the specifically industrial ministries were eliminated, and instead 105 regional economic councils were established (later reduced to 47). In September 1965 his successors abolished these councils and restored the ministries in Moscow, but with a difference— the Economic Reform.[5] The new Soviet leadership took a whole year to decide the terms of this reform, whose execution Kosygin described to the Central Committee as unthinkable without significant worker participation in management. In the event the scope of the reform was modest; its success was limited; and a most important measure—the formation of regional or all-union corporations, operating on the basis of autonomous profit-making—was not finally approved until April 1973.[6] By the end of the Five-Year Plan, not only had the notoriously inefficient and wasteful Soviet system of agriculture achieved a far smaller increase in production than had been hoped, because it had been starved of the capital investments and the quantity of machinery laid down in the plan (as Brezhnev reported to the Central Committee in July 1970), but many key Soviet industrial products had failed to achieve their planned targets, even though the industrial output plan as a whole was fulfilled.[7]

How was it that Soviet industry could produce hundreds of SS-9 intercontinental ballistic missiles and put the *lunakhod* vehicle on the moon, and yet find it difficult to cover the Soviet Union with a chain of

modern hotels (as was done in the space of a few years in the impover-
ished Italian *Mezzogiorno*)? In its article reporting the Central Committee meeting of December 1969, *Pravda* admitted that the key
problem was an increase in productivity; the quantitative approach to
the Soviet economy was no longer good enough; new methods and new
decisions were required. This was true. But there were many other
things that *Pravda* did not, or could not, say. Among these, six may be
singled out. The first is the growing technological gap between East
and West, which Sakharov described in the passage quoted above, and
which was to be publicly admitted later within the Soviet Union. The
second is the managerial gap. The reasons for both these gaps are
complex. They became evident at a time when the pace of change in
industrial and in management techniques in the West was so great that
it amounted to a second Industrial Revolution. One of the essentials of
the technological revolution—the ability of an industrial society to
diffuse new technology swiftly through all sectors of its economy—is
discouraged by the very nature of the Soviet system, partly for reasons of
security. As for management, to the sheer size of the Moscow bureaucracy must be added what has been described by a Soviet critic as the
greatest single obstacle: the absence not only in the political system, but
also in the economy, of an effective mechanism for renewing management.[8] Third, in a non-market economy, a qualitative as opposed to a
quantitative approach depends on its planners' ability to identify
success indicators that will encourage a prompt response to demand:
this is something that Soviet planners have found hard, even though the
economic reform of 1965 modified the cult of gross output—the
essence of Stalinist economics.[9] Fourth, the Soviet economy no longer
has at its disposal the reserves of labour which—through a concentration of effort on key sectors of the economy—helped it to win its
greatest successes in the past. (In the construction industry in September 1972, Kosygin revealed that the volume of investments immobilized
in uncompleted projects had almost trebled in four years, to reach a
total of 61·4 billion roubles.)[10] Fifth, the aspirations of the Soviet
consumer are at last beginning to make themselves felt: for example, the
meat shortage—the consequence of the deficiencies of Soviet livestock
production—could in 1970 no longer be ignored. Finally, whatever the
statistical doubts mentioned in an earlier chapter, it must be concluded
that at least part—perhaps a major part—of the strain imposed on the
entire Soviet economy by the end of the 1960s was caused by the over-
commitment of resources to its defence sector.

At the same time there was a profound political malaise in the Soviet Union. Just when their country's military power had grown to a size which—for example—enabled them to carry out the military intervention in Egypt in 1970, the Soviet leaders seemed to see themselves as the embattled defenders of Marxist-Leninist orthodoxy in the Kremlin, assailed alike by any new idea put forward within the boundaries of the Soviet Union, by the schismatic Chinese, by the reformist Czechoslovaks, and by the New Left in the West. The Soviet Communist Party showed no sign whatsoever of sympathy with the perpetrators of the Parisian *chie-en-lit*[11] of 1968. Marcuse was described as an ideologist of *petit-bourgeois* rebels and an old fool. At first sight it may seem strange to find the General-Secretary of the CPSU devoting a whole paragraph of his report at the XXIVth Party Congress to an attack on a group of Marxist 'renegades' so disparate as Roger Garaudy, Ernst Fischer, the Italian 'Manifesto Group', and Teodoro Petkoff (formerly a member of the Venezuelan Communist Party), until one recalls that the heretic appears to the faithful to pose a greater threat than the infidel.[12] As if to break the monotony, the Soviet leadership decided to make a major event of Lenin's centenary year. Few of the thousands of words written and spoken about this extraordinary man in 1970 would have given him pleasure—certainly not *Pravda*'s misquotation of a passage from one of his works, which did not escape Chinese ridicule.

New ideas within the Soviet Union covered a wide spectrum. The connecting link was the conviction that scientific and industrial progress was inseparable from intellectual freedom. Sakharov emerged as the leader and co-founder of the first, unofficial, civil rights movement[13] in the Soviet Union. A group was formed of individuals resolved to see that the rights conferred on the citizen by the Soviet Constitution were observed to the letter. What these dissidents regarded as illegal acts began to be publicized in 1968 in the *Samizdat* news-sheet *Khronika Tekushchych Sobytii*—passed from hand to hand (like Akhmatova's lyric poems during the war)—and from 1970 in the *Ukrainian Herald*. Copies of these news-sheets regularly reached the West. This movement[14] arose in protest against constraints which have been interpreted by some observers as neo-Stalinism. If by neo-Stalinism is meant the arrest of liberalizing tendencies, coupled with the fact that, since his total eclipse under Khrushchev, Stalin has been partly rehabilitated in official statements (he is now depicted as a wise and benign leader in Soviet war films), there is no need to quarrel with this assessment. But there can be no question of a return to historical Stalinism, if for no other reason than that this involved the physical destruction of the CPSU, including most of the senior members of the Soviet officer corps.* Under the collective leadership, the literary freedom allowed under Khrushchev had been steadily eroded. True, Tvardovsky did what he could, so long as he was editor, to defend the literary journal *Novyi Mir* as a bastion of liberalism. Dimitri Shostakovich was allowed to compose as he wished: the performances of his tragic Fourteenth Symphony cannot have pleased the censors. And, after several years' delay, Moscow audiences were allowed to see Andrei Tarkovsky's politically ambivalent and intensely religious film *Andrei Rublev*. But what the regime found intolerable was the growing habit of publication in the West of works[15] banned in the Soviet Union. Thus, in February 1966 Andrei Sinyavsky and Yuli Daniel were sentenced to seven and five years' forced labour respectively for having published abroad, under pseudonyms, allegedly anti-Soviet writings; two years later Alexander Ginsberg and three others were convicted on charges based, *inter alia*, on their having compiled a White Book on the Sinyavsky-Daniel case; and in 1969 Solzhenitsyn, the heir to the great tradition of the Russian novel, all but one of whose major works have been published abroad, was expelled from the Writers' Union. In the same year Piotr Grigorenko, a dissident General who had espoused the cause of the Crimean Tartars (deported from their homes during the war by Stalin's order), was committed to a mental home—a way of dealing with political opposition which has since been repeated with other dissidents.[16]

The Soviet leadership could not accept the link between the solution of their country's economic problems and that of its political problems, in the sense advocated by men like Sakharov and Medvedev. To have done so would have led them down the path of pluralism, which the Czechoslovak reformers had followed and to which they themselves were adamantly opposed. But they were seized of the necessity to seek to meet the needs of the Soviet consumer and to close the economic gaps between East and West—technological and managerial. Their solution was a compromise: at home, an intensification of ideological discipline; abroad, an intimate economic cooperation with the Soviet Union's cold war adversary, the United States, and with its former enemies, Germany and Japan, which would, they hoped, make ultim-

---

* 'History never repeats itself—historians repeat themselves.' But if any analogy is to be drawn, the atmosphere of the reign of Tsar Alexander III (1881–94) offers a closer parallel than that of the Great Terror. For the important distinction between neo-Stalinists and moderate conservatives in the CPSU, see Medvedev, op. cit., pp. 55 ff.

ately possible the development of the vast resources of Siberia, such as the Tyumen' oil-field and the copper deposits of Udokan. A start in the direction of economic cooperation had already been made by one of the most forward-looking departments of the Soviet bureaucracy, the State Committee for Science and Technology, a new agency established under the collective leadership. It was this committee which was primarily interested in the conclusion of inter-governmental agreements for the exchange of scientific and technological know-how (a word now transliterated into cyrillics to form part of the Soviet vocabulary). The French Government led the way in 1965, followed by the Italian Government in 1966, and the British Government in 1970; by then Britain, France, and Italy all had considerable numbers of men helping to establish industrial plants in the Soviet Union, the biggest of which was the giant Fiat factory already mentioned. But at a time when Western firms were not yet allowed to open permanent offices for their representatives in Moscow, this was only a beginning.

The compromise solution was presented to the XXIVth Congress of the CPSU on 30 March 1971, by which time the Soviet leadership was also influenced by the events leading to the fall of Gomulka three months earlier (discussed in Chapter 10). The supreme aim of the Party's economic policy was described to this Congress as the raising of the Soviet standard of living, the planned increase in real income per head of the population being almost one third. For the first time priority for consumer goods was written into the Five-Year Plan, although this did not mean that concern for heavy industry was being slackened (the planned increase was 42–46 per cent). Kosygin made it clear that 80–85 per cent of the entire planned increase in material income during the period of the plan would have to be derived from increased productivity. And Brezhnev added two interesting footnotes: the first at the Congress, when he stated that 42 per cent of the defence industry's output was used for civilian purposes, and the second in the course of an electoral speech delivered in a Moscow constituency on 11 June, when he said that socialism was powerful enough to secure both reliable defence and the development of the economy, although the Soviet economy would have advanced much more quickly, had it not been for large defence expenditures.[17]

In the field of foreign policy, the basic tasks were reiterated in Brezhnev's report to the Congress, when he spoke of 'the great alliance of the three basic revolutionary forces of our day—socialism, the international workers' movement, and the peoples' national-liberation struggle'.[18] As is expected of a communist party leader on such an occasion, he described the general crisis of capitalism as deepening (accurately, in the event, since the dollar crisis finally erupted the following August). The conduct of affairs with the United States was, he said, complicated by the 'frequent zigzags of American foreign policy', which he attributed to internal political manoeuvres. Nevertheless, he left the door ajar. Soviet policy towards the United States was based on the premise that an improvement in relations between the two countries was possible: 'our line of principle in our relations with capitalist countries, including the USA, is consistently and fully to realize in practice the principles of peaceful coexistence. . . .'

About China Brezhnev pulled no punches. The CCP's ideological-political platform on the fundamental questions of international relations and the world communist movement was condemned as incompatible with Leninism. The talks about frontier questions were going slowly; if they were to be concluded successfully, a constructive attitude was required from both sides. The Chinese slanderous inventions about Soviet policy, instilled into the Chinese people from Peking, were rejected absolutely. Nevertheless, the CPSU and the Soviet Government were profoundly convinced that an improvement in relations between the Soviet Union and the Chinese People's Republic would correspond to the long-term interests of both countries; they were therefore ready to cooperate across the board not only in order to normalize relations, but also to restore good-neighbourliness and friendship; and they were certain that in the final reckoning this would be attained.

A last word had to be said about Czechoslovakia. The network of Soviet bilateral treaties with its Eastern European allies, taken together with the latter's treaties with each other, was described by Brezhnev as a comprehensive system of mutual commitments of a new, socialist type. Czechoslovakia had received international assistance in defending socialism against the forces of imperialism and counter-revolution in the exceptional circumstances of 1968, for reasons of 'class duty, loyalty to socialist internationalism, concern for the interests of our states and for the fate of socialism and peace in Europe'.

International communist attendance at the Congress must have satisfied the CPSU. Most Asian communist parties were represented; the North Vietnamese delegation repeated their 1966 practice of stopping in Peking on the way to Moscow, but they praised the CPSU, with only a passing reference to China. This time the Cuban delegate,

President Dorticòs, described his country's friendship with the Soviet Union as indestructible and he thanked the Soviet Government for its aid to Cuba.

The policy approved by the XXIVth Congress was presented by the leadership to the Soviet people and to the world as a Programme of Peace. True, the Soviet Government had, in August 1970, concluded its negotiations with the Federal German Government by signing the Moscow Treaty. But there was nothing essentially new in the programme; and it was not until 1972-3 that Soviet foreign policy underwent changes that proved to be as important as those of 1956. It is arguable that these changes would have taken place in any case. But they were, at the very least, greatly accelerated when, a few weeks after the Congress had ended, the Soviet leadership suddenly found themselves outflanked by the Metternichian diplomacy of Henry Kissinger.

The language of international relations is the poorer for its wealth of dead metaphors: bombshell, landmark, watershed. None of these is strong enough to describe the effect[19] of the announcement on 15 July 1971, that the United States President intended to accept an invitation from Mao Tse-tung to visit Peking the following year, with the object of restoring normal relations between the United States and China. This decision, secretly prepared by Kissinger during a 49-hour visit to Peking, which he reached from Pakistan, paved the way for the lifting of the ostracism imposed on the People's Republic of China by the United States for a quarter of a century, and for China's assumption of its seat in the UN Security Council. It was particularly dangerous for the Soviet Union, for which the worst of all possible worlds would be a nuclear China and a unified Western Europe—the Chinese make no secret of their wish to see Western Europe unite against the Soviet Union—backed by the United States, in alliance with Japan. The Soviet leadership lost little time in making the best of a bad job. In October of the same year, they invited Nixon to Moscow: the first visit ever paid to the Soviet Union by a US President.

NOTES

1. *Kniga o sotsialisticheskoi democratii*, Alexander Herzen Foundation, Amsterdam/Paris, 1972.
2. Circulated first in *Samizdat*; and the translation was published in London, in 1969, by Penguin Books; see p. 66.
3. *Pravda*, 13 January 1970. As late as July Brezhnev said that the Party Congress would be held during 1970.

4. Oscar Lange, who used this description in a lecture given in 1957 in Belgrade, quoted in Alec Nove, *The Soviet Economy*, George Allen and Unwin, London, 1968, p. 162. The closest quotation in Lange's collected works is in an article entitled *O niektorych zagadnieniach polskiej drogi do socjalizmu* (1957), reprinted in vol. 2 of his collected works, *Socjalizm*, Warsaw, 1973, p. 499.

5. The most important measures introduced in 1965 were some devolution of planning and decision-making to enterprise level and changes in the success criteria of enterprises, followed in 1967 by a revision of prices. Much has been written on this subject: see, for example, Medvedev, op. cit., pp. 287 ff., and Nove, op. cit., ch. 9.

6. *Pravda*, 3 April 1973. *Pravda* of 19 June foresaw the formation of transnational corporations.

7. Brezhnev, op. cit., vol. 3, p. 66. See ibid., pp. 62–9 for a strongly worded exposition of the shortcomings of Soviet agriculture. Cf. Nove, *The Soviet Economy*, p. 335. For an analysis of the 1965–70 Plan, see Nove, *The Soviet Five Year Plan*, Hong Kong Economic Papers, no. 6, 1971.

8. Medvedev, op. cit., p. 302.

9. The cult of the gross output, *kul't vala*, is a quotation from D. Kondrashev, *Tsenoobrazovanie v promyshlennosti*, Moscow, 1956, p. 32. The translation of *pokazatel'* as 'success indicator' is Nove's: see *The Soviet Economy*, *passim*.

10. Quoted by Alain Jacob in *Le Monde*, 15 February 1974: an example of the defect known by Soviet economists as *raspylenie sredstv*.

11. De Gaulle's own description of the students' revolt of May 1968.

12. For this attack, see Brezhnev, op. cit., p. 215. The description of Marcuse is in B. Bykhovskii's article *Filosofia mel'koburzhuaznogo buntarstva*, *Kommunist*, no. 8, 1969, pp. 114–24.

13. In November 1970. The text of the declaration of the programme of the *Committee for the Rights of Man* is given in Medvedev, op. cit., p. 91.

14. This movement has in effect performed the same gadfly function for Soviet society as the emigré intellectuals did for nineteenth-century Russia. For a description of how *Samizdat* (literally, 'self-publishing house') works, see Julius Taleshin's article in *Encounter*, February 1973.

15. An extreme case was *Can the Soviet Union Survive until 1984?* by Andrei Amal'ryk, Harper and Row, New York; Allen Lane, London, 1970.

16. Grigorenko was not released until 1974, despite the publicity given to his case in the West. A reply from a group of Soviet psychiatrists to Western criticism of this method of treatment was sent to the *Guardian*, which published their letter on 29 September 1973.

17. Brezhnev, op. cit., vol. 3, p. 390. All subsequent quotations from, and references to, this speech will be taken from this source.

18. Ibid., pp. 195–6.

19. The announcement came as an especially rude shock for the Japanese, who were not consulted in advance and took even longer than the Russians to absorb it; they had to adjust themselves not only to the US-Chinese rapprochement, but also to American economic demands. There had indeed been signs that the US and Chinese governments were moving towards a new relationship (such as the resumption of the US-Chinese talks at ambassadorial level in Warsaw, in December 1969, and the ping-pong diplomacy earlier in 1971), but the secret was well kept until 15 July 1971.

10

THE YEAR 1970

Europe

So far the evolution of Soviet foreign policy has been treated thematically, each chapter covering a span of several years. The next five chapters will seek to record, baldly, and with the minimum of comment, the conduct of Soviet foreign policy during the period 1970–3 (up to the end of October 1973), in roughly chronological order. This method may make the swift unfolding of events during these four years harder for the reader to follow, but it reproduces the kaleidoscopic effect that they presented to the leadership in the Kremlin as they occurred. My own assessment will be largely reserved for Part Four of this book.

In Europe, the critical date—from which everything that has followed in Europe stems—was 12 August 1970. Exactly thirty-one years to the day after the signature of the Soviet-Nazi Non-Aggression Pact,[1] the Soviet Union and the Federal Republic of Germany concluded the Treaty of Moscow. The preamble and the five articles that make up this brief document[2] formed the basis of what today amounts to a *de facto* European peace settlement. It was welcomed by most Europeans, Western as well as Eastern, although in the Federal Republic the Opposition remained unconvinced of the wisdom of the whole concept of Brandt's *Ostpolitik* and therefore opposed the treaty with all the means at their disposal. (The Bundestag did not ratify it until nearly two years later.)

At first reading, this treaty may appear to be no more than the mutual renunciation of force and the recognition of existing frontiers in Europe, including those between the two Germanies and the western frontiers of Poland. Indeed, on his return to Bonn after signing the treaty, the

Federal Chancellor claimed in a televised statement that with this treaty nothing had been lost which had not been gambled away long before. This remark, however, referred to the German loss of what are known as the Western Territories of Poland; a loss rendered virtually irrevocable by the fourth paragraph of Article 3 of the treaty, under whose terms the German signatories 'regard' the Oder-Neisse line as 'inviolable now and in the future'. But the wording of the treaty is subtle. At least in the Federal Government's view, the specific reference in the preamble to the Adenauer-Bulganin Agreement of 1956 and the implied reference in Article 4 to the Paris Agreements of 1954, coupled with the opening words of Article 3, provided sufficient legal backing to preserve the right of the ultimate reunification of Germany in the text of the treaty, in spite of the commitment to regard the frontier between the two German Republics as inviolable. And to make doubly sure, Scheel simultaneously wrote a letter to Gromyko, published five days later, stating that the treaty did not stand in contradiction to the political aim of the Federal German Republic; this remained a peaceful European settlement in which the German people would regain its unity through self-determination.

The Federal German side made it clear to the Soviet side that their ratification of the treaty was conditional on a satisfactory conclusion of the Four-Power talks on Berlin, which had opened in March, and that the question of Allied rights and responsibilities with regard to Germany as a whole and to Berlin was not affected by the treaty. This second statement—together with Gromyko's oral acknowledgement of it—was recorded in an exchange of notes between the Government of the Federal Republic and the British, French, and US governments. The treaty was also regarded by both sides as part of a package of other related agreements, the first of which was the Treaty of Warsaw,[3] signed between the Federal Republic and Poland in December. And both sides saw it as the prelude to a large expansion of trade; in the preceding February the two governments had already concluded an agreement whereby West Germany was to supply the Soviet Union with large-diameter pipe in return for future delivery, by pipeline, of large quantities of natural gas.

The Moscow Treaty was the cornerstone of Brandt's *Ostpolitik*. For the Russians it was a radical turning point not only in their relationship with the Federal German Republic, but also in the post-war history of Europe.[4] Two years after accusing the Czechoslovaks of yielding to the blandishments of German revanchists, why did the Soviet Union itself enter a close bilateral relationship with the Federal Republic—and this (suspected at the time and evident in April 1971, when Ulbricht was succeeded by Erich Honecker) in the teeth of the opposition of the redoubtable East German communist leader, one of the few survivors of the old guard who had known both Lenin and Stalin personally? It is significant that two meetings of the Warsaw Pact Political Consultative Committee were held, one in Moscow a week after the signature of the Moscow Treaty and the other in Berlin on 2 December, both of which set the seal of all the Eastern European governments' approval on the treaty. The turn of the decade may have seemed to the Soviet leadership to have constituted one of Hegel's unique moments in history: Brandt's electoral victory in 1969; his government's signature of the Nuclear Non-Proliferation Treaty;[5] and Soviet recognition of their country's urgent need of German capital and technology. A rapprochement with the West Germans may well have been considered a different matter in the Kremlin provided that it was made clear to the world that the way to it lay through Moscow, not through the capitals of the Soviet Union's Eastern European allies. And it was not at all untypical of Soviet diplomacy that the news of the rapprochement was broken to the Soviet public with little advance preparation, nearly eight months after talks had begun in Moscow with the Federal Chancellor's personal representative, Egon Bahr, and three years after the beginning of the earlier round of talks between the two governments. Yet the fact remains that it was one of the most dramatic changes in post-war history, which cannot have been decided on by the Soviet leadership without much debate. Even now it is still too early to answer the Leninist question *kto kogo*?* The nearest historical parallel is the seventeenth-century Treaty of Westphalia; and it is to be hoped that the compromise enshrined in the Moscow Treaty of 1970 will be found by later historians to mark the beginning of the end of the twentieth-century European civil wars.

The Soviet Government succeeded in forming this new relationship with Bonn without disturbing the relationship with Paris that had developed steadily since de Gaulle's visit to Moscow in 1966. Indeed, in

---

* The question can roughly be translated as 'who is top dog?' Brezhnev's own answer, given in the course of a speech delivered to the Central Committee of the Azerbaijan Communist Party and the Azerbaijan Republic Supreme Soviet on 2 October 1970, was 'everyone won equally': Brezhnev, op. cit., vol. 3, p. 145. Apart from acquiescing in the legal niceties described, the main Soviet concession, which did not become effective until the conclusion of the Quadripartite Agreement on Berlin, related to the question of West Berlin.

October 1970, during a visit paid to the Soviet Union by his successor, Pompidou, the two governments signed a protocol whereby they agreed, should a critical situation arise, to 'enter into contact with each other without delay with the object of agreeing their positions'.[6] Britain, the Soviet Union's major trading partner in the late 1960s, was not included in the new set of bilateral relationships established by the Soviet Union both with its major opponents and with leading countries of the Third World, in spite of the comparatively successful visit paid to the United Kingdom by the Soviet Prime Minister in 1967. The fact that the negotiations following Kosygin's public—and unexpected—proposal of a new Anglo-Soviet friendship treaty during this visit subsequently petered out is hardly relevant. The coolness between Britain and the Soviet Union which lasted off and on from August 1968 until 1973 was due to a range of issues, some of which aroused strong feelings on both sides; one of these was the question of Soviet espionage, which finally erupted in September 1971.

In the summer of 1970 the proposal for a European Conference took what proved to be a decisive step forward, when the two alliances reached the point of exchanging memoranda on a possible agenda. In the communiqué issued after their meeting in Rome in May, the NATO Foreign Ministers suggested that (subject to progress in the talks already being conducted, especially on Germany and Berlin) the subjects to be explored should include: 'the principles which should govern relations between states, including the renunciation of force' and 'the development of international relations with a view to contributing to the freer movement of people, ideas, and information and to developing cooperation in the cultural, economic, technical, and scientific fields as well as in the field of human environment'. In a separate declaration (from which the French abstained, as at Reykjavik) NATO ministers laid down certain principles for their proposed negotiations on mutual balanced force reductions. The NATO proposals, which were communicated to the Warsaw Pact governments by the Italian Government, in its capacity as host at the Rome meeting, met with a rapid response. In a memorandum approved in Budapest on 21–22 June, the Warsaw Pact foreign ministers suggested three questions for the agenda of a very early meeting: 'the safeguarding of European security and renunciation of the use of force or the threat of the use of force in inter-state relations in Europe; expansion on an equal basis of trade, economic, scientific, technical, and cultural ties, directed towards the development of political cooperation between the European states; and creation at the all-European conference of a body for questions of security and cooperation in Europe'. Although they continued to refer to the conference as all-European, they envisaged for the first time participation by the United States and Canada, as well as by both Germanies; and they also made another concession: the 'question of reducing foreign armed forces on the territory of European states ... could be discussed in a body whose creation is proposed at the all-European conference, or in another form acceptable to the interested states'.[7]

These quotations make the difference in the objectives of the two alliances evident. What the NATO countries had in mind was the Brezhnev doctrine and an opening up of Eastern Europe, including the Soviet Union, to Western ideas. The first objective was made still more explicit in the final communiqué of the Brussels ministerial meeting of December 1970, which listed three principles[8] which must in their view be respected as the basis for any genuine and lasting improvement in East-West relations in Europe. They were also well aware of the growing pressure in the US Congress, stemming from Senator Mansfield's resolution, first moved in 1966, for a reduction of the 300,000 American troops deployed in the European theatre.

The Warsaw Pact countries' original objectives in calling for a conference in the sixties are clear enough. They are listed in the History of Soviet Foreign Policy as: first, recognition of frontiers, including the Oder-Neisse line and the frontier between the two Germanies; second, recognition of the German Democratic Republic as a sovereign state; and third, denial of all nuclear armament whatever to the Federal Republic of Germany.[9] Each of these aims had either already been attained, or was on the point of being attained, by the time of the Budapest meeting. Why then did the Soviet Government in particular continue to press for the holding of a European conference, as it did again in Berlin the following December, after both the Moscow and the Warsaw Treaties had been signed, when it must have realized that once a conference was convened, it could not expect to avoid discussion of subjects which were sensitive for the Soviet Union? The least convincing explanation is that the idea of a conference had achieved such momentum through the years, thanks largely to Soviet effort, that the Soviet Government could no longer reverse it, especially as some of its allies wanted the conference to further their own national interests. Soviet diplomacy was fully capable of having made such an abrupt change of course, even later than 1970, if the Soviet leadership had

judged this to be in the national interest. If so, we are left with two
explanations, which do not exclude each other. Soviet diplomacy is not
only flexible; it is also formal. However an agreement involving the
Soviet Union may be arrived at, it must be recorded in black and white
at the end of the day. The Soviet leadership may therefore have wanted
some kind of overarching agreement, witnessed by the signatures of all
Europe, as well as by Western Europe's trans-Atlantic allies, which
would directly or indirectly constitute general approval of the *de facto*
settlement of post-war Europe. They may also have been searching for
some kind of all-European framework, jointly guaranteed by both the
Soviet and the United States governments, within which they and
their Eastern European allies would be able to contain the enlarged
Western European Community, a factor that must have begun to loom
large in the planning of Soviet foreign policy at the very latest after
Edward Heath's agreement with Pompidou during his visit to Paris in
May 1971. Some colour is lent to this interpretation of Soviet motives
by the proposal made in the communiqué[10] issued on 19 April 1974 in
Warsaw by the Warsaw Pact ministers, calling for the establishment of
'a permanent security council for Europe aimed at building new relations between all states'.

It has been argued by some that the main Soviet object in holding a
conference in the 1970s was part of a wider plan to remove the United
States forces from Europe, and to secure for the Soviet Union due
recognition as the most powerful country in Europe; once the American
forces were out of the way, the rest of Europe would, in effect be
'Finlandized'. It is questionable whether an immediate withdrawal of all
US forces from Europe would be in the Soviet interest. In any case, the
term 'Finlandization' does less than justice to the Finns, the one people
of the former Russian Empire who have succeeded in remaining outside
the borders of the Soviet Union ever since 1917.*

In the course of 1970 the Soviet Union also completed its network of
bilateral treaties with its allies by signing new treaties of friendship with
Czechoslovakia and Romania, in May and July respectively. Whereas
the latter was worded to take account of Romanian susceptibilities, the
former reflected the Brezhnev doctrine. Its preamble described the
'support, strengthening, and protection of the socialist achievements of

---

* The 1948 Soviet-Finnish Treaty (renewed for another twenty years in 1970
—see *Pravda* of 21 July 1970) is unique, as are Soviet-Finnish relations. It
obliges Finland to defend its own territory in the event of an attack against the
Soviet Union being directed across it: an echo of 1941.

the people' as 'the common international duty of socialist countries';
under Article V of the treaty the parties undertook to take the necessary
measures to this end; and in the words of the History of Soviet Foreign
Policy,[11] the treaty re-affirmed the principles of the Bratislava Declaration of 3 August 1968, regarding the collective defence of socialism in
any country of the socialist commonwealth. But at the very end of a year
which must otherwise have given the Soviet leadership much satisfac-
tion, this commonwealth was shaken once again, in Poland, where the
government was overthrown—literally in the streets—for the second
time in fourteen years.

Unlike 1956, when the issues at stake were both political and economic,* this time they were chiefly economic—the mismanagement of
the economy by the Gomulka regime, culminating in increases in the
price of essential food items, tactlessly introduced just before Christ-
mas. The battles between strikers and police, reinforced by the army,
that followed in the Baltic cities were so severe (a total of 45 dead and
over 1,000 injured was officially admitted),[12] that Gomulka was obliged
to resign after over fourteen years as Party Secretary. Fortunately for
the Soviet Union, he was swiftly succeeded by Edward Gierek, who
rescinded his predecessor's economic measures, made concessions to
the workers, and—so it was rumoured—received Soviet economic aid
to help him meet his country's difficulties. Like Gomulka in 1956,
Gierek both admitted the errors committed by the previous Party
leadership and made it clear that there was no question of Poland seeking to break loose from the Soviet alliance. And unlike Dubcek, he not
only succeeded in restoring a measure of popular confidence but also
reassured the Soviet Union that the rule of the Party would be upheld in
Poland. Nevertheless, the Soviet leadership, however relieved they may
have felt at the outcome of the Polish crisis, must have asked themselves
how they would have reacted had it developed according to the Czechoslovak model. Poland lies athwart the lines of communication between
the Soviet Union and its forces in East Germany. Another invasion,
little more than two years after the invasion of Czechoslovakia, and only
a few days after the conclusion of the Treaty of Warsaw with the
Federal Republic of Germany, would have presented an appalling
prospect. The Polish crisis passed without any official Soviet comment;
but it left the Kremlin with food for thought; and as we have noted in
the preceding chapter, it may well have affected the decision of the

* 'Bread and freedom' was the demonstrators' slogan in Poznań in 1956.

XXIVth Party Congress to give priority to the needs of the consumer for the first time in the history of the Soviet Union.

Relations between the super-powers

Relations between the Soviet Union and the United States at the beginning of the decade could already be described as edging towards the 'middle ground of peaceful, if somewhat distant, coexistence ... lying somewhere between the intimacy we cannot have ... and the war there is no reason for us to fight'.[13] That this is how things seemed in the Kremlin is suggested by an article which appeared in the journal of the Soviet-USA Institute,[14] written by Lyudmila Gvishiani, an historian and daughter of the Soviet Prime Minister. The article consisted of an account of Bullitt's ill-fated mission to the Soviet Union in 1919, and quoted George Kennan's favourable verdict in his memoirs (that the peace proposals put to Bullitt by Lenin offered an opportunity that should not have been let slip by the Allied Powers). The chief interest of the article, however, lay in its opening and concluding paragraphs. The former described the principle of peaceful coexistence of states with different social systems as one of the basic principles of the Leninist foreign policy of the Soviet State, and went on to say that the 'realistic approach' of the Soviet Government and of Lenin personally appeared with the greatest clarity in the history of Soviet-American relations in March 1919. The article ended:

Lenin demonstrated the possibility of reaching agreement with capitalist countries, and first and foremost with the United States. To dogmatists the decisions of Vladimir Ilyich Lenin in the sphere of foreign policy might appear too bold, or, as G. V. Chicherin wrote, 'for all of us the sudden change from the early opinions of an underground revolutionary party to the political realism of a government in power was extremely difficult'.[15]

In the light of subsequent developments it is not fanciful to regard this as a prescription, inspired at a high level, for a new Soviet-American relationship, on a basis of equality, half a century after Lenin's death. But who were the dogmatists—the Chinese, or opponents within the CPSU Politburo of such a relationship, or both? This the author did not explain.

Meanwhile both sides continued their SALT talks—in Vienna from mid-April to mid-July and again in Helsinki from 2 November to 18 December, after which they were adjourned until the following March.

The Nuclear Non-Proliferation Treaty was brought into force in March 1970, when Great Britain, the Soviet Union, and the United States simultaneously deposited their ratifications. Over Indo-China, there could be no meeting of minds, particularly after the American–South Vietnamese 'incursion' into Cambodia in April-June (a similar operation was conducted in Laos in 1971). This followed the deposition *in absentia* of Prince Sihanouk, the Cambodian Head of State. It was the Chinese Government which acted as his host and sponsor in March, and in the following month joined with him in convening a summit conference of Indo-Chinese peoples. By comparison, Kosygin's denunciation of the incursion—although carried on television, the first such appearance by a Soviet Prime Minister within the Soviet Union— seemed a mild reaction; and the Soviet Union retained diplomatic relations with the new Cambodian Government for the next three and a half years.

In Latin America, both Chile and Cuba might have caused trouble between the two super-powers had the Soviet-US relationship still been as it was eight years before: Chile, when its electorate voted the Marxist leader of the Chilean Socialist Party, Salvador Allende, into power in September, and Cuba, when (following a visit by the Soviet Defence Minister to Havana) a Soviet submarine tender was anchored at Cienfuegos, accompanied by special barges for the storage of effluent from submarine reactors. As it was, the Soviet Government made no attempt to make Chile into a second Cuba, although it welcomed the new Chilean Government's nationalization measures and the swift re-establishment of Chilean diplomatic relations with Cuba; and the following May a modest Soviet-Chilean credit and technical assistance agreement was signed in Moscow,[16] which was visited by a Chilean trade delegation. The Soviet Government denied that it was building a base for ballistic-missile submarines in Cuba: an assurance that the US Government appeared disposed to accept.

By far the most difficult area was the Middle East, which in 1970 replaced South-East Asia as the principal source of conflict in the world, despite the fact that American involvement in Indo-China was to drag on for another three years. Here, while officially adversaries, the Soviet Union and the United States cooperated in practice, both in multilateral (together with the British and the French) and in bilateral talks, and notably by persuading Egypt and Israel to accept a cease-fire in August. In January, the Israeli Air Force's deep raids came within five miles of Cairo. Nasser could not be expected to survive a challenge on this scale. Following a hurried visit which he paid to the Soviet Union on 22 January, the Soviet Government took a major decision: to deploy in Egypt a force of about the same size as that despatched to Cuba in 1962 —150 Mig-21J aircraft and over 300 mobile and modern SAM-3 (surface to air) missiles.[17] This force, together with six Soviet-controlled airfields, was led by a Soviet air defence commander, General V. V. Okunev, from his headquarters in Cairo.

The Soviet Government took pains to assure the other governments concerned that the role of this force, which was sent to Egypt by air, was purely defensive and that the Soviet objective in the Arab-Israeli dispute remained a political settlement. Unlike 1962, on this occasion Moscow's assurances were accepted, as was the fact that the Soviet Defence Ministry could hardly forego side-benefits for Soviet national interests conferred by the operation that they had mounted: extra naval facilities at Mersa Matruh and an increased ability to keep watch on the US Sixth Fleet and allied navies in the Mediterranean from the air. The operation was successful, at a cost of the lives of four Soviet pilots shot down on 30 July. After mid-April Israeli deep raids virtually ceased; and the air defence of Cairo, the Nile valley, and the Delta was thus assured. The Israeli Air Force, which had hitherto enjoyed undisputed command of the air, now began to suffer losses, and by taking advantage of the cease-fire in August, the Russians were finally able to establish a complete air defence both of the Suez Canal itself and of a narrow stretch of Israeli-occupied Sinai immediately to the east of it.

Meanwhile, both advocates were exercising pressure on their clients, the United States Government by refusing, in March, to supply Israel with more Phantom aircraft, and the Soviet Government by applying pressure on Nasser in July, during another visit to the Soviet Union, to accept the American proposal for a cease-fire on the Canal and a military stand-still fifty kilometres either side of it. Unfortunately, the negotiations through Jarring, the UN mediator, that should have followed the cease-fire (which came into effect on 7 August), never got off the ground, because the Israeli Government withdrew from them in protest against the Soviet-Egyptian violations of the stand-still agreement. Had the Soviet Government resisted the temptation to move the SAMs forward to the Suez Canal in August, Jarring might have been able to make progress. As it was, an opportunity was missed, given the conciliatory statements made by both Golda Meir and Nasser before the cease-fire began. (Six months later, Soviet forces were withdrawn from the Canal, leaving the SAM-3 sites substantially in Egyptian hands.)

However, during the Jordanian civil war in the following month, both Nasser and the Soviet Government exercised a moderating influence, the former on the *fedayeen* and the latter on the Syrian Government, which was persuaded to withdraw the armoured force that had crossed the Jordanian frontier.[18] An anxious moment passed; this final exertion may well have hastened Nasser's death; but the cease-fire between Egypt and Israel, originally intended to last ninety days, held good. Nasser was succeeded as President of Egypt by Sadat, who in the course of the next three years was to set his country on a new course and, in the process, to bring the super-powers—for a few hours—closer to a nuclear confrontation than they had been at any time since the Cuban missile crisis of 1962.

NOTES

1. A Western European, especially from Britain, old enough to recall the events of 1938/9, might expect his Soviet contemporaries to prefer to forget this treaty, rather as he would prefer not to be reminded of the Munich Agreement: yet it appeared in posters displayed prominently in Moscow at this time, with a Nazi boot kicking through it.
2. Text in *Pravda* of 13 August 1970, translated in *Survival*, vol. XII, no. 10, October 1970.
3. Translated in *Survival*, vol. XIII, no. 2, February 1971.
4. The latter point was rammed home by Brezhnev again and again in his subsequent speeches: see, for example, the many references to the Moscow Treaty in Brezhnev, op. cit., vol. 3, indexed on p. 506.
5. Although the Federal Republic did not ratify this treaty for over four years after signing it: a measure of its importance.
6. *Istoriya Vneshnei Politiki SSSR*, vol. 2, p. 460. A similar protocol was signed during the Canadian Prime Minister's visit to Moscow in May 1971.
7. The texts of these two communiqués were reproduced in *Survival*, vol. XV, no. 8, August and no. 9, September 1970, respectively.
8. *Keesing's Contemporary Archives 1969/70*, p. 24348. These principles were 'sovereign equality, political independence and territorial integrity of each European state; non-interference and non-intervention in the internal affairs of any state, regardless of its political or social system; and the right of the people of each European state to shape their own destinies free of external constraint'.
9. Op. cit., vol. 2, p. 352.
10. See *The Times*, 20 April 1974.
11. Op. cit., vol. 2, p. 350.
12. In *Krajowa Agencja Informacyjna*, XII–XVI, no. 7/579, pp. 1, 3–13: Gierek's report to the Polish Central Committee, submitted early in February 1971.
13. George Kennan, in his article published in *Foreign Policy*, Summer 1972, p. 21, edited by Huntington and Manshel, National Affairs Inc., New York, 1972.

14. 'The Year 1919, the Mission of William Bullitt', *SShA*, Moscow, January 1970.
15. G. V. Chicherin, *Articles and Speeches*, Moscow, 1961, p. 227.
16. *Izvestiya*, 31 May 1971.
17. *Strategic Survey 1970*, IISS, London, pp. 46–9; the same source estimates the free market value of Soviet military equipment supplied to Egypt since the 1967 War as having increased during 1970 from 2,000 million to 4,500 million dollars.
18. Units of the US Sixth Fleet also moved eastwards towards the Syrian Coast. It is not clear whether this pressure on the Syrian Government was exerted by the super-powers acting in concert or in parallel.

11

THE YEAR 1971

The Middle East and the Mediterranean

On paper, the Soviet relationship with the new Egyptian President began well. In May, four months after the opening of the Aswan High Dam, the financing of which had first been undertaken by the Soviet Government in 1958, Podgorny signed a treaty of 'unbreakable' friendship between the Soviet Union and Egypt,[1] which provided for even closer cooperation between the two governments than did the Soviet-Indian Treaty concluded three months later. But its military clauses were carefully balanced. Article 7 laid down:

in the event of the development of situations creating, in the opinion of both sides, a danger to peace or violation of peace, they will contact each other without delay in order to concert their positions with a view to removing the threat that has arisen or to the reestablishing of peace;

while Article 8 stated that military cooperation, developed on the basis of 'appropriate agreements', would:

provide specifically for assistance in training the United Arab Republic military personnel, in mastering the armaments and equipment supplied to the UAR in order to strengthen its capacity, to eliminate the consequences of aggression as well as to increase its ability to stand up to aggression in general.

The phrase 'to eliminate the consequences of aggression' suggested the possible provision of more sophisticated offensive weapons by the Soviet Union than hitherto, while the phrases 'in the opinion of both sides' and 'appropriate agreements' seemed to safeguard the Soviet Union from being drawn into an adventure by Sadat, who had announced that 1971 was to be the Year of Decision.

Despite the treaty, it was a difficult year for the Russians in Egypt. Although Article 2 described Egypt as having 'set itself the aim of reconstructing society along socialist lines', it was in May that Sadat liquidated the pro-Soviet faction in Egypt, led by Ali Sabri. Worse still, soon afterwards the Sudan Government, which was being supplied with Soviet arms, executed the Sudanese Communist Party leader, Abdel Khalik Mahgoub. (The Chinese profited from the quarrel which arose between the Russians and the Sudanese by signing a 34 million dollar aid agreement with the latter in August.) Already perhaps sensing something of what was to follow in Egypt in 1972, the Soviet Government reinsured elsewhere. In the course of 1971 they supplied Syria with aircraft and surface-to-air missiles, accompanied by military advisers. The first Soviet arms deal with the Lebanon was announced in November, and in the following month the Soviet Prime Minister visited Morocco and Algeria—Morocco's armed forces being partly, and Algeria's wholly, supplied by the Soviet Union.

Although there were some anxious moments in the Arab-Israeli dispute, the cease-fire was maintained, amid a series of negotiations which were complicated by the fact that they were at times being simultaneously conducted by the Soviet and the US governments bilaterally; by the Russians with the Egyptians and by the Americans with the Israelis; and by Jarring with both the Egyptians and the Israelis. The idea which held the field at any rate in the earlier part of the year, was one which had first been floated by Moshe Dayan the previous October, namely that the Israelis should withdraw a certain distance from the Suez Canal, which would then be re-opened by the Egyptians. The negotiations foundered; in November Sadat said that he would go to war by the end of the month; once again both the super-powers were able to exercise restraint on their clients; but the Soviet Union was to pay the price for this in 1972.

Seen from Moscow, Cyprus is part of the Middle East. The island ended the year in a state of unrest, primarily because of the return of Grivas, the EOKA guerrilla leader, from Athens, where he had been living under surveillance since his recall from the island by the Greek Government nearly four years before. Despite the strength of the Greek Cypriot Communist Party, the immediate aim of Soviet policy in Cyprus was largely negative: to prevent the partition of the island between Greece and Turkey. While preserving its policy of friendship with the governments of both Turkey and Cyprus, it took the opportunity of the election of the new Moscow Patriarch to invite Archbishop Makarios to pay a state visit to the Soviet Union, which he did in June. As for the other former British colony in the Mediterranean, Malta (whose government had issued an ultimatum to the British Government), so far from the Soviet leadership emulating the Tsar Paul I,[2] it was the Chinese who granted the Maltese Government an interest-free loan of nearly £17 million, in April 1972. The Soviet Union was content to keep a watching brief on both these islands.

Europe

Notwithstanding the importance of the Soviet treaties with Egypt and India, by far the most significant agreement signed by the Soviet Government during the year 1971 was the Quadripartite Agreement on Berlin of 3 September. (The city was described as 'the relevant area' in the preamble and the first article of Part I of the agreement, in order to bridge the gap between the Soviet Government, mindful of its East German ally, and the other three governments.) The agreement,[3] which was expressly stated not to affect the Four Powers' quadripartite rights and responsibilities and their 'corresponding wartime and post-war agreements and decisions', was, like the Moscow Treaty, a compromise. It provided for unimpeded traffic between the western sectors of Berlin and the Federal Republic, for improved communications between these sectors and the rest of Berlin and the German Democratic Republic, and for the maintenance and development of the ties between the western sectors and the Federal Republic. Even though the western sectors of the city were not to be regarded as part of the Federal Republic, it was also agreed that the latter's government might perform consular services for permanent residents of the western sectors and might represent the interests of these sectors in international organizations and conferences; in return, the Soviet Union was authorized to establish a consulate-general in the western sector of Berlin.

In order to overcome the legal difficulty that the German Democratic Republic had not yet been formally recognized by the three Western signatories, or by the Federal German Government, the Quadripartite Agreement delegated the detailed arrangements for traffic and communications to be agreed by 'the competent German authorities'; and it was stated that these arrangements would be brought into force by a final quadripartite protocol when the latter had been concluded. These, broadly, were the legal niceties thanks to which the problem that had bedevilled East-West relations for twenty-three years was now in sight of solution. That the negotiations took eighteen months was, at least in part, the result of the opposition of the East Germans, whose object remained the complete *Abgrenzung** of the two Germanies.

The Berlin Agreement also opened the way for the first practical steps towards the holding of a European Conference. At their meeting held in Brussels in December, NATO ministers suggested four areas of discussion for an eventual meeting in Helsinki: 'questions of security, including principles governing relations between states and certain military aspects of security; freer movement of people, information and ideas, and cultural relations; cooperation in the fields of economics, applied science and technology, and pure science; and cooperation to improve the environment'.[4] And, following a remark about tasting the wine made by Brezhnev in a speech at Tbilisi in May (which perhaps helped to defeat the Mansfield amendment calling for US troop reductions), they also appointed Manlio Brosio, the former Secretary-General of NATO, to engage in exploratory talks about mutually balanced force reductions with the Soviet and other interested governments. To this offer there was no Eastern response; and there was no meeting in Helsinki for another year.

In 1971 Western and Eastern Europe each made what, at the time at any rate, seemed important advances towards closer unity. In the West, the enlargement of the European Economic Community was in sight. In the East, the COMECON Council approved in July its 'Complex Programme for the Development of Socialist Economic Intregration', with a time-scale of fifteen years for its execution. The lengthy text of the programme makes it clear at the outset that socialist economic integration is 'completely voluntary and does not involve the creation of supernational bodies; it does not affect questions of internal planning or of the financial and self-financing activity of organizations'. Given this restriction, which was essential for the Romanians (who had temporarily abstained from the previous year's decision to set up an Eastern European Investment Bank), integration meant the coordination by the member governments of their Five-Year Plans, through agreed decisions on product specialization, and implemented both by trade agreements for an equivalent period and by flows of capital, and in particular by the exchange of scientific and technological information between members. The basis of intra-COMECON trade remained the

---

* The concept of two German states, each with a completely different, irreconcilable, social system.

provision by the Soviet Union of long term supplies of raw materials in return for equipment manufactured by the Eastern European countries under specialization agreements.[5] But in deference to the smaller members of the organization, the programme included a schedule whereby the 1980 unit of COMECON accounting would become mutually convertible at unified exchange rates. The organization's principal task was defined as being gradually to bring closer and level up the economic development of member countries.[6] By Western European standards of the time the scope of this Eastern European economic programme was modest; and was, in the event, destined to be watered down still further.

Asia

The dramatic impact of the American decision to mend fences with China led the Soviet leadership to invite the US President to visit their country as well. But the Soviet response was not as clear-cut as this invitation may suggest. Some idea of the Kremlin's thinking may be derived from a comparison of the speech made by Brezhnev to the XVth Soviet Trades Union Congress, five months after the invitation was announced, with an article that appeared in *Kommunist* in January 1972. Having reaffirmed the need for a collective security system in Asia—a proposal that he had first launched in 1969—Brezhnev spoke with caution about the new Sino-American relationship: only time, perhaps the near future, would show how matters really stood, but the Soviet Union did not welcome the thought that the American and Chinese peoples held the future of our world in their hands.[7] According to the Chinese, Sino-Soviet relations should be based on principles of peaceful coexistence.[8] So be it, he said; and went on to recall Soviet proposals to the Chinese for non-aggression and the settlement of the frontier questions.[9] As for the United States, the key to success in the SALT negotiations was the recognition by both participants of the principle of identical security of both parties and their readiness to abide by this in practice—a Soviet formulation of the American concept of essential equivalence?

There was not yet, however, any public recognition of the responsibilities imposed on the two super-powers by their ability to blow up the globe. On the contrary, the *Kommunist* article repeated to its readers the conventional warning against the ideas, current in the bourgeois scientific world, of super-power, convergence, and bridge-building.

None the less, in February 1971 the Soviet Union joined with Great Britain and the United States in signing the Sea-bed Treaty; and on 30 September 1971 the United States and the Soviet Union signed two bilateral agreements, one to improve the hot line, which was converted to communication by satellite, and the other to reduce the risk of accidental nuclear war. Under the terms of the latter agreement, both sides agreed to do everything in their power to render harmless or destroy any nuclear weapon launched accidentally or without authority; each undertook to inform the other not only if its warning systems detected a possible missile attack, but also if warning or communication systems were themselves interfered with; and they committed themselves to give advance notice of any missile flights beyond their national territory.

On the ground in Asia, the Soviet leadership did all that they could to counter the Sino-American rapprochement. Whether they did indeed seek to influence some of their Chinese opposite numbers cannot be judged from Soviet sources; but two years later the Chinese Prime Minister publicly accused Mao Tse-tung's former right hand man, Lin Piao, of treason, plotting an armed *coup d'état* and fleeing 'surreptitiously . . . as a defector to the Soviet revisionists in betrayal of his party and country'.[10] (Lin Piao's death in an air crash in Mongolia in September 1971 was made officially public in August 1972.) Certainly, by the end of the year nearly a third of the two-year-old CCP Politburo had been dismissed by Mao. The number of Soviet divisions stationed along the Chinese frontier and in Mongolia was estimated to have risen to forty-four (from fifteen in 1968)—more than the number in Central Europe. Soviet support for India was given legally binding form by the Indo-Soviet Treaty concluded in August 1971,[11] on the eve of the Indo-Pakistan War, in which China and the United States both found themselves backing Pakistan—unsuccessfully, as it turned out.[12] There was a delicate moment in December when elements of the US Seventh Fleet were sent to the Bay of Bengal and elements of the Soviet squadron were sent northward from the Indian Ocean; but the war ended quickly with an overwhelming Indian victory. Soviet support for India was also diplomatic: two vetoes of cease-fire resolutions in the Security Council, where the representatives of the world's two great communist powers at once became engaged in a slanging match. As a Soviet commentator claimed, 'events in the Indian sub-continent led to the first joint defeat of the USA and China in the struggle with the national-liberation movement'.[13]

The Indo-Soviet Treaty looked like the first link in the Soviet system for containing Chinese power in Asia, which the Russians adopted just as the Americans were in the process of giving it up. (The number of US troops in Vietnam was halved in the course of 1971.) Its preamble affirmed both sides' belief in the principles of peaceful co-existence and of cooperation between states with different political and social systems. Could this have been designed to justify whatever agreements the Soviet Union intended to conclude with the United States in the following year? It was, however, balanced by Article 10, in which the parties declared that they 'shall not undertake any commit-ment, secret or open, towards one or more states imcompatible with the present treaty'. In essence, the treaty provided India with a Soviet umbrella against China for as long as India chose to stay out of the nuclear club: under the terms of Articles 8 and 9 respectively, each party solemnly declared that it would not enter into or participate in any military alliances directed against the other, and undertook to:

refrain from giving any assistance to any third party taking part in an armed conflict with the other party. In case any of the parties is attacked or threatened with attack, the High Contracting Parties will immediately start mutual consultations with a view to eliminating this threat and taking appropriate effective measures to ensure peace and security for their countries.

The message to China was clear enough.

NOTES

1. Full text in *Pravda*, 28 May 1971. In fact, Egypt was still called the United Arab Republic at that time, but it has seemed simpler to use the shorter form throughout.
2. In 1798 the Tsar Paul I accepted the Grand Mastership of the Order of the Knights of Malta.
3. *The Times*, 4 September 1971.
4. *Keesing's Contemporary Archives 1971/2*, p. 25015. The NATO communiqué was still cautious about the proposal for a meeting in Helsinki, expressing readiness 'to begin multilateral conversations intended to lead to a Confer-ence on Security and Cooperation in Europe'.
5. As examples, Brezhnev mentioned at the XXIVth Party Congress the prospect that by 1975 the *Druzhba* pipeline would ship nearly fifty million tons of oil to Eastern Europe (as compared with 8·3 million tons in 1964), and that a gas pipeline would carry natural gas from Siberia to European Russia, thus facilitating the supply to Eastern European countries.
6. This analysis of the Complex Programme is indebted to Michael Kaser.
7. Brezhnev, op. cit., vol. 3, pp. 495 ff., contains the text of his speech. This

passage referred to Nixon's remarks, made on 21 and 27 February 1972, at
the banquets given in his honour in Peking and Shanghai respectively: 'what
we do here can change the world', and 'this is the week that changed the
world'. For the 1969 proposal, see Brezhnev, op. cit., vol. 2, p. 413.

8. Not a flattering proposal, since in Leninist theory peaceful coexistence
applies only to countries 'with different social systems'—i.e. between
Marxist and non-Marxist countries.

9. At the end of the same year Brezhnev revealed that the proposal for a non-
aggression pact with China, including nuclear weapons, had been put
forward by the Soviet Union as early as January 1971.

10. *The Times*, 1 September 1973.

11. Full text in *Pravda*, 10 August 1971.

12. On the other hand, China supported the Government of Ceylon—as did the
Soviet Union, among other countries—against the Maoist rebels there.

13. *Kommunist*, 'The Programme of Peace in Action', January 1972. But, in my
view, Soviet policy in the sub-continent was aimed primarily against China.
Soviet relations with Pakistan were restored in March 1972.

12

THE YEAR 1972

The year 1971 had been a transitional one for Soviet foreign policy. At the outset of 1972—the year in which Peking and Moscow were, each in turn, visited for the first time by the President of the United States—the concept in Washington of the structure of world power emerging in the late twentieth century seemed to resemble the nineteenth-century concert of the great powers, described as an even balance[1] between the United States, China, the Soviet Union, Japan, and Western Europe. In the event, things worked out differently. But the foundations of a new world power structure were laid during this memorable year.

China

Nixon visited China from 21 to 28 February 1972. Despite the American rear-guard action, fought only a few weeks beforehand in New York and many of the world's capitals, as a final attempt to retain Taiwan's seat in the United Nations, this visit came very close to achieving its stated objective, the normalization of relations between the United States and China. (Initially, diplomatic contact was maintained through their ambassadors in Paris, but liaison missions were exchanged in 1973.) The joint communiqué[2] consisted partly of points agreed by both sides and partly of statements of each side's position on the Taiwan question. The Chinese categorically described Taiwan as a province of China; its liberation was a Chinese internal affair; and they were opposed to concepts such as the two Chinas and an independent Taiwan. The Americans acknowledged that 'all Chinese on either side of the Taiwan Strait maintain that there is but one China and that Taiwan is a part of

China'; they affirmed as their ultimate objective the withdrawal of all US forces and military installations from Taiwan; meanwhile they would reduce them progressively, as tension in the area diminished. Both sides agreed to conduct their relations on the basis of the Five Principles;[3] neither would seek hegemony in Asia and the Pacific; each was opposed to efforts by any country or group of countries to establish such hegemony; major countries should not divide up the world into spheres of influence; and the Chinese declared that China would never be a super-power, and that it opposed hegemony and power politics of any kind.

The Soviet Union

This done, Nixon visited the Soviet Union from 22 to 30 May. Any doubt that by May 1972 the Soviet leadership had reached the conclusion that they must agree, at the highest level, the framework of a new Soviet-American understanding, was removed by the welcome that they gave the US President in Moscow, in spite of his decision (announced only a fortnight previously) to mine seven North Vietnamese ports and to attack supply routes from China to Vietnam.[4] Of the Soviet-American bilateral agreements concluded in 1972, by far the most important were the Treaty on the Limitation of Anti-Ballistic Missile Systems (ABMs), the interim agreement (lasting five years) on certain measures with respect to the limitation of strategic offensive arms, both signed during Nixon's visit, and the three-year grain agreement, signed in Washington on 8 July.[5]

The first of the SALT agreements is clear, the second less so. It will be recalled that one of the major destabilizing factors in the nuclear strategic equation by the end of the 1960s was the prospective deployment by both the super-powers of ABM systems. Under the terms of the treaty limiting such systems, each side was permitted to deploy them in two areas only: one centred on its capital and the other, at its own choice, containing some part of its ICBM force. Launchers so deployed must be capable of firing one missile with one warhead only; they must be static; and they must be land-based. These conditions, coupled with restrictions on the associated radar systems, meant that the Soviet Union could expand the existing ABM defences of Moscow to a total of 100 launchers, and also construct another site for the defence of some of its ICBMs.

The interim agreement was a holding operation, designed to set the ring for the second round of SALT talks, which were resumed in Geneva—their venue from then on—in November. Under its terms, each side was permitted a total of ICBM and SLBM launchers based on the number either operational or under construction on 1 July and 26 May respectively, although both sides were allowed to modernize and replace these launchers, subject to certain conditions. Quantitatively, this agreement sanctioned what had in the previous three years become a marked Soviet superiority: about 1,530 operational ICBMs (with another 90 under construction) as against 1,054 American ICBMs; and about 560 operational SLBMs (with another 245 under construction) as against 656 American SLBMs.[6] The Soviet Union had achieved an equally marked superiority in megatonnage, each of its 290 SS-9s having an estimated warhead yield of between 20 and 25 megatons, as opposed to the *Titan* 2's estimated yield of between 5 and 10 megatons. In order to assess the balance of the interim agreement, it is important to bear in mind not only that in strategic nuclear weapons systems accuracy matters more than megatonnage, but also that the agreement mentioned neither strategic bombers—an arm in which the US Air Force had retained its superiority—nor the so-called forward based systems (FBS)—US strike aircraft based on the territory of the United States' allies or on aircraft carriers stationed in the Mediterranean Sea and the Pacific Ocean—between two and three thousand in all—capable both of carrying out conventional attacks and of delivering nuclear warheads on Soviet targets.[7] Moreover, the ceilings on permitted numbers of American missile launchers were based on programmes laid down at the outset of the Kennedy Administration and had been accepted by successive US Administrations since 1967. Five years later, by which time both governments were probably spending about twenty-five billion dollars annually on strategic armament,[8] the US Government was already concentrating its efforts on quality rather than on quantity. In consequence, in 1973 US *Poseidon* submarines and *Minuteman-3* ballistic missiles were being deployed as quickly as possible, equipped with MIRVs, capable of doubling the number of Soviet targets at which, at any rate in theory, American missiles could strike by mid-1977.[9] MIRVs, which are unidentifiable by satellite, were not mentioned in the interim agreement, which was signed at a time when they had not yet been deployed by the Soviet Union.

The passage of the interim agreement through the US Senate was not an easy one. Ratifications were finally exchanged by the two governments in October, after the Senate had adopted an important amendment, submitted by Henry Jackson, urging the President to seek a further treaty with the Soviet Union—i.e. in SALT II—'which would not limit the United States to levels of intercontinental strategic forces inferior to the limits provided for the Soviet Union'.

The significance of the two strategic arms agreements of May 1972 is described by Soviet writers as difficult to overestimate.[10] Even though they did not mark a breakthrough towards the kind of disarmament to which both super-powers had been committed since their ratification of the Nuclear Non-Proliferation Treaty over two years previously, they did mark a potential beginning; and this must be assessed against the new kind of language used in the twelve points of the Joint Declaration on Basic Principles of Relations between the USA and the USSR, which formed part of the agreements signed in Moscow. In this declaration the two sides agreed that in the nuclear age there was no alternative to conducting their relations with each other on the basis of peaceful coexistence; they attached 'major importance to preventing the development of situations capable of causing a dangerous exacerbation of their relations'; they would therefore do their utmost to avoid military confrontations and to prevent the outbreak of nuclear war; they would always exercise restraint in their relations with each other and would be prepared to negotiate and settle differences by peaceful means; efforts to obtain unilateral advantage at the expense of the other, directly or indirectly, were inconsistent with these objectives; and the prerequisites for maintaining and strengthening peaceful relations between the USA and the USSR were 'the recognition of the security interests of the parties based on the principle of equality and the renunciation of the use or the threat of force. . . .'

These principles of parity were reaffirmed by Nixon in his speech at the Kremlin banquet given in his honour on 22 May, when he said that there was no longer such a thing as security in a preponderance of strength; the nuclear great powers had a solemn responsibility to exercise restraint themselves in any crisis, to take positive action to avert direct confrontation, and to exercise a moderating influence on other nations in conflict or crisis.[11] As if to play down the closeness of the special relations between the two super-powers implied by such language, he declared in his televised broadcast from the Kremlin on 28 May that it was not their aim to establish a condominium. And the joint communiqué ended by affirming that the Moscow agreements and understandings were not in any way directed against any other country.

Unlike the strategic agreements, the two commercial agreements, one covering the Soviet purchase of American grain and the other setting up a Joint Trade Commission, could be assessed in hard cash. Of these, the former came into immediate effect, whereas the Trade Commission, which held its first meeting in Moscow in July, could not exert its full impact on the Soviet-US economic relationship until Congress was willing to pass the legislation required to grant the Soviet Union most favoured nation treatment. Nevertheless, the Commission succeeded in settling the long outstanding Soviet Lend-lease debt to the United States; and the Trade Agreement contemplated that the volume of trade during its three-year period would be at least three times as much as over the 1969–71 period, to an aggregate of at least 1,500 million dollars; American business was on the point of making an assault on the Soviet market, which had previously been largely a West European and Japanese preserve.

The dimensions of the grain agreement were a measure of the Soviet crop failure. During the three-year period beginning on 1 August 1972 the Soviet Union was to buy at least 750 million dollars' worth of US grown food grains, at least 200 millions' worth of which was shipped in the first year. The US Government undertook to make available a line of credit not exceeding 500 million dollars for these purchases, repayable in three years from the date of delivery. The conclusion six days later of a five-year agreement with the Soviet Government by the Occidental Petroleum Company, for the joint development of Soviet oil and natural gas, seemed to open up a prospect of a longer term economic relationship between the two super-powers, with the Soviet Union an importer of American grain and the United States an importer of Soviet oil and natural gas.

One subject in the joint communiqué on which the two sides were able only to record their agreement to differ was Vietnam. Did the Soviet leadership use their influence in Hanoi on behalf of the US Government in the closing stages of the latter's painful negotiations with the North Vietnamese? The American bombing was halted while Podgorny visited North Vietnam in June; in August the last US combat unit was withdrawn from Vietnam; and by December (although it did not appear so at the time, when American bombing of the North was temporarily resumed) the end was at last in sight. In his televised address to the American people during his visit to the United States a year later, Brezhnev spoke of Soviet-US cooperation in halting the war in Vietnam.[12] Just how much ice Soviet representations cut with a government that had already held out so long,[13] and with the Chinese offering Hanoi free military equipment and materials for 1973, is questionable. In any case by January 1973, when Kissinger finally reached agreement with Le Duc Tho in Paris, the sigh of relief in the Kremlin must have been as deep as in every other country.

Japan

The political pattern that had been familiar for so many years in Asia was beginning to break up. The immediate[14] response of Kakuei Tanaka, the new Japanese Prime Minister, to the American announcement of 15 July 1971 had been to reinsure both with China and with the Soviet Union: in the words of the Japanese Foreign Minister, Japan must adapt to the multipolar age and pursue a foreign policy divorced from ideology. In September 1972 Tanaka visited Peking. The Japanese Government expressed its 'respect' for the Chinese position on Taiwan; the Chinese Government renounced its claims to war reparations; and the two governments re-established diplomatic relations. (In consequence Taiwan broke off diplomatic relations with Japan.) In October the Foreign Ministers of Japan and the Soviet Union began to discuss the negotiation of a peace treaty in Moscow.[15] Although the Japanese Government had earlier agreed to study positively the Soviet proposal for an Asian collective security system (during a visit paid to Tokyo in January by Gromyko), the only territorial concession that the Soviet Government felt able to offer Japan, no doubt with Chinese territorial claims in mind, was the return of two of the four Kurile Islands occupied by the Soviet Union in 1945—not enough for Japan, for whom half a loaf was unacceptable. This deadlock did not prevent a rapid expansion of trade. This had already increased in both directions from a mere 40 million dollars in 1958 to 822 millions in 1970; a new trade agreement concluded in 1971 had provided for an increase of nearly double over the next five years; and in June 1972 the two governments seemed to be nearing agreement in principle to engage in immense projects, the joint development of the Tyumen' oil field in Western Siberia and other areas, including Sakhalin, possibly with American participation, and natural gas resources at Yakutsk.

Japanese-Soviet participation in projects such as the Tyumen' development was viewed with suspicion by the Chinese Government, because this would in their view increase the potential Soviet military threat to China. By the end of the year, during which there had been another alleged clash on the Sino-Soviet border (this time between

Kazakhstan and Sinkiang, in which five Soviet border guards were believed to have been killed), China had built up, or was on the point of building up, a nuclear *force de frappe*[16] directed against the Soviet Union: 20–30 MRBMs probably deployed, mainly in north-eastern China, and an IRBM developed and possibly deployed with a range long enough to reach Moscow. No Siberian agreement was to be concluded between Japan and the Soviet Union for another two years.[17]

Europe

This was a year of fruition, both within Western Europe and between West and East. On 22 January the new members of the European Economic Community signed the Treaty of Accession in Brussels; on 18 October Great Britain ratified this treaty; on 19–20 October the heads of the Western European Governments, meeting in Paris, set themselves the goal of Western European unity by the end of the decade; and on 1 January 1973 the Treaty of Accession came into force.

It was against this background that on 17 May the Federal German Bundestag finally approved the ratification of the Moscow and Warsaw Treaties; on 26 May the treaty on traffic questions between the two Germanies was signed in East Berlin, thus opening the way for the foreign ministers of the Four Powers to sign the final Quadripartite Protocol of their 1971 Agreement on Berlin, which then came into force; and the West and East German governments went on—in December—to sign their Basic Treaty on relations between the two countries, which was signed in East Berlin.[18] Like the Moscow Treaty, from which this whole network of treaties stemmed, this agreement was a *de facto* compromise, which did not purport to settle the German problem *de jure*; indeed the rights and responsibilities of the Four Powers (who alone are legally entitled to bring about a *de jure* settlement) were expressly affirmed by both sides. Its most important practical consequences were threefold; preservation for the German Democratic Republic of its privileged position under the European Economic Community's Protocol on inter-German trade, whereby East German exports to West Germany are excluded from the EEC common tariff; the exchange of permanent missions—not described as embassies—between the two states; and application by both for membership of the United Nations (which they finally entered in September 1973).

Towards the end of the year the two conferences that had formed the subject of so many communiqués issued by the NATO Alliance and the Warsaw Pact, at last entered the phase of practical preparation: the Conference on Security and Cooperation in Europe (CSCE) at the level of heads of mission in Helsinki, in November; and in the same month— following Kissinger's discussions in Moscow two months earlier— seven NATO countries invited five Warsaw Pact countries (the USSR, Poland, Czechoslovakia, Hungary, and the German Democratic Republic) to preparatory talks on Mutual Balanced Force Reductions on 31 January 1973.[19] On 30 November, in a speech[20] delivered during a visit to Hungary, Brezhnev declared his belief that it would be possible to solve the problem of reducing armed forces and armaments in Europe, and in his address to a joint session of the CPSU Central Committee and the Supreme Soviet, on the occasion of the fiftieth anniversary of the formation of the Soviet Union, he raised for the first time the possibility that COMECON and the EEC might cooperate.

The Third World

Soviet multilateral diplomacy was impelled in 1972 both by the momentum which it had gathered during the two previous years and by the Soviet understanding with the United States. In March, the Soviet delegate to the Geneva Disarmament Conference presented a draft treaty banning chemical weapons; in April, the convention banning the production or possession of biological weapons was opened for signature in London, Moscow, and Washington; and in May, the Seabed Treaty banning the location of arms on the ocean floor was brought into force by the ratifications of Britain, the Soviet Union, and the United States. But in the Third World the Soviet leadership found their traditional policy hard to reconcile with this new understanding. In the Middle East,[21] Egypt became a test case. Having failed to make 1971 his Year of Decision, Sadat paid two visits to Moscow in February and April 1972, doubtless in the hope of securing arms that would enable Egypt to 'eliminate the consequences of aggression' as defined in Article 8 of the Soviet-Egyptian Treaty of May 1971. The Soviet Defence Minister visited Egypt in May. The Soviet-American agreements concluded in that month induced a mood of despair in Egypt. On 18 July Sadat demanded the withdrawal of all Soviet military advisers and experts, estimated to number about 17,000. The Soviet Government took this blow (the forerunner of Sadat's decision, nearly two years later, to adopt a policy of 'positive neutrality' between the super-powers) on the chin. Within a fortnight the withdrawal had substantially been completed;

only a few hundred Soviet advisers were thought to have remained; and the Soviet Union lost the use of Egyptian airfields, although their Mediterranean naval squadron retained some facilities on the northern Egyptian coast.

The Soviet response was to reinforce success further north. Soviet naval activity along the Syrian coast increased; the return of Soviet-trained military to Syria was accelerated; further arms were delivered; and a SAM-3 system was brought into operation. On 9 April the Soviet Prime Minister had visited Iraq to sign a fifteen-year Treaty of Friendship and Cooperation.[22] As in the Egyptian model, the friendship was unbreakable. The only military commitment was cautious, being to the effect that each side would assist the other in strengthening its defences and that they would coordinate their positions in the event of a threat to peace. The Iraqi armed forces had been largely dependent on Soviet arms since 1963 and wholly so since 1969. Soviet arms supplies were now increased; and a few SAM-3 sites were brought into operation by the end of the year. Equally important, the Soviet Union undertook to help to distribute oil from the Iraq Petroleum Company field at Kirkuk, which the Iraqi Government had at last nationalized on 1 June, and to bring the North Rumaila oil field into large-scale production (Soviet imports of oil from Iraq appeared for the first time in the statistics of Soviet foreign trade in 1972, published one year later). This tightening of Soviet-Iraqi relations suggested that the Soviet Government was seeking to make the Gulf, from which British troops had been withdrawn at the end of 1971, a new focus of its policy in the Middle East. Diplomatic relations had already been established with Kuwait, although not yet with the Union of Arab Emirates that had been formed after the British withdrawal. As long ago as November 1940, during Molotov's last round of negotiations with Hitler and Ribbentrop, the German side had described the natural tendency of the USSR as being to move in the direction of the Indian Ocean. But thirty-two years later there was an important difference in the political geography of this immensely rich area: although Britain had withdrawn its military presence, Iran was on the way to becoming a formidably armed country, using part of its vast oil revenues to buy sophisticated modern weapons. The Soviet Union's need to remain on good terms with Iran, therefore, acted as a restraining influence; and in October the Shah, while on a visit to Moscow, signed a fifteen-year treaty of economic cooperation and trade.

The Soviet dilemma in the Third World was presented to the

Kremlin personally by the leaders of the two Latin American Marxist governments, those of Cuba and Chile, both of whom visited Moscow in December 1972, in order to seek financial aid. The Soviet answer to their requests for aid was given in blunt terms: to Cuba, a great deal, to Chile, very little. Cuba had five months earlier become a full member of the COMECON, thus qualifying—like Vietnam—for aid within the socialist commonwealth. But by any standards the terms of the deal[23] secured by Castro were generous: deferment of the repayment of the Cuban debt (estimated at nearly three billion dollars, excluding military aid) until 1986, after which it would be repaid free of interest; Soviet credits to cover Cuban trade deficits in 1973–6, also to be repaid after 1986 without interest; and a 330 million dollar development loan, to be repaid at a low rate of interest after 1976. The Russians also agreed to buy Cuban sugar and nickel for the rest of the decade at prices well above the world prices then obtaining.

The joint communiqué[24] issued after Allende's visit to the Soviet Union could hardly have offered a greater contrast. It had much to say about the two governments' identity of views on the problems of the rest of the world and little about either Chile itself or Latin America—a recognized Moscow method of dealing politely with a distinguished visitor who has not been granted what he hoped for. Having made it clear early in his presidency that he would not accept a Soviet military presence in Chile, Allende did not seek military aid. But by the end of 1972 he was in desperate financial straits, with agricultural production lowered in the wake of the Chilean agrarian reform, and inflation already soaring at a rate of 160 per cent per annum. (The World Bank, the Export-Import Bank, and the Inter-American Development Bank had all suspended lines of credit to Chile, mainly because of the Chilean Government's decision to nationalize, without compensation, US copper interests in Chile.) Having received Soviet trade credits the previous June worth 260 million dollars and obtained Soviet agreement to import 130,000 tons of Chilean copper (despite the fact that the Soviet Union is a net exporter of copper itself), Allende was believed at the time[25] to have come to Moscow in search of 500 million dollars in hard currency loans. The paragraph in the joint communiqué relating to Soviet aid was not explicit, referring to Soviet agreement to extend aid to Chile for a number of stated purposes, but subject to the conclusion of 'corresponding agreements' reflecting the 'concrete measures for implementing this agreement'. All that Allende seems to have received by way of immediate help was 30 million dollars' worth of credit for

Soviet deliveries of food and of cotton for the textile industry, and agreement to reschedule the repayment of Chile's debt to the Soviet Union, amounting to 103 million dollars.

Once bitten, twice shy; after the Cuban experience, the Soviet leadership did not, as *Le Monde* gently put it, consider that the Chilean experiment should be defended by all available means. A Soviet apologist for his government's treatment of Allende—the CPSU Central Committee responded to the military *coup d'état* that overthrew his government with no more than a brief expression of sympathy— would no doubt recall the fact that, instead of heeding the economic advice given him by the Chilean Communist Party, Allende followed the ruinous path preferred by the extremists of his own, socialist, party. Yet if he had accepted communist advice and thus strengthened his claim to Soviet support (which even then would have had to be on a huge scale in order to keep Allende's regime afloat), would this claim have been met, given the Soviet experience in Cuba and the new Soviet understanding with the United States?[26] As it was, the award of the Lenin Peace prize, although a compliment to a septuagenarian socialist, cannot have been much consolation to Allende as a president who needed far more than that in order to stay in power, or, as it turned out, to stay alive (he committed suicide after being deposed by the Chilean armed forces on 11 September 1973).

So ended 1972, a year of great change for the international status of the Soviet Union, now formally acknowledged by the world's first super-power as its equal: a change that was to be reflected in the following spring by the first new formulation in the doctrine of Soviet foreign policy for nearly two decades.

NOTES

1. In an interview published in *Time* magazine of 2 January, Nixon said: 'I believe in a world in which the United States is powerful. I think it will be a safer world and a better world if we have a strong, healthy United States, Europe, Soviet Union, China, Japan, each balancing the other, not playing against the other, an even balance.' The President was echoing a remark made by Kissinger in 1968, in 'Central Issues of American Foreign Policy', Brookings Institution, Washington: 'in the years ahead the most profound challenge . . . will be . . . to develop some concept of order in a world which is bipolar militarily, but multipolar politically'.
2. *Keesing's Contemporary Archives 1971/2*, pp. 25150 ff.
3. Respect for the sovereignty and territorial integrity of all states; non-aggression against other states; non-interference in the internal affairs of other states; equality and mutual benefit; and peaceful coexistence.

4. The mines were laid and activated on 11 May.
5. *Keesing's Contemporary Archives 1971/2*, pp. 25309 ff. and p. 25291. Subsequent quotations from other documents signed in Moscow are derived from the same source.
6. *The Military Balance 1972/3*, IISS, London, 1972, Appendix I, pp. 83 ff., analyses the effect of the SALT agreement on the strategic balance.
7. *Strategic Survey 1972*, IISS, London, 1973, p. 15.
8. Ibid., p. 14.
9. Ibid., p. 16.
10. *Diplomatiya Sotsializma*, Moscow, 1973, p. 171.
11. Cf. Brezhnev's remark, quoted in ch. 1, made a year later in Washington.
12. *Pravda*, 25 June 1973.
13. The United States Air Force is estimated to have dropped three and a half times as many bombs on Vietnam as it did on all the United States' enemies in the Second World War. For rough estimates of the cost, in blood and in treasure, of the Vietnam War, see *Strategic Survey 1972*, IISS, London, 1973, pp. 48 ff.
14. For a Japanese assessment of the range of responses open to Japan in the longer term, see Kiichi Saeko, 'Japan's Security in a Multipolar World', *Adelphi Papers* no. 92, IISS, London, 1972.
15. The Soviet Union had refused to sign the Japanese Peace Treaty negotiated at San Francisco in September 1951, under Article 2 of which Japan renounced all claim to the Kuriles. The state of war between the Soviet Union and Japan was nevertheless brought to an end in October 1956, by the re-establishment of diplomatic relations between the two countries.
16. *The Military Balance 1972/3*, IISS, London, 1972, p. 44.
17. The 1972 agreement in principle led in the end to Japanese participation on a modest scale, a $450 million loan from Japan for the development of Siberia, not including Tyumen': see *The Times*, 23 April and *Pravda*, 27 June 1974.
18. An account of the three-cornered manoeuvres that preceded the momentous vote of 17 May is given in Kulski, op. cit., pp. 428 ff. The text of the Basic Treaty is in *Survival*, January/February 1973, vol. XV, 1, pp. 31–2.
19. At their meeting in Prague in January 1972, the Warsaw Pact ministers had declared that the interests of European security would be served by reaching an agreement on the reduction of armed forces and armaments in Europe, although it could not be 'an exclusive matter for the existing military and political groupings in Europe to consider and determine the way in which to solve that problem'.
20. *Keesing's Contemporary Archives 1971/2*, p. 25676.
21. In Africa south of the Sahara, on the other hand, Soviet policy, although troubled by fierce Chinese competition for influence, notably in Tanzania (whose armed forces were exclusively trained by the Chinese), could afford to be long term. In Southern Africa the principal source of the supply of arms for the major guerrilla movements remained the Soviet Union. The Soviet Government also made some well-judged offers to African governments: for example, field artillery to Nigeria, which made an important contribution to the ending of the civil war in 1970 (*New York Times*, 21 January 1970: 'Nigeria says Russian help was vital to war victory'); and cash ($7,500,000) to Somalia for the development of the Port of Berbera, which was to become a valuable port of call for the Soviet Navy's squadron in the Indian Ocean. And the Soviet Navy patrolled the coast of Guinea after that country had been attacked from Portuguese Guinea in 1971.
22. In turning to Iraq, the Russians did the same as the British had done twenty-

four years earlier, when the future of their Egyptian base began to look insecure.

23. Summarized in *The Economist*, 13 January 1973.

24. Text in *Pravda*, 10 December 1972.

25. For contemporary assessments of his mission, see *The Economist* of 9 December and *Le Monde* of 7 December 1972.

26. For a Soviet posthumous criticism of Allende's economic mistakes, see A. Sobolev's article in *The Working Class and the Contemporary World*, no. 2, Moscow, 1974. The CPSU's expression of sympathy was carried in *Pravda*, 14 September 1973.

13

1973—ANNUS MIRABILIS?

At the Moscow summit meeting in 1972 Brezhnev had accepted an invitation to visit Washington the following year. Before he paid this return visit, and before he visited Bonn—the first time that the General-Secretary of the Soviet Communist Party had ever set foot in the Federal Republic of Germany—the Central Committee held a meeting on 27 April 1973, which took two major decisions. The first of these was to set the seal of the Committee's formal approval on a foreign policy that had become more and more identified with Brezhnev personally. The second was to make the first important changes in the composition of the Party Politburo for eight and a half years. Two members of the Politburo were dropped: Voronov and Shelest, the latter having already been removed a year before from his powerful post as head of the Ukrainian Communist Party (perhaps because he was opposed to receiving Nixon, just as he had allegedly been the leader of the hawks over Czechoslovakia in 1968). The three newcomers were Andrei Gromyko, the Foreign Minister, Marshal Andrei Grechko, the Defence Minister, and Yuri Andropov, the head of the KGB. None of the holders of these three offices would normally qualify for membership of the Politburo; the last time that any of the incumbents had done so had been in the 1950s. Brezhnev was thus able to embark on his two delicate missions in the summer backed both by the maximum of departmental expertise concentrated inside the Politburo and by a fresh mandate of the Central Committee of the CPSU.

This mandate was expressed in a resolution, to which the Soviet press gave especial publicity, entitled 'On the international activity of the Central Committee of the CPSU regarding the realization of the decisions of the XXIVth Party Congress'. The resolution[1] began by describing the Party's international policy in conventional terms: active and thrusting, relying on Soviet strength, power, and authority. Although imperialist aggression against Vietnam had been brought to a halt, constant watchfulness was required against any intrigues of the aggressive, reactionary circles of imperialism; in particular, the legal rights of the Arab peoples in their struggle against imperialist aggression must be supported. So far, no change. But the nub of the resolution was its emphasis on the principle of peaceful coexistence 'as a general rule'* of relations between states with different social systems. From this rule stemmed the switch from cold war to *détente* and the need to 'ensure that the favourable changes achieved in the international sphere should acquire an irreversible character'. The value of summit meetings was affirmed; so was the role of foreign trade as a way to help peace as well as the interests of the Soviet people. The resolution ended with an attack on the CCP leadership's alleged opposition to the unity of the world communist movement and to international *détente*. The emphasis on peaceful coexistence as a general rule in this declaration, and the link between foreign and domestic policy, were both pointed up by Brezhnev during his visit to the Federal Republic the following month, when he declared, in the course of his televised address to the German people, published in full by *Pravda* on its front page on 22 May: 'our peace-loving foreign policy is the expression of the very essence of our society, the expression of its deep internal needs ... our aim is to ensure that the Soviet people live better tomorrow than they do today'.

Europe

Brezhnev visited Bonn from 18 to 22 May.[2] The chief fruit of the visit was economic: a ten-year agreement on the development of economic, industrial, and technological cooperation between the Soviet Union and the Federal Republic. (An agreement on cultural cooperation was also

---

* A literal translation of the three Russian words *v kachestve normy* will not suffice, because of the different significance of the word 'norm' in the two languages. Their inclusion in the resolution was an important doctrinal innovation, whose significance was made clear by their appearance among the officially approved slogans for the October Revolution celebrations six months later (see *Pravda*, 14 October 1973). On 26 October Brezhnev described the principles of peaceful coexistence as 'gradually becoming converted into the generally accepted role of international life' (*Pravda*, 27 October 1973) and on 15 August, in his speech at Alma Ata, he defined the aim of Soviet foreign policy as 'to render irreversible the phenomenon of *détente*' (*Pravda*, 16 August 1973).

signed.) Six months previously the two sides had signed a declaration of intent concerning the construction of an integrated steelworks using the direct reduction process on the Kursk ore-fields in central Russia, the largest Soviet-West German project so far (a further long-term agreement for the supply of Soviet natural gas to the Federal Republic had been signed in 1972). Its total cost was estimated at DM3,000 million, including orders from West German firms worth at least DM2,000 million, to be financed by long-term credits granted by a West German consortium, which were to be repaid by the supply to West Germany of the product of the plant. The joint statement issued on 21 May welcomed the current negotiations[3] on industrial projects, including the Kursk steelworks; agreed to promote cooperation in the development of advanced technology and the creation of new production facilities in the USSR; while, for its part, the Federal Government declared its interest in receiving large supplies of crude oil from the Soviet Union.

At the opening banquet on 18 May, the Federal Chancellor made it clear where he stood politically: 'the Federal Republic is a member of the Atlantic Alliance. It is embedded in the community of Western Europe, which has now grown beyond the Common Market.' As for Berlin, it was still not all plain sailing. Although both the Ten-Year Agreement and the Cultural Agreement contained clauses applying them to West Berlin 'in accordance with the Four Power Agreement of 3 September 1971', the joint statement referred to a detailed exchange of views on questions concerning that agreement, and the two sides agreed that strict observance and full application of the agreement were essential to lasting *détente* in Central Europe and to the improvement of relations 'between the states concerned', especially between the Federal Republic and the Soviet Union. Speaking in the Bundestag afterwards, the Federal Chancellor denied that there was any question of altering the Four Power Agreement on Berlin, or of giving it a special interpretation for the Federal Republic's bilateral relationship with the Soviet Union. It had become clear as the result of Brezhnev's visit that practical difficulties existed between the two governments regarding the application of the agreement, which must be, and indeed could be, solved, by using the facilities offered by the agreement. Brandt went on to say that the situation in Berlin was the touchstone of West German-Soviet bilateral relations, and that so far as economic relations were concerned, no negotiations on specific projects had been conducted or decisions taken. The difficulty to which Brandt referred concerned the

precise nature of the consular representation of West Berlin to be undertaken by the Federal German authorities under the terms of the 1971
Agreement. This was not resolved until November, when a compromise
was agreed in Moscow between the Federal German and Soviet
Foreign Ministers.[4]

In June, after five months of preparatory talks in Vienna, the NATO
and Warsaw Pact governments concerned agreed to begin negotiations
on 30 October, again in Vienna, regarding 'mutual reduction of forces
and armaments in Central Europe', with what amounted to an open
agenda. Thus the adjective 'balanced' that had occurred in every NATO
pronouncement on this question since the ministerial meeting at Reykjavik in 1968, was dropped, although the communiqué[5] recorded agreement that specific arrangements would have to be carefully worked out
in scope and timing in such a way that they would in all respects and at
every point conform to the principle of undiminished security for each
party. On the NATO side, the participants did not include France; and
the Warsaw Pact side succeeded in securing agreement to the exclusion
of Hungary, which would have only observer status, along with Romania
Bulgaria, Norway, Denmark, Italy, Greece, and Turkey.

In the United States, Congressional pressure for a reduction in the
number of US troops stationed in Europe, excluding the Sixth Fleet,
mounted steadily. On 25 July Mike Mansfield proposed that the half
million US ground forces overseas should be cut by half within three
years, the axe to be applied most sharply to the 300,000 troops in
Europe. In the event, he changed the 50 per cent to 40 per cent shortly
before the Senate voted on his amendment, which was carried, by three
votes, for the first time in a decade. Although the amendment was
defeated in a subsequent vote,[6] and although the President could in any
case delay cuts in Europe by beginning with a reduction of the 168,000
US troops stationed in the Far East and South-East Asia, substantial
cuts seemed inevitable sooner or later in Europe, where, in the crucial
central sector, the Soviet Union retained its massive margin of numerical superiority in conventional forces. Leaving aside the number of
formations, Soviet—as opposed to Warsaw Pact—forces in this sector
had more tanks than all the NATO forces in the sector put together,
and the total number of Soviet tactical aircraft was slightly larger than
the NATO total, excluding France.[7]

When the thirty-five foreign ministers—from all Europe, except
Albania, and from the United States and Canada—convened on 3
July in Helsinki to prepare for the Conference on Security and Coopera-

tion in Europe, they adopted an agenda,[8] hammered out by their ambassadors over the previous six months, which bore a closer resemblance to what NATO ministers had suggested in the past than to what had been put forward by the ministers of the Warsaw Pact, although it was they who had launched the idea of a conference in 1965 and persisted in promoting it ever since. In particular, although the third section of the agenda, entitled 'cooperation in humanitarian and other fields', did not explicitly refer to the freer movement of ideas, it did contain several phrases which, if translated into action, would have that effect. The preparatory talks were notable both for Soviet resistance on this sensitive issue, and for a Romanian attempt to secure the inclusion of the phrase 'irrespective of membership of military and political groupings' in the list of principles which each participating country was committed to respect and apply in its relations with other participating states, by the terms of the first section of the agenda, entitled 'questions relating to security in Europe'. In the end, the words used were 'irrespective of their political, economic, and social systems'—less than the Romanians wanted and more than the Russians were at first prepared to concede. In his speech on 3 July,[9] Gromyko tried to claw this back, saying that cultural cooperation should observe fully 'the principles designed to govern relations between states', particularly those of sovereignty and non-intervention; and he pressed for a rapid conclusion of the conference before the end of the year. It was none the less agreed that the second stage of the conference should meet in Geneva on 18 September, and with such issues at stake, there was every indication that it would last for at least another year.

Thus, after years of bargaining, the Soviet Union and its allies got their European Conference and the United States and its allies got their negotiation on the reduction of forces in Central Europe, although both had to make concessions in order to secure their objectives. Meanwhile, Western Europe began 1973 with a bang—the signature of the Treaty of Accession by the three new members of the European Economic Community, Britain, Denmark, and Ireland—although by the end of the year the Community had been thrown into disarray. In Eastern Europe, COMECON's target of economic integration by 1985 had receded. This target, and the Complex Programme, remained a slogan, but in the course of 1973 the time-scale began to lengthen to twenty or twenty-five years. This was not simply the result of the four-fold increase in world oil prices at the end of the year, against whose effects Eastern Europe could not be immunized. The old idea of a crisis-proof

Eastern European monetary system was beginning to give way to a new concept of Eastern European cooperation, commercial and financial, with the Western economic community. The impulse for this change came from the needs of the Soviet economy, as much as from the desire of Eastern European governments for greater freedom to pursue their national interests. The old basis of the COMECON structure— broadly, an exchange of Soviet raw materials for Eastern European manufactured goods—weakened as the Soviet Union looked increasingly to the United States, Japan, and West Germany for help in the joint development of its natural resources, especially those located in Siberia. In consequence, Eastern European countries were, for their part, beginning increasingly to look westwards for sources of raw materials, for technical assistance in modernizing their industries, and for finance. Romania had become a member of the International Monetary Fund in 1972; Hungary joined Czechoslovakia, Romania, and Poland as a member of GATT; Eurodollar bank consortium loans to Eastern European countries rose sharply; the COMECON clearing bank itself raised loans in Western Europe; and there was even the prospect of joint ventures controlled by COMECON countries in Western countries. This loosening of COMECON made it increasingly important to establish some form of relationship between COMECON and the EEC. After Brezhnev had told the Luxembourg Foreign Minister (who happened to be visiting Moscow at the time) that COME-CON wanted to begin working together with the Community on monetary, financial, and investment questions, on 27 August the COMECON Secretary-General formally proposed to the Chairman of the EEC Council of Ministers that both organizations should appoint delegations to discuss cooperation.[10]

The Washington Agreements

It has been suggested in the opening chapter that one of the agreements signed by Brezhnev during his visit to Washington may be regarded as terminating the cold war: the Agreement on the Prevention of Nuclear War of 22 June 1973. The contrast between the circumstances in which Brezhnev visited the United States, from 18 to 25 June 1973, and those of Khrushchev's visit fourteen years earlier could scarcely have been greater. True, in the intervening fourteen years the brave new communist world prophesied by Khrushchev had not materialized—the gap in living standards and gross national product between the two countries remained enormous. Militarily, however, the dialogue between the two leaders was now conducted between equals; and it was not just a dialogue, but—as in Moscow the year before—a negotiation expressed in written agreements. Moreover, by the time Brezhnev arrived in Washington, events there had reached a point where the visit of the most powerful leader in the communist world served to strengthen domestically the most powerful leader in the capitalist world, by diverting the attention of the American public for one week from the televised hearings of the Senate Watergate Committee, which suspended its activities while Brezhnev was in the United States as the government's official guest. This paradox was unknown to the rank and file of the Soviet public, who learned nothing about the Watergate scandal from Soviet sources until the second half of August, when Moscow radio broke the official silence by attributing it to the fears of Nixon's opponents that he might 'go too far in his steps towards the relaxation of international tension'.[11]

The key-note of the Washington agreements was the use of the word 'permanent'. The preamble of the communiqué issued on 25 June[12] recorded the decision of both sides to turn the development of friendship and cooperation between their peoples into a permanent factor for world-wide peace; and the United States President accepted Brezhnev's invitation to pay a second visit to the Soviet Union, in 1974. In spite of the constraints of Watergate, the 'broad network of constructive relationships' between the two super-powers—the aim of the new American diplomacy—was further strengthened.

Three nuclear agreements were signed, one relating to the peaceful use of atomic energy and the other two to the prevention of nuclear war and to the limitation of nuclear weapons. Under the terms of the first, for a duration of ten years, both sides agreed to expand and strengthen their cooperation in the fields of controlled nuclear fusion, fast breeder reactors, and research on the fundamental properties of matter, and to set up a joint committee to this end. The second agreement[13] was a Soviet initiative. It is of unlimited duration; its second article binds the Soviet Union and the United States to 'proceed from the premise that each party will refrain from the threat or use of force against the other party, against the allies of the other party and against other countries, in circumstances which may endanger international peace and security'. These last nine words provide a possible loophole, which Kissinger was at pains to close when, in an explanatory news conference held after the agreement's signature, he urged that the document should not be approached with the eye of a sharp lawyer; and he conceded that in the light of history, if either signatory wanted to go to war, it would, as before, find an excuse to do so.[14] This agreement also included an article (IV), which—although Kissinger said it did not make the United States an arbiter between the Soviet Union and China—defined the special relations between the super-powers in the strategic field in the following terms:

If at any time relations between the parties or between either party and other countries appear to involve the risk of a nuclear war between the USA and the USSR or between either party and other countries, the United States and the Soviet Union . . . shall immediately enter into urgent consultations with each other. . . .

The third agreement[15] committed the two governments to make serious efforts to work out the provisions of a permanent agreement on the limitation of strategic offensive arms, with the objective of signing it in 1974. They described the prospects for a permanent agreement in 1974 as favourable. The events of the following year proved them wrong. Among the weaknesses of this agreement are the inadequacy of the national technical means of verification envisaged, and the contrast between the third and fifth articles, the former stating that limitations 'can apply' to the quantitative aspects of strategic weapons as well as to their qualitative improvement, and the latter envisaging their modernization and replacement, under conditions to be agreed between the parties. The present prospect is that by 1975 Soviet SS-18 rockets, the most powerful in the world, will be deployed, equipped with MIRVs, which have since been developed by the Soviet Union; meanwhile the United States has been reported to be developing a more sophisticated version of MIRV, known as MARV—manoeuvrable re-entry vehicle— the flight path of whose individual warheads can be influenced from the launching-point, instead of being pre-determined.[16] This technology is intended for use in the *Trident* submarine, whose rapid construction was approved by the US Senate in September 1973.[17] The first of these vessels should be ready by 1978, at a cost of 1,300 million dollars. Carrying 24 missiles, each armed with 10–14 independently targetable warheads with a range of 6,000 miles, it will be both faster and quieter— and therefore harder to hunt and destroy—than previous submarines, and will have a displacement larger than that of a modern British cruiser.

In the commercial field, American firms had governmental encouragement to work out concrete proposals on specific projects involving the participation of American companies, including the delivery of Siberian natural gas[18] to the United States. A sign of the times was the front page of *Pravda* on 24 June, which devoted a few lines to the CPSU General-Secretary's meeting with American Communist Party leaders, but the whole of the rest to his meeting with American businessmen, whose names and firms were spelled out in full. It was on this occasion that he spoke with candour both about the origins of the cold war—leaving it an open question which side had been responsible for it in the first place—and about deficiencies in the Soviet economy generally and in the handling of Soviet foreign trade in particular. In his televised address to the American people, which text took up the front page of *Pravda* of 25 June, Brezhnev reverted to the question of the cold war, describing it as 'a miserable substitute for real war', whose 'sombre influence is unfortunately preserved to some extent even to the present day'. He emphasized that both the Soviet Union and the United States respected the fact that each had its own allies and obligations to other governments. But the chief significance of what he and the President had discussed and agreed was the determination of both sides to make good relations between the USSR and the USA a permanent factor of international peace. He might well have added that this new relationship between the super-powers was symbolized by the plan for the meeting of their astronauts in space in July 1975.

Apart from the Watergate affair and related scandals, whose drama was resumed as soon as Brezhnev left America, two other shadows hung over the visit: the failure of the two governments to make any headway over the Middle East, their only point of agreement being that it caused both of them deep concern—with good reason, as events were soon to prove—and the question whether Congress would approve the granting of most-favoured-nation treatment to the Soviet Union. Two months later, a Soviet periodical[19] carried an abridged version of an article entitled 'USSR–USA and the Contemporary World', written by the chief editor of the Soviet journal *USA*, who had remained in the United States for some time after Brezhnev's visit, in order to sound the opinions of leading figures across the whole range of the American political spectrum. Basing himself on the premise that the changes both in Soviet-American relations and in the world as a whole were due to the decisive change in the Marxist correlation of world forces, which had obliged the leaders of the capitalist powers to carry out ' "an agonizing re-appraisal" of their foreign policy doctrines', the writer of this article went on to observe that the question that now interested many people both in the United States and in other countries was whether stability in US-Soviet relations was possible. So far as the Soviet side was concerned, the answer was clearly affirmative. As for the American side, it was not merely a matter of the good will of the present Administration or of external factors, but also of internal political problems in the United States which had necessitated new approaches and concepts both in the international and in the domestic field. The conclusions drawn were that the Administration's policy towards the Soviet Union had bipartisan support to a remarkable degree and that there were grounds for hoping that the world really was entering an era of *détente*.

What was significant in this article was the evident anxiety that this assessment should prove to be correct. By the autumn pressures were building up in the Western world with the object of making any concessions to the Soviet Union in the field of foreign policy dependent on Soviet willingness to modify internal policy—this in spite of the appeal of Kissinger, newly appointed Secretary of State,[20] for a fresh consensus behind US foreign policy and Brandt's statement that his government would have pursued the same *Ostpolitik* even if Stalin had still been head of the Soviet Government.[21] In the United States these pressures focused on the clause* in the Trade Reform Bill granting most-favoured-nation treatment to the Soviet Union, that is to say, the termination of the existing tariff discrimination against Soviet goods to which the Administration stood committed by the Moscow commercial agreement of 1972. Under the leadership of Jackson and Vanik, overwhelming support was secured in Congress for withholding not only MFN treatment but—more important—American credits and credit guarantees backed by the US Government, from countries denying free emigration or imposing more than nominal taxes on emigrants. This support was reflected in a non-binding resolution, passed in the Senate by an unopposed vote of eighty-five on 18 September, condemning Soviet treatment of political dissidents and calling on the President to use current negotiations to secure its end. As Jackson remarked, 'now, at the beginning of the road to *détente*, is the time to test the direction we are asked to travel'. Further evidence of Soviet awareness of the significance of the Jackson amendment was supplied by the description of Jackson as the darling of the military-industrial complex in *Pravda*,

* The object of this bill was to give the US Administration a mandate to negotiate further liberalization of world trade with other countries in the GATT framework. The clause relating to MFN treatment for the Soviet Union was tacked on to the bill by the Nixon Administration as an afterthought.

which accused him of interfering in the Soviet Union's internal affairs for purely political motives.[22] Soviet anxieties were deepened by the dramatic news of the President's dismissal of the Watergate Special Prosecutor and the consequent resignation of the US Attorney-General in October,* when the Fourth Arab-Israeli War had been raging for nearly a week.

* *Novoe Vremya* gave the Soviet public this news at the end of October—by Moscow standards, promptly—but it was not until this periodical appeared on 2 November 1973 that Soviet readers were informed for the first time of the possibility that Nixon might be impeached by Congress, the word 'impeachment' being transliterated into cyrillics. No comment was offered.

NOTES

1. Text in *Pravda*, 28 April 1973.
2. Once again, the Soviet leadership took pains to preserve their links with France: Brezhnev received Pompidou in January, before the French parliamentary elections, and he stopped in France for talks on his way back from Washington in June. He also visited the German Democratic Republic and Poland immediately before his visit to the Federal German Republic, and at a meeting of bloc party leaders, held in the Crimea at the end of July, he obtained their approval of his summit diplomacy: see *Pravda*, 1 April 1973.
3. *Keesing's Contemporary Archives 1973*, pp. 25975 ff. The Kursk negotiations came to fruition two years later.
4. As a result of this compromise, the Federal German and Czechoslovak governments were able to sign a peace treaty on 28 November. Signature had previously been held up by this disagreement.
5. Text in *The Times*, 29 June 1973.
6. Ibid., 28 September 1973. The lobby for the cut in American forces abroad rests its case partly on political and partly on financial grounds. The latter can be summarized in a single statistic: the average cost of US military pay per man rose from 5,081 dollars in 1967/8 to 8,533 dollars in 1972/3. For leaked reports of an American plan for a 15 per cent cut in US troop levels in Europe, see *The Times*, 15 September 1973.
7. *The Military Balance 1973/4*, IISS, London, 1973, Appendices I and II, pp. 87 ff.
8. *The Times*, 2 and 3 July 1973.
9. Ibid., 4 July 1973.
10. Ibid., 28 August 1973: and for an assessment of the changes in COMECON, see *The Times*, 24 September 1973, 'Eastern Europe: Changing Priorities' by Kurt Weisskopf.
11. *The Times*, 21 August 1973, 'Mr Nixon Gets a Little Help from His Friends' by Victor Zorza. Soviet citizens able to listen to foreign broadcasts would of course have followed the affair throughout.
12. Text in *The Times*, 26 June 1973. The phrase was also used by Brezhnev in his televised address to the American people: see *Pravda*, 25 June 1973.
13. Text in *The Times*, 23 June 1973.

14. Ibid., 23 June 1973.
15. Ibid., 22 June 1973.
16. For MIRVs, see ibid., 18 August 1973, quoting James Schlesinger's press conference of the previous day. For MARVs, see *The Economist*, 26 January 1974, p. 56.
17. *The Times*, 28 September 1973.
18. Ibid., 22 June 1973, reported that an annual figure of 200 million dollars worth of natural gas, over twenty years, was being mentioned in Washington at the time, together with Export-Import Bank finance for a part of the cost of a 400 million dollar fertilizer plant.
19. Berezhkov in *Literaturnaya Gazeta*, no. 35, 29 August 1973. pp. 9 and 14.
20. Kissinger retained his post as Special Assistant to the President for National Security Affairs.
21. *The Times*, 10 October and 13 September 1973 respectively.
22. Ibid., 19 September, and *Pravda*, 7 October 1973.

14

1973: THE TEST

In October 1973, less than four months after the signature of the Washington Agreements, the new relationship between the super-powers was subjected to its first serious test, when war broke out between their clients in the Middle East, for the fourth time in a quarter of a century.

On the eve of this war, whose profound consequences are still being felt today—not only by the participants and the super-powers—how would the international scene have appeared to a well-informed observer in the Kremlin? Since anniversaries have a special attraction in Moscow, he might have begun his reflections by recalling that it was almost thirty years since what were then the world's Three Great Powers met at the Teheran Conference; just over twenty years since Stalin died; sixteen years since the first *sputnik*; eleven years since the first Soviet ballistic missiles were installed in Cuba; just over ten years since the Sino-Soviet dispute was publicly acknowledged in the Soviet Union and since the Soviet Government joined with the governments of its two former partners in the Grand Alliance in signing the partial Nuclear Test Ban Treaty; and not quite nine years since the resignation of Khrushchev and the explosion of the first Chinese nuclear device. What would have struck him most about the past decade was the increasing intimacy of his country's relations with the leader of the capitalist world, the United States, and the increasing acrimony of those with the leader of the great Marxist heresy, China. The Soviet Government was still theoretically* bound by the defence obligations of the

* *Pravda*, 16 October 1973, included, among Soviet proposals that the Chinese had rejected, 'confirmation of the validity of the Treaty of 1950'.

thirty-year Sino-Soviet Treaty of Alliance and Friendship signed in 1950. But by now dependable Chinese missiles could reach Moscow and other targets in European Russia.

It was no doubt with an eye to the Xth CCP Congress that, in a speech delivered on 15 August in Central Asia, at Alma Ata, Brezhnev repeated the offer that he had made to the Chinese Party leadership two years earlier at the XXIVth CPSU Congress (to normalize Sino-Soviet state relations and restore good-neighbourliness and friendship). Speaking on 24 September at Tashkent, again in Central Asia, he reveal-ed that as recently as mid-June the Chinese Government had not even replied to a renewed Soviet offer of a non-aggression pact, although he simultaneously warned third parties against trying to make capital out of the Sino-Soviet dispute.[1] The Chinese response to the Soviet Union was not encouraging. At the end of August, the New China News Agency, after accusing the Soviet Union of having dismembered Romania and subjugated Bulgaria, concluded: 'The Romanov dynasty and the Khrushchev-Brezhnev dynasty are linked by a black line, that is, the aggressive and expansionist nature of Great Russian chauvinism and imperialism. The only difference is that the latter dons a cloak of "socialism"—"social imperialism" in the true sense of the term.'[2] The Chinese radio broadcast at length a speech made by the Chinese Prime Minister at the CCP Congress, in the course of which he went so far as to compare Brezhnev with Hitler and accused him of trying to get money from capitalist countries as a reward for opposing China.[3] On 28 July he said that both the contradictions between the two super-powers and their contention were ceaselessly intensifying, and that their temporary compromise and collusion would in no way change the nature of either of them.[4] Chinese opposition to the monopoly of world affairs by the super-powers was repeated by the Chinese Prime Minister at the banquet given in honour of Pompidou on 11 September, when he also reaffirmed Chinese support for the cause of Western European unity.[5]

The strength of the language used by the Chinese, who again spoke of the danger of a Soviet pre-emptive nuclear strike, may have been partly attributable to trouble on the Sino-Mongolian border (little more than 300 miles from the Chinese capital). In September a fresh element was injected into the Sino-Soviet dispute by a Mongolian press allega-tion that China had been violating this frontier.[6] (Of the forty-five Soviet divisions stationed in the Sino-Soviet border area, two are in the Mongolian Republic.)[7] But the two major attacks on Chinese policy that appeared in *Pravda* in August over the pen-name Aleksandrov provided enough explanation in themselves. The second[8] of these left nothing unsaid. The CCP, which represented the Soviet Union as its principal enemy, preached:

a reactionary pseudo-theory borrowed from bourgeois ideologists, according to which the march of historical development allegedly determines a 'conflict' of all small and medium states of the world with the two 'super-powers' . . . the absurd thesis of the 'two intermediate zones',[9] according to which the oppressed peoples of Asia, Africa and Latin America (the 'first zone') are allegedly not only 'linked by common interests' with certain basically capitalist countries of West and East (the 'second zone'), but they should and can unite with this 'zone' in a struggle against the 'super-powers'.

Thus China portrayed itself as the defender of the interests of small and medium countries and the leader of the Third World, to which it claimed to belong, instead of to the communist world. In spite of this, at the same time the Chinese leadership were forcing forward their country's conversion into a nuclear super-power, with the object of controlling the destinies of other countries. The chief proof of China's ideas of hegemony cited by Aleksandrov was Chinese policy in South-East Asia, where the Chinese aim was to establish a group of states under the aegis of Peking. China had aligned itself in an opportunistic alliance with the most aggressive circles of imperialism against the socialist countries, and had reoriented its foreign trade at the expense of its links with the communist world. China not only opposed the Soviet Union's European policy—the Moscow and Warsaw Treaties and the European Conference—but even pronounced panegyrics of NATO and the 'principles of Atlantism', and favoured the maintenance of the American military presence in Europe and a new Atlantic charter.[10] While opposing the Soviet suggestion of Asian collective security, China supported the US-Japanese security agreement and the US nuclear zone in the Far East; it had also tried to propagate the illusion in Tokyo that China had chosen Japan as its permanent partner for the joint decision of all Asian issues; it had encouraged Japanese territorial claims[11] against the Soviet Union; and had sought to dissuade Japan from pursuing a policy of peaceful coexistence with the socialist commonwealth.

China was further reproached for its refusal to sign the nuclear treaties;[12] for its refusal to consider the Soviet proposal for a treaty renouncing the use of force and its rejection of repeated proposals for the settlement of frontier questions; and for Chou En-lai's description of the Washington Agreement on the prevention of nuclear war as a mere scrap of paper. The absurd claims to broad areas of Soviet territory, false allegations about plans for a Soviet pre-emptive nuclear strike, and insinuations about an alleged 'threat from the North' were all spread by the Maoist leadership not only in order to work up a war fever and to justify the nuclear arms race, but also to divert popular attention from internal difficulties. Maoist ambitions of great power hegemony were described as being in contradiction with the needs of the Chinese people, whose interests did not coincide with the great power chauvinism of its leaders—a clear appeal to Chinese public opinion over the heads of the party leadership. For its part, the Soviet Union would continue its struggle against the theory and practice of Maoism, a trend hostile to Leninism, although it stood ready to restore its inter-state relations with China to normal.

Brezhnev's speeches and *Pravda*'s anathemas may have been aimed at a future Chinese leadership, rather than at the CCP Congress. So long as Mao Tse-tung remains in office, any normalization that goes beyond the courtesies required by the presence of ambassadors in the two capitals is hardly conceivable. What therefore is the best that our imaginary observer in the Kremlin could reasonably hope for? Anything resembling a renewal of the Sino-Soviet bloc would require a reconciliation between the two major communist parties that would resolve both the ideological and the state issues dividing the Soviet Union and China. By 1973 these divisions were so profound and so numerous that, from the Soviet viewpoint, the optimum goal had become simply an agreement to differ: perhaps something on the lines of the principles of the Belgrade Declaration of June 1955* (when Khrushchev made his Canossa journey, after seven years of Soviet-Yugoslav hostility), or at any rate a restoration of relations between the two governments to a state that would leave each party free to compete for world leadership—but not at the current level of mutual vituperation—and would enable both governments to devote less effort to preparing for a war that could benefit no one, and that would do incalculable harm.

Within the Soviet Union, our observer would have been aware that in spite of the Central Committee's April mandate for Brezhnev's

---

* The relevance of this declaration, which has served the Yugoslav leadership as the touchstone of their oscillating relationship with the Soviet Union ever since, is that it was an agreement of principles reached between the two governments, not the two parties: see Brzezinski, op. cit., pp. 177 ff., and Kulski, op. cit., pp. 339 ff.

foreign policy, of which the new concept of foreign trade formed an integral part, there were still autarkic voices prophesying woe among the planners trained in methods of the Stalinist era, who either could not or would not adapt themselves to the new model of compensation agreements, whereby credits from Western countries are devoted to producing commodities in the Soviet Union, part of which are used to repay the credits, over a long period of years. That these voices were audible in the Kremlin is suggested by the appearance of two articles in May 1973, defending the credit-barter compensation model. (In one of these[13] *Pravda* even felt obliged to cite Leninist principles to justify economic links with capitalist countries.) The natural allies of such critics of the new foreign policy would be those who feared its effects within the borders of the Soviet Union. Such fears would have been lessened by the tightening of the bonds of internal discipline and the steady weakening of the dissident movement in the Soviet Union.

The last edition—the twenty-seventh—of the *Samizdat* chronicle of current events had appeared in October 1972. At the end of August 1973—just before the second stage of the European Conference on Security and Cooperation was due to open in Geneva—two Soviet dissidents, Yakir and Krasin, pleaded guilty to offences under Article 70 of the Russian Federation's penal code, allegedly linked with the activities of organizations in the West. In the course of this trial, the names of Sakharov and Solzhenitsyn were implicated by the defendants. Both reacted forcefully. Solzhenitsyn said in a press interview in August that so long as permission to print his works in the Soviet Union was withheld, he would continue to have them printed by Western publishers; on 21 September he announced that he had begun underground circulation in the Soviet Union of two hitherto unpublished chapters of *The First Circle*;[14] and in the same month he decided to publish, in Paris, the most damaging attack on the Soviet system that he had ever written— *Gulag Archipelago*—for this reason:

with an uneasy heart I refrained for years from printing this book that was already completed; my duty towards those still alive outweighed my duty towards the dead. But now that the State Security has in any case seized this book nothing remains for me but to publish it at once.[15]

Adding what must have seemed to the Soviet leadership insult to injury, on 5 September Solzhenitsyn sent them a letter,[16] which was later published in the West. In this he put forward a programme of proposals aimed at preventing war with China, which he regarded as the chief danger facing the Soviet Union abroad, and at preserving the

Russian environment and the Russian nation: these proposals included repudiation of official support both of Marxism as a state ideology and of national liberation movements, termination of Soviet tutelage over Eastern Europe, permission for national republics to leave the Soviet Union, a Soviet agrarian reform on the Polish model, and concentration of Russian effort on domestic problems, especially development of the Siberian north-east. Five months later Solzhenitsyn was arrested by the KGB, and deported to the Federal Republic of Germany, on 12 February 1974.

For his part, Sakharov gave a long press conference on 21 August 1973 in his flat in Moscow, the full text of which was published in the West.[17] In the course of this he lamented the much stronger reprisals taken against Soviet political dissidents during the previous two years; he described the Soviet elite as having a 'sort of separate thinking' which prevented them from reacting differently from the way in which they did; and he declared:

a rapprochement while the West accepts our rules of the game . . . would be very dangerous . . . would not solve any of the world's problems, and would mean simply a capitulation to our real or exaggerated strength. It would mean an attempt to trade, to get gas and oil from the US, neglecting all other aspects of the problem . . . *détente* without any qualifications would mean the cultivation and encouragement of closed countries . . . no one should dream of having such a neighbour, especially if this neighbour is armed to the teeth.

The subsequent campaign in the Soviet press against these two world-famous figures caused a wave of indignation in the West. Ironically, this happened at a time when, following the outcry aroused by the Leningrad trials[18] of December 1970, an unprecedented number of Soviet Jews received permission to emigrate to Israel (70,000 in the period from 1971 to September 1973), and when the stiff emigration tax on Soviet Jews applying for exit visas was suspended, in deference to American pressure in April 1973. Moreover, in Marc Chagall's old age an exhibition was at last allowed of his works, which had lain for years in the cellars of Soviet museums; and just before the Geneva Conference opened, the Soviet authorities stopped jamming Western broadcasts in Russian. Nevertheless, when Soviet policy towards the dissidents was clearly intended either to silence them at home or to force them into exile, Sakharov had come uncomfortably close to the heart of the matter.

To sum up, in the autumn of 1973, although an observer in the

Kremlin would have been well satisfied with the Soviet-American agreements of the previous two years, he could not have ignored the shadows threatening the super-power relationship; and he would have been acutely conscious that the country that would gain most from a breakdown of this relationship would be China. In these circumstances it is hard to believe that on 6 October the Syrian and Egyptian combined attack on Israel, which achieved complete tactical surprise, can have been welcome to the Soviet leadership.

The Arab-Israeli War

The course of the war has been described in detail by other writers.[19] The war, which lasted from 6 to 25 October, was longer, more evenly balanced, more bitterly contested, and more costly in loss of life and of material than any of the three previous Middle Eastern wars. The Arab attack was launched on two fronts: the northern, on the Golan Heights, and the southern, in the Sinai Peninsula, both of which had been occupied by Israeli forces since the Six Day War of 1967. In the north, the Syrian forces were helped by Arab allies from as far afield as Morocco. Both attacks achieved initial success. But by 12 October the Israeli counter-attack on the northern front had reached a point twenty miles from Damascus, and on the southern front their counter-attacking force west of the Canal was about fifty miles from Cairo when the fighting stopped. Nevertheless, in strong contrast with previous Arab-Israeli wars, in this one neither side emerged as the victor; and because Israel had won the wars of 1948, 1956, and 1967 outright, this time it was the Arabs who acquired a new feeling of military confidence on the battlefields, whereas Israel's invincibility was called in question for the first time. This war also differed from earlier Middle Eastern wars in two other, highly significant ways: the use of economic warfare by the Arab oil-producing countries, and the involvement of the two super-powers, which culminated in the nearest approach to a nuclear confrontation between them since the Cuban missile crisis, exactly eleven years before.

In October 1973, for the first time, the Arabs used the power of their oil resources to apply political pressure to Israel's principal protector, the United States: an embargo on oil supplies to the United States, a cut-back in production and—above all—an increase in oil prices, which led to the world energy crisis of 1974 (a crisis which the war did not cause, though it hastened its onset).

The super-powers' intervention took two forms. As adversaries, the Soviet and United States governments each delivered vast supplies of arms by air to the combatants in the Middle East, to replace the losses incurred in battle. As partners, they conferred, both with each other and with their allies. At any rate so far as the public record is concerned, the first Soviet reaction to the Arab attacks was one of reserve. On 8 October the Soviet Union was warned by the United States that it could not disregard the principles of *détente* in any area of the world 'without imperilling its entire relationship with the United States.'[20] Brezhnev responded the following day with a message to the Algerian President suggesting that all possible aid should be sent to Egypt and Syria; and on 10 October the Soviet airlift of military supplies to the Middle East began. The American airlift to Israel was announced on 13 October; and on 19 October a bill was presented to Congress seeking 2·2 billion dollars military aid for Israel.

The day after the Israeli bridgehead had been established on the west bank of the Suez Canal, Kosygin arrived in Cairo, where he spent three days. On 20 October Kissinger visited Moscow, where agreement was reached between the two governments to sponsor jointly a resolution in the Security Council calling for an immediate cease-fire and for the implementation of the Council's Resolution 242 of November 1967. After Kissinger had flown from Moscow to Tel Aviv, both sides accepted the resolution, which brought the cease-fire into force on 22 October. The cease-fire soon broke down, with the prospect that the Egyptian Third Army, established in force on the east bank of the canal, would be cut off by the Israeli force that had by then reached Suez. After the super-powers had co-sponsored a second resolution in the Security Council, calling for a withdrawal to the positions of 22 October, the Egyptian Government pressed the Soviet and US governments to intervene militarily on the spot to ensure Israeli withdrawal. This was followed on 24 October by a personal message from Brezhnev to the US President, which was interpreted in Washington as a Soviet threat to intervene unilaterally in Egypt unless Israel observed the cease-fire of 22 October. For a few hours, in the early morning of 25 October, the American response took the form of a world-wide Defence Condition Three alert. Later on the same day, a third Security Council resoluton[21] was passed, which finally brought the war in Egypt to an end. It was agreed to send a United Nations Emergency Force to the Middle East, from which troops not only of the super-powers, but of all five permanent members of the Security Council, were excluded. On 28 October

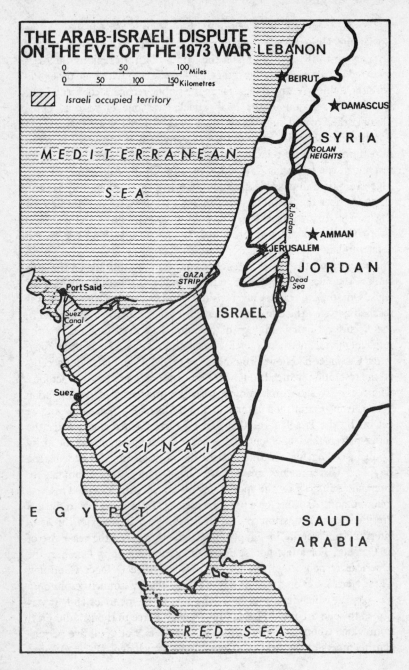

146

THE ARAB-ISRAELI DISPUTE
ON THE EVE OF THE 1973 WAR

LEBANON

0   50   100 Miles
0   50   100 150 Kilometres

Israeli occupied territory

BEIRUT

DAMASCUS

SYRIA

GOLAN
HEIGHTS

MEDITERRANEAN

SEA

R. Jordan

AMMAN

JERUSALEM

JORDAN

GAZA
STRIP

Dead
Sea

ISRAEL

Port Said

Suez
Canal

Suez

S I N A I

E G Y P T

SAUDI

ARABIA

RED SEA

the first meeting between Egyptian and Israeli officers for seventeen years took place, at Kilometre 101 on the Suez-Cairo road. Thus Soviet military intervention in Egypt was prevented; the encircled Egyptian Third Army was saved; and Sadat succeeded in making 1973 his year of decision.

To this brief account must be added a complicating factor: that the Middle Eastern crisis coincided with major developments in American domestic politics. On 10 October Spiro Agnew resigned as Vice-President under threat of indictment; two days later Gerald Ford was appointed Vice-President in his place; and on 12 October, by dismissing the Special Watergate Prosecutor, Nixon took a decisive step on the road that was to lead to his resignation nine months later as President of the United States.

Future historians will no doubt seek to provide the answers to four questions arising from the October war. First, in their attitudes towards the Middle East, where the temperature mounted steadily during the three and a half months that followed the signature of the Agreement on the Prevention of Nuclear War in Washington, to what extent did the Soviet and the US governments 'act in such a manner as to prevent the development of situations capable of causing a dangerous exacerbation of their relations, as to avoid military confrontations, and as to exclude the outbreak of nuclear war between them'? Second, once unmistakable signals that the Arab attack on Israel was imminent were received in Moscow (earlier, but perhaps not much earlier, than in Washington), did the Soviet Government act in the manner prescribed by the Treaty of June 1973, in relation both to the Arab governments concerned and to the US Government? Third, once the war had begun, how quickly did the Soviet and US governments 'enter into urgent conversations with each other'? (The meeting between the US Secretary of State and the Soviet leadership in Moscow did not take place until after two weeks of fighting and after both the Soviet and the US governments had started their air-lifts.) Fourth, what was the precise chain of events between the meeting in Moscow and the second cease-fire five days later; and in particular did the Soviet and United States governments misunderstand each other's intentions at any point during that critical period?

Without awaiting the full evidence required to answer these specific questions, some preliminary conclusions can be drawn with a fair measure of confidence. In general, although the strain to which the Middle Eastern War subjected the new relationship between the super-powers was severe, what matters is that their relationship survived it unimpaired. In particular, even in the early hours of 25 October what Soviet theorists call the *nekontroliruemyi element** in crisis management was contained. Each of the two governments achieved its immediate aim on that day. Moreover, the political outcome of the war was something completely new: the opening of negotiations between Arabs and Israelis at last—in December, in Geneva, under the co-Chairmanship of the Soviet and US governments. The contrast between the crisis of 14–28 October 1962 and that of 6–25 October 1973 speaks for itself.

* Literally translated, 'the uncontrollable element'—the factor of miscalculation—quoted from V. V. Zhurin and E. M. Primakov, *Mezhdunarodnye konflikty*, Moscow, 1972, p. 21, by Hannes Adomeit in *Adelphi Papers*, no. 101, p. 5, IISS, London, 1973.

NOTES

1. *The Times*, 25 September 1973.
2. Ibid., 27 August 1973.
3. Ibid., 1 September 1973.
4. Ibid., 30 July 1973.
5. *Glasgow Herald*, 12 September 1973.
6. *The Times*, 13 September 1973.
7. However, only about one-third of these Soviet divisions are 'first category' (between three-quarters and full strength and with complete equipment), whereas in Eastern Europe all thirty-one Soviet divisions are in this category: see *The Military Balance 1973/4*, IISS, London, 1973, p. 6.
8. *Pravda*, 26 August 1973. Both articles had been cleared at the highest CPSU level.
9. This concept, otherwise known as the 'changing geographical vortex of the revolution', had indeed been evolved by the Chinese in the early sixties, when they first began publicly to attack what they regarded as a Soviet-American attempt to establish a global hegemony: see Brzezinski, op. cit., pp. 403 ff.
10. A reference to Nixon's proposals for making 1973 the 'year of Europe', put forward on his behalf by Kissinger in a speech on 23 April 1973. By the end of the year the US and its allies were to have worked out 'a new Atlantic charter setting the goals for peace'. For the nine EEC governments' draft of such a declaration, agreed at Copenhagen in September, see *The Times*, 25 September 1973.
11. On 20 September the Japanese Diet voted unanimously, including the Communist Party, in favour of a demand for the return of the four southern Kurile islands.
12. The text in fact reads: 'the Nuclear Weapons Non-Proliferation Treaty of 1963'. The writer presumably had had both the Non-Proliferation and the Test Ban treaties in mind.
13. *The Times*, 12 June 1973, published an article by Nove summarizing it. In an article published by *The Times* on 11 July, 'Telling Omissions in Soviet Economic Performance', Nove pointed out that, for the first time ever in any

year in which Soviet foreign trade figures were published, those for 1972 (published in mid-1973) contained no word whatsoever about any grain, except rice.

14. A brief statement made it clear that Solzhenitsyn's purpose was to test how the Soviet authorities would in practice adhere to the international copyright convention, which the Soviet Government had at last signed in May: see *The Times* of 22 and 28 September 1973.

15. *Archipelag Gulag*, YMCA Press, Paris, 1973, on the fly-leaf.

16. This letter has since been published in paperback by Fontana, 1974.

17. See *The Times*, 22 August and 5 September 1973.

18. When several Soviet Jews were condemned to death for having tried to hijack an aircraft in order to fly to Israel.

19. For example, *Strategic Survey 1973*, IISS, London, 1974, examines the war in all its aspects. See also *Survival*, May/June 1974, 'Soviet Aims and the Middle East War', pp. 106 ff., by Galia Golan.

20. Kissinger's words at the *Pacem in Terris* conference, to which he added 'coexistence to us continues to have a very precise meaning: we will oppose the attempt of any country to achieve a position of predominance either globally or regionally'.

21. For texts of the three resolutions, nos. 338, 339, and 340, see *Survival*, January/February and May/June 1974.

PART FOUR

The Future of Soviet Foreign Policy

15

THE MOTIVATING FORCE

This reappraisal of Soviet foreign policy took as its starting point the Cuban missile crisis, or the Caribbean crisis as it is known in Moscow. Had this book been written in the immediate aftermath of that crisis, its author might reasonably have been expected to foresee both the limited *détente* that followed between the Soviet Union and the United States, based on a temporary coincidence of national interests, and at least the broad perspectives of the Sino-Soviet schism, although in public it had not yet led to a direct confrontation. Nevertheless, no study of Soviet foreign policy written eleven years before could have foreseen what would have happened by October 1973: on the one hand, Khrushchev long since obliged to resign from public life—he died, unforgiven and unhonoured by the Soviet state, seven years after his resignation—leaving his successors, at the zenith of Soviet military power, to grapple with the same domestic problems as he had himself, to seek an intimate, long term, political and economic relationship with the United States, and to extend their country's conflict with China to the military field; on the other hand, John Kennedy and his principal adviser during the Cuban crisis—his brother, Robert—both assassinated, the Camelot legend of the New Frontier cast on the scrap-heap of history, the United States brought to the brink of a constitutional crisis, the American people scarred by the self-inflicted wounds of a war in Indo-China that bore some resemblance to the Syracusan expedition of ancient Athens,*

---

* Although this analogy cannot be pressed too far—the Americans were not defeated in the field and American prisoners of war in Hanoi did not have to win their liberty by teaching their captors the choruses of Euripides—the points of resemblance are striking. The Syracusan expedition was undertaken outside the main strategic theatre; it was justified on the domino theory; its original purpose was to respond to a request for military aid from a weaker city (Segesta) against a stronger one (Syracuse); the ensuing war sucked a vast commitment of Athe-

and the hatchet buried between the United States and China after the rancour of quarter of a century. Nor could it have been foreseen in 1962 —the year of the Berlin crisis as well as of the Cuban crisis—that the focal point of the world conflict of interests, economic and strategic, would have shifted from Central Europe to the Middle East and that this conflict would have shaken the structure of the alliance between the United States and Western Europe.

Moreover, these examples must be viewed against the wider background of change over the past decade: the demographic explosion and the north–south economic gap (the poverty of many underdeveloped countries being still further increased by the new growth in the financial power of the oil-producing countries); the liquidation of the remainder of their empires by the Western European states; the accumulation of wealth in Japan and in Western Europe, the latter groping its way towards a closer unity within the European Economic Community; the collapse of the Bretton Woods international monetary system; the energy crisis; and the vertiginous pace and the complexity of scientific and technological innovation. In the strategic field, lead-time for modern weapons systems is now anything from ten to fifteen years. This means that so far as the systems which the super-powers will deploy in the 1980s are concerned, the initial decision to finance their Research and Development* was already taken by about 1970, and the decision to commit resources of men, money, and materials to their mass production and deployment must be taken not later than 1975. In the field of energy, the parameters of world demand for energy by 1985 can already be established with stark clarity, but precisely how this demand will in practice be met from then until the end of the century depends on a wide range of variables, political, strategic, financial, and technological, which is at the present moment anybody's guess. Nevertheless, a history of the past which is not written with at least half an eye on the future runs the risk of becoming no more than a literary or a statistical exercise. Therefore the attempt to see through the glass, however darkly, must be made.

There are those who argue that the recent change in Soviet foreign

nian manpower, materials, and money into a country of which the Athenians had little first-hand knowledge; it divided Athenian society (the mutilation of the Hermes and the trial of Alcibiades); and the Athenian withdrawal was followed by the establishment of a right-wing government in Athens.

* The process of Research and Development can best be defined as combining basic and applied research with the development of research into new products and processes, up to and including the prototype stage.

policy is only superficial, and that its underlying reality remains unchanged. Those who hold this view concede that the current decade has
so far been a period of *détente*, but they compare it with the period of
temporary *détente* that followed the Cuban missile crisis. They then
divide into two opposed schools of thought. According to the first of
these, Soviet foreign policy is devoid of principle, the lineal descendant
of Russian foreign policy under the Empire, of which Curzon wrote,
nearly a hundred years ago: 'so far from regarding the foreign policy of
Russia as consistent, or remorseless, or profound, I believe it to be a
hand-to-mouth policy, a policy of waiting upon events, of profiting by
the blunders of others, and as often of committing the like herself.'[1]
Even those who, like myself, find this view unacceptable, have to admit
that some colour is lent to it by the fact that the most up-to-date Soviet
book on Soviet foreign policy still stoutly defends the conclusion of the
Soviet-German Non-Aggression Pact of 1939.* The second, more
plausible, school of thought recalls Lenin's early definition of Soviet
foreign policy in 1920, in which he ridiculed refusal 'to temporise and
compromise with possible (even though transient, unstable, vacillating
and conditional) allies' and defended the idea that 'at times we might
have to go in zigzags, sometimes retracing our steps, sometimes abandon-
ing the course already selected and trying out various others'.[2] For the
adherents of this view, the whole history of Soviet foreign policy for the
past half century reveals a grand design, which includes the zigzags
recommended by Lenin in 1920; such a policy is the logical corollary of
the doctrine of the correlation of forces; strategic nuclear parity with the
United States is for the Soviet Union no more than a temporary halting
place on its 'ascent of an unexplored and heretofore inaccessible
mountain' (as Lenin described the path of Soviet foreign policy in the
same passage); this ascent must sooner or later be resumed, with the
ultimate aim of turning the correlation of forces, with the aid of the
forces of history, to the advantage of the Soviet Union; in other words,
to substitute a *pax sovietica* for the *pax americana* under which the
peoples of the world lived, for the most part better than they had ever
lived before, from 1945 until the beginning of the current decade; and
meanwhile the Soviet leadership will, to allow time for modernizing
their country's economy, rest content with a Soviet-American equilibrium. In short, the Soviet national game is chess.

An objective assessment of Soviet foreign policy suggests two replies.

---

* *Diplomatiya Sotsializma* (with a foreword by the Soviet Foreign Minister) in
a paragraph explaining the flexibility of Soviet foreign policy: p. 38.

First, study of the past decade indicates that the parameters of the next decade (examined in the next chapter) will indeed continue to be different from those of the cold war, although the unstable equilibrium that has recently been established between the two super-powers could be upset. The second reply is related to the vexed question: what is the determining force that motivates the men who formulate and carry out Soviet foreign policy? To put it at its simplest, if the motivating force is Marxist-Leninist ideology pure and simple, the prospects of the existing equilibrium between the super-powers being maintained for long are more tenuous than they would otherwise be. If, on the other hand, the motivating force is Soviet national interest, the Soviet-American equilibrium may not only be maintained but rendered less insecure. This is a crude antithesis. We may not know much about the deliberations of the Soviet Politburo, but we do know enough to realize that it consists of politicians who share the motives of politicians the world over, such as the need to survive, physically and politically, which in turn involves a complex interplay of factors extending far beyond the sphere of foreign policy. Nevertheless, the manner in which they see their own motivation is of great importance; and this question has been given a new dimension by Sakharov's statement[3] commenting on Solzhenitsyn's letter to the Soviet leadership of 5 September 1973. The main thrust of this statement, after expressing his admiration for Solzhenitsyn as an author and as a man, was directed against over-estimation of the role of ideology in present-day Soviet society and the Russian nationalistic and isolationist direction of Solzhenitsyn's thinking, which—for Sakharov—made his proposals Utopian and potentially dangerous.

For the official historians of Soviet foreign policy Marxism-Leninism and the interests of the Soviet state coincide. Soviet foreign policy is said to 'reflect the harmonious concurrence of the national interests of the Soviet state and the Soviet people with the international obligations of the working class which has come to power'.[4] Yet a conflict of interest between the two seems to have been recognized from the outset of the Russian Revolution. Although Lenin's initial reaction to foreign policy was that of an old Bolshevik—'What! are we going to have foreign relations?'[5]—he swiftly adapted himself to the realism of a government in power. This transition from the earlier opinions of an underground revolutionary party, observed by foreign diplomats serving in Moscow in the 1920s, was later described by Chicherin as having been difficult for other members of the Bolshevik Party.[6] Lenin was an exceptionally bold man, who had both the audacity and the wisdom not to keep to the rules; for him Marxism was the science which made possible the fearless prediction of the future and the daring needed to bring it about. What of his successors?

It is hard to conceive of a Soviet leader adopting a policy likely to damage the interests of the Soviet state while furthering those of the world communist movement. The history of the first half century of the Soviet Union's existence is rich in examples of the interests of fraternal parties being sacrificed to those of the CPSU. And the most notorious case of all—Stalin's conclusion of his pact with Hitler not only did grave damage to the world communist movement but almost led to the destruction of the Soviet Union. And yet Soviet historians and statesmen are guilty neither of dishonesty nor of cynicism when they claim, in effect, that what is good for their country is good for world communism. (A similar infallibility has been claimed at some time or other—often for long periods—by other European states, not to mention the United States during its messianic epoch.)

An analytic tool devised by two American writers[7] has shown that in selected public statements of Soviet leaders in the early 1960s, the impact of Marxist-Leninist ideology was weakest in their short-range formulations and their specific conclusions and perceptions, whereas it was at its strongest in their long-range thinking and their broad generalizations. This finding corresponds with everyday experience. In a private conversation a Soviet statesman or official appears to a non-Marxist observer to think and reason in the same manner as he does himself. But when time permits, or the occasion—such as a Party Congress—requires, the same statesman or official will speak in a different tongue. To take a concrete example, the Soviet Prime Minister may indeed have told his Japanese interlocutor in September 1968 that the invasion of Czechoslovakia in the previous month was unavoidable because the national survival of the Soviet Union was at stake[8]—an argument derived from pure *Realpolitik*—but publicly the invasion was justified by an appeal to the Marxist concept of proletarian internationalism. Without such a justification the Soviet leadership would have felt embarrassed, because their mandate to rule at home and to act abroad depends on the ultimate sanction[9] of Marxist-Leninist doctrine. In the last analysis—not always in the heat of a crisis,* but whenever

* Nevertheless, in his 'Friday' letter, written to Kennedy at the height of the Cuban missile crisis, Khrushchev found time to justify himself by the doctrine of peaceful coexistence.

action is being prepared or recollected in tranquillity—the general framework and guidelines of Soviet foreign policy must be seen to be justified by the doctrines of Marxism-Leninism: the ultimate sanction which gives those who formulate and carry out this policy the sense that they are moving forward with the forces of history and that their success is predicated on the truth of this ideology.

If this is how Soviet leaders think and how events in the Soviet Union are moulded, what happens when the Soviet Union reaches a point in history, as it did in 1956, when the inadmissible gap between Marxist-Leninist theory and Soviet practice becomes blatant? Sooner or later this gap must be closed—not by changing the practice, which will continue to be dictated, in Marxist terms, by Life Itself, but by changing the theory. Officially, theory never changes in the Soviet Union. In 1956, it was simply given a new formulation. But—as a Polish Marxist remarked to the author—all great communist leaders have been revisionists, from Lenin and Stalin onwards.[10] The adjective 'great' is an essential condition, because radical revision demands the courage to break the horizon—a quality that does not seem to be any more abundant in the Soviet Union than in other countries at the moment. Nevertheless, who could have foreseen Khrushchev's speech at the XXth Party Congress?

To sum up, the foreign policy of the Soviet Union, like that of any modern state, is conducted in the interests of the state, as perceived by its leaders. Their perception of Soviet state interests is at most only slightly distorted by the lens of Marxism-Leninism, whose doctrines provide the leaders with their ultimate sanction. And an eloquent contrast with the Curzonian thesis is afforded by comparing the principal characteristics claimed by Soviet apologists for their foreign policy—flexibility, firmness, and circumspection—with the source to which Tolstoy, writing not long before Curzon, ascribed traditional Russian self-confidence: 'a Russian . . . neither knows anything nor wants to know anything, because he does not believe in the possibility of knowing anything'.[11] Half a century of Soviet rule may not have altered the fundamental scepticism of the Russian character; the Soviet claim to have evolved a new, Soviet type of man cannot be sustained; but the outward manifestation of the Russian character, observable in the conduct of Soviet foreign policy, has surely changed. A Soviet writer might trace this change back to the Marxist proposition[12] that one and the same idea in different, concrete, historical circumstances may be either reactionary or progressive.

NOTES

1. G. N. Curzon, *Russia in Central Asia*, Longmans Green, London, 1889, p. 315.
2. Lenin, *Left-Wing Communism—an infantile disorder*, Moscow, 1920: *Collected Works*, vol. 31, p. 70.
3. Full text in translation in *The Times*, 16 April 1974.
4. *Istoriya Vneshnei Politiki SSSR*, introductory chapter.
5. Leon Trotsky, *Moya Zhizn'*, Granit, Berlin, 1930, vol. 2, p. 64. Cf. Trotsky's own remark, when appointed Commissioner for Foreign Affairs, that he would issue some revolutionary proclamations to the peoples and then shut up shop.
6. See ch. 10, n. 15. For the views of foreign observers, see, for example, Arthur Hodgson's report to Austen Chamberlain of 6 May 1926, *Documents on British Foreign Policy*, Series IA, vol. I: 'the Soviet Government has been continually in conflict with the conceptions to which it owes its being—to cope with practical exigencies it has had to recede little by little from the ideas which inspired the Revolution . . . Moscow . . . has to deal with precisely the same problems as any of its neighbours—and is dealing with them in very much the same way.'
7. Jan F. Triska and David D. Finley, *Soviet Foreign Policy*, Macmillan, New York, 1968, pp. 118 ff.: the 'doctrinal stereotype quotient', representing the number of doctrinally stereotyped words or phrases in proportion to the total number of words in the statement being analysed.
8. Quoted by Hayter, op. cit., p. 63.
9. Compare Sakharov's description of 'ideological rituality' as a substitute for 'an oath of loyalty': *The Times*, 16 April 1974.
10. Julian Hochfeld, in conversation in 1959.
11. Leo Tolstoy, *War and Peace*, Bk. III, pt. I, section X.
12. See, for example, Andrei Zhdanov, *Essays on Literature, Philosophy, and Music*, p. 58, International Publishers, New York, 1950.

16

PARAMETERS AND VARIABLES

Soviet parameters[1]

The assumptions made in this chapter and the next will relate to the ten-year period 1973–83, a time span comparable with the years reviewed in this book. It is rather less than the period covered by the fifteen-year economic plan now being prepared in the Soviet Union, and far shorter than the twenty or thirty years of peaceful coexistence of which Brezhnev has been reported to be thinking.[2] But to look further ahead runs the speculator into a new era in which account must be taken of an entirely new factor in the world power structure, the possible emergence of China as a super-power. The span of ten years from 1973 onwards should include three congresses of the CPSU, one of which may be expected—in the course of nature—to produce a fresh Soviet leadership.

Since April 1973 personal responsibility for Soviet foreign policy has been attributed, both within the Soviet Union and abroad, to Brezhnev. However, with the world in the heat of the second industrial revolution and in the grip of the great bureaucratic age, the concept of the state as a rational actor is even less appropriate than half a century ago, when the image of states as individual characters or anthropomorphized animals —the Russian Bear, Uncle Sam, and John Bull—had already ceased to bear much relation to reality. As early as August 1914, when asked why the First World War had broken out, the German Chancellor Beth-mann-Hollweg replied: 'if only I knew!' In a crisis today the ruler of a modern state reaches a decision for which he will be held responsible before history not as a lonely figure, weighing up the pros and cons of the advice submitted to him by his personal staff, his specialist advisers, and his colleagues, but as the hub of a many-spoked governmental wheel and sometimes as the passenger, rather than the driver, of a bureaucratic machine carried forward by the momentum of its own procedures.[3] Nevertheless, the Soviet regime is nothing if not centralized. True, the growing complexity of Soviet society is reflected by the fact that, even though Brezhnev has long been *primus inter pares* in the Politburo, it still remains a collegiate body. A return to the Stalinist system of government, in the sense that every decision of importance was handed down by a single man, is inconceivable; and even a return to the Khrushchevian concentration of offices is improbable. But if we concede that the leading member of the Politburo, like any other national leader, is obliged to build up his majority round a consensus, the fact remains that during the ten years which we are now considering, he will wield immense power.

The first question is therefore this: if an alternative Soviet leadership were to accede to power tomorrow, either naturally or in the style of 1964, could it reverse the Brezhnev foreign policy? Given the intimate links between Soviet domestic and foreign policy, the answer is, theoretically, yes. But in my view such a leadership, however much it might commit itself publicly to a reappraisal of Soviet foreign policy, would sooner or later find itself constrained by the basic parameters of this policy.

The first parameter stems from nuclear logic. The statement that the nuclear bomb does not adhere to the class principle remains as valid today as when it was included in the CPSU Central Committee's Open Letter of 1963. By the end of 1973, the Soviet Union and the United States had already travelled some way towards a SALT II agreement; and eventually their negotiators are likely to reach the crossroads, where they must either put some trust in each other or abandon hope of preserving a civilized society. No Soviet leadership will opt out of the Great Game of strategic nuclear power; it will remain a vital national interest of the Soviet Union to preserve a strategic balance with the United States; but a way will have to be found of acknowledging the fact that strategic nuclear superiority for either super-power is a chimera.[4]

The second parameter is twofold: the East-West technological gap, which has been discussed in an earlier chapter, and the problem of the development of the natural resources of Siberia. Even if the gap could be closed in ten years, which seems improbable at the present pace of technological advance, the Siberian problem would remain for the rest of this century. Whatever Soviet ministers may say from time to time in public, no Soviet leadership can escape the fact that without Western help, the Soviet Union will not have the capital, the know-how, and the management techniques to solve it. Add to this the congenital weakness of Soviet agriculture and its climatic disadvantage—grain imports are likely to be needed in years of poor harvests—and it is clear that it will become increasingly difficult for the Soviet Union to avoid becoming an integral part of the world economic system. In Sakharov's words, 'not a single key problem can be solved on a national scale'.[5]

Because the Soviet leadership are well aware of this economic logic and of the greatly increased personal contacts between East and West that it is bound to involve, they are determined to do everything in their power to prevent these contacts from contaminating the ideological purity of the Soviet system. Hence, for example, Soviet opposition to concessions over the free exchange of ideas and information at the Geneva negotiations. As the Soviet Diplomatic Dictionary puts it, 'peaceful coexistence has nothing whatsoever to do with peace in the sphere of ideology ... those principles do not in any way exclude ideological struggle. Such a struggle goes on continually and is unavoidable. ...'[6] One need only reflect on the impact that modern Western managerial techniques—let alone actual Western management —would have on the Soviet Union in the longer term, to wonder for how long the Soviet leadership will be able in effect to have its cake and eat it.

American parameters

The first of the three parameters described above (Mutually Assured Destruction) applies equally to the United States. As for the second, the United States could, in theory, revert to its previous policy of withholding from the Soviet Union both advanced technology and long term credit to finance the exploitation of Soviet natural resources. But is such a reversal now practical economics? However vast the resources that lie within its own boundaries, can the United States afford to play no part in the development of the largest known reserves of raw materials in the world?

Until the close of 1973 the obvious example was energy. The Soviet Union claims one third of the total sedimentary basins in the world; expert estimates of the ultimately recoverable oil, gas, and coal vary; not only are exact statistics lacking, but there are also problems of climate (permafrost) and distance (6,600 kilometres from the Tyumen' oilfield in Western Siberia to the Pacific port of Nakhodka). Until the world price of oil was quadrupled, it had seemed likely that by 1980 the United States, which consumes one third of the world's energy, would be as dependent on imported oil as Western Europe is today; that Saudi Arabia, whose estimated oil reserves are the greatest in the world, would become the world's 'swing' oil producer,[7] and that given the political uncertainties of the Middle East, a logical consequence for the United States would be large-scale investment in Siberian oil and natural gas. Today, it is now theoretically economic for the United States to develop alternative sources of energy (tar sands, shale, and coal), of which North American reserves are almost as large as those of the Soviet Union. Yet even Project Independence—the immense new American energy pro- gramme—would still leave room for a flow of oil and natural gas from the Soviet Union.*

In any case, the sudden increase in the cost of energy is only one aspect of the explosion in commodity prices which is central to the world inflationary crisis of today. Now that the Soviet Government has taken the plunge, by inviting Western firms to participate in major Siberian ventures in the energy field, it can only be a matter of time before Western investment is attracted to the rest of the Soviet Union's natural resources. It would be surprising if American capital were not in the van. This brings us back to American domestic politics, and in particular the Jackson Amendment, which in 1973 was linked with the conflict between President and Congress, with the Arab-Israeli dispute, and with the problem of Soviet Jewry—all three delicate issues in the United States. It is possible to construct scenarios in which Soviet resistance to concessions of the kind for which Jackson has pressed will continue for some years. No one knows how many[8] Soviet Jews wish to emigrate, nor at what pace Israel could absorb them, even assuming a crash programme. But given the strength of the logic, both strategic and economic, pulling any US Administration and any Soviet leadership down the path traced in 1972–3 by Kissinger and Brezhnev, a compro-

---

* Just how much will depend on a number of related but unpredictable factors: the success of the American programme (whose original target of complete oil self-sufficiency by 1980 is generally regarded as unattainable); the extent to which the Soviet Union decides to become a major oil and natural gas exporter; the extent to which Western oil and natural gas importers are prepared to become dependent on Soviet supplies; and the future reliability of Middle Eastern exporters, which is in turn connected with the outcome of the Arab-Israeli dispute.

mise solution of the problem of Soviet Jewry is by no means impossible, although it will take time.

Variables

This twilight world may be more easily explored by the political scientist than by the historian. There are at least four major factors that could, over the next ten years, upset the existing equilibrium between the super-powers.

The agreements concluded between the Soviet Union and the United States in 1972–3 established the ground rules of this equilibrium. However, whereas the rules of international behaviour by the super-powers have at last been established in South-East Asia, and have long been understood in Central Europe, they are less so in the rest of Europe, and above all in the Middle East—witness the US nuclear alert of October 1973. In Europe, Yugoslavia's non-aligned stance has allowed Tito to maintain close links with Moscow and Eastern Europe on the one hand, and with Washington and Western Europe on the other. But Yugoslavia's ability to combine the two has owed much to the unique position in the communist world that its leader has occupied since he out-faced Stalin a quarter of a century ago. Will his eventual successor have the strength and the stature to prevent outsiders from fishing in what could become troubled waters, as the Croatian troubles of 1971 showed?* What would be the Kremlin's reaction if the Italian Communist Party were, after a quarter of a century in opposition, at last to succeed in obtaining portfolios in central government? An attitude of caution, one would hope, as also towards the re-emergence of Marxism in Portuguese and Spanish political life. But can one be certain that counsels of caution would prevail if the Politburo were to find itself suddenly presented with a target of opportunity? Equally, given the importance of Israel in American domestic politics, how much effort will it cost any US Administration to recognize the Soviet claim (repeatedly put forward over the years, and reiterated by Brezhnev immediately after the Arab-Israeli War of October 1973)[9] that the Middle East and the eastern Mediterranean constitute an 'area in the immediate vicinity' of the frontiers of the Soviet Union, which is regarded in Moscow in much the same light as the Caribbean is in Washington?

* The trials of 'Cominformists' in Yugoslavia three years later pointed in the same direction.

Second, however high a degree of mutual trust may be established between the governments of the super-powers in whatever agreement flows from their SALT negotiations, this may not be enough to persuade either the scientific or the military community in both countries to resist technological temptation. The process of Research and Development of new nuclear weapons systems has an in-built momentum* that cannot be arrested at a stroke of the pen. The overall directive, on both sides, might well be to work towards the eventual deployment of such systems not against each other, but against China. But any technological break-through by one super-power must have a destabilizing effect on the other, particularly if the nuclear innovation is of a kind that cannot be verified by what are termed national technical means. The best con-temporary example is the multiple independently targetable and the manoeuvrable re-entry vehicle; but what would be the effect, either in the Kremlin or in the White House, if one or other side were to succeed in deploying an effective system of anti-submarine warfare?

Third, if political and military constraints are once set aside, the economic obstacles in the way of developing and deploying a simple nuclear weapons system are less formidable than might be supposed. Indeed, a recent article[10] on this subject included the sobering state-ment that, given unlimited time, there is no country obviously in-capable of a nuclear weapons programme. In 1968, a United Nations consultative group of experts estimated that an expenditure of 1,280 million dollars spread over ten years would allow an industrial country with a civil nuclear programme to develop and build a force of 100 plutonium weapons and 50 medium-range missiles, and to buy 30–50 aircraft as well. As the same article concluded, after allowing for infla-tion, in 1973 there were about sixteen countries capable of carrying that financial burden over the remaining years of the current decade, by diverting less than one per cent of GNP. These countries included India, Japan, and Italy, all of which have indigenous uranium and reactor capacity and which also have, or will have, reprocessing plants. Egypt would, according to the same estimate, need to divert 3·6 per cent and Israel about 4 per cent of GNP for this purpose.

---

* In the valedictory address which made famous the term military-industrial complex, Eisenhower added this warning: 'we must also be alert to the equal and opposite danger that public policy could itself become the captive of a scientific-technological elite'. The combined power of the two interest groups, in an advanced industrial society, is formidable.

If the super-powers succeed in persuading their clients in the Middle East to reach some kind of agreement, perhaps they will also be able to dissuade them from the folly of embarking on a nuclear programme. But could the accusation of folly be levelled at India or Japan if, in the second half of this decade, they decided that the growing strategic nuclear power of China obliged them no longer to rely on the nuclear umbrellas hitherto held over them by the Soviet Union and the United States respectively, especially if the 1975 review of disarmament required by the Non-Proliferation Treaty had borne no fruit? By exploding a nuclear device on 17 May 1974, India has become a member of the nuclear club. Japan's extreme vulnerability and the strength of public feeling against nuclear warfare in Japan are powerful constraints. Yet Japan will shortly become the second industrial state of the world, utterly dependent on long sea routes for its supply of raw materials. It will certainly wish to postpone the nuclear option, leaving it open, but no more, for as long as possible. But if it does finally decide to continue to rely either on the protection or the benevolence of others for the security of its life-line, it will prove to be the first great trading country in history to do so. Moreover, beyond such deliberate decisions of national policy, there is also the nightmarish possibility of a do-it-yourself nuclear, biological, or chemical device, in the hands of a guerrilla group, using it as an instrument of political blackmail, but this time with the survival of a whole capital city, not an airliner, or a team of athletes, at stake. It has been rightly said that the trouble with nuclear ploughshares is that they can be beaten into nuclear warheads.

Fourth, the most volatile variable of all is the pace of political change in Eastern Europe. We have noted the present Soviet leadership's dislike of anything new in Marxist thought; and we have taken as one of the Soviet parameters for the next ten years their determination to preserve Soviet society in its present form. Now that the Moscow Treaty and the agreements which followed it have removed the German bogey, in order to hold their Eastern European allies together, the Soviet leaders seem to be relying on a policy of *enrichissez-vous:* a pale image of the consumer society of the West, but a marked improvement, if measured against the standard of living which Eastern Europeans had experienced in the Stalinist period after the Second World War. Stalin needed Eastern Europe in the late 1940s as a defensive barrier, behind which he could glower or thunder at the West during the years of the Soviet Union's extreme weakness, with twenty million dead, European Russia ravaged by the most terrible campaign since the Mongol invasion in the thirteenth century, and the power of the Red Army rendered nugatory, in the eyes of Stalin and his advisers, by the American monopoly of the atomic bomb. Khrushchev, on the other hand, while not ignoring the military value of Eastern Europe, realized the political importance of its leaders as allies in his ideological struggle against the Chinese. Whichever of the two factors—political or military—weighed more in the present leadership's decision to invade Czechoslovakia in 1968, as the present decade advances, it will surely be the value of the Eastern European political frontier, beyond the administrative borders of the Soviet Union, that will be uppermost in the minds of Soviet policy-makers. The great political difference between the Soviet Union and its Eastern European allies (with the possible exception of Bulgaria) is that whereas in the USSR the Communist Party has deep roots, in Eastern Europe the Communist Parties consist of small oligarchies, brought to power, or the successors of men brought to power, by Soviet arms in 1944–5. The fragility of the socialist commonwealth has been proved repeatedly, most recently in Czechoslovakia in 1968: that a force of half a million men should have been required for the invasion of a country whose government had made no plan whatsoever for armed resistance speaks for itself.

What matters for the future is whether the pace of change in the Soviet Union will continue to be so slow as to exasperate one or more of the Eastern European peoples once again. Soviet society is not impervious to change; nor are Soviet political institutions; but they cannot be expected to evolve towards the Western model. The Warsaw Pact includes countries, notably Poland, Hungary, and Czechoslovakia, whose society remains rooted in the Western European tradition. Understandably, the Soviet fear is that if Pandora's box is once opened in Eastern Europe, the lid will sooner or later have to be lifted in the Soviet Union, which includes almost all the territories ruled by the Tsars. The Soviet constitution allows for any of the republics (some of which were independent countries[11] for over twenty years after the First World War) that compose the Union to secede; the official formula governing the principle of nationality within the Soviet Union is that it is 'nationalist in form, socialist in content'; but Lenin was not mistaken when he remarked in 1919, having concluded a treaty granting independence to Finland, 'scratch some communists and you will find Great Russian chauvinists'; and the last Soviet census, taken in 1970, gave the Russians a very narrow majority: 53·3 per cent.

Under the present Soviet leadership any radical change in the Soviet internal political system is inconceivable. The question therefore is, what will be the policy of their successors? A story was going the rounds in the summer of 1973 that Brezhnev had told a distinguished American visitor that he hoped to be succeeded by a man twenty years younger than himself. What would such a Soviet politician be like? A well educated man, perhaps a pious agnostic where Marxism was concerned, and a professional politician (the distinction sometimes drawn between conservative *apparatchiki* and liberal technocrats is not helpful). But above all he would be a man without any feeling of guilt. Not through any fault of their own, but simply because of their age, the triumvirs who ousted Khrushchev, like Khrushchev himself, owed their first steps on the ladder of success to the Great Terror. It is impossible to believe that this fact has not affected their attitudes profoundly: the importance of guilt in the Russian character is amply attested. John Rickman, who witnessed the Russian Revolution from a unique vantage point,[12] wrote in an essay that was published over thirty years later:

the Russian attitude towards guilt has always seemed strange alike to Western and Eastern peoples. In the religion of the old regime it was a central theme; in that of the new it is denied in relation to everything except the State. In the place of the old blasphemy . . . there is now the sin of not believing in the perfect suitability of the present rulers . . . for the needs of the Russian people. Discontent is taken as a sign of the unpardonable sin working in a diseased mind.

This prophetic passage is followed by the statement that, although violence may be necessary in politics, 'it generates feelings of guilt which may be unconscious. It is foolish and . . . in the long run politically imprudent to deny a factor so important in mental—or political—life.'[13] Khrushchev's revelations about Stalin at the XXth Party Congress may be regarded as a controlled attempt to free Soviet society from guilt and to release the energies of its people—including those of the millions of political prisoners who were then set free—for the task of working for a better life, by acknowledging, three years after Stalin's death, the extent of the trauma that the Soviet people had suffered from their leader's systematic use of violence on a titanic scale. It is the essence of the case pressed by men like Solzhenitsyn and the Medvedevs that this process, once begun, should have been allowed to run its full course. Perhaps the younger Soviet generation, unburdened by the nightmare of the purges, may feel able to allow some fresh air, and with it some new ideas, into the Soviet Union. If they do, it may help to lift the malaise that hangs over Eastern Europe and so contribute to the all-

European cooperation which has for so long been a primary aim of Soviet policy.

NOTES

1. In the Oxford English Dictionary's definition of this much misused term: 'a quantity which is constant (as distinct from the ordinary variables) in a particular case considered'.
2. Sadat, in his address to the Central Committee of the Arab Socialist Union on 16 July 1973, as reported by Cairo Home Service radio.
3. For an application of these three concepts to an historical process of decision-making, see Allison, op. cit.
4. Giles Bullard drew my attention to 'the Great Game', a phrase which his researches show to have been used for the first time in J. W. Kaye's *History of the War in Afghanistan*, in 1851, after which it became a shorthand for Anglo-Russian rivalry. The doctrine of Mutually Assured Destruction 'rests on two pillars: strength and vulnerability. Each side must be seen to have the strength to retaliate adequately for any attack. Each side must also permit the other to have the confidence that it too can retaliate intolerably. In other words, a sufficient retaliatory force must always remain invulnerable, and a sufficient hostage must always remain vulnerable. If A believes that B is trying either to reduce the invulnerability of A's retaliatory force or the vulnerability of B's hostage, A is driven either to strengthen his own forces or, *in extremis*, to attack before the tendency has gone too far.' This quotation comes from Ian Smart's 'Advanced Strategic Missiles', *Adelphi Papers* no. 93, IISS, London, 1969, p. 27.
5. Quoted from the statement translated in *The Times*, 16 April 1974. For a do-it-yourself line, see the remarks by the Soviet Minister of the Oil Industry, reported in *The Times*, 29 May 1974, but subsequently denied.
6. *Diplomaticheskii Slovar'*, vol. 2, Moscow, 1964, p. 176.
7. For the critical position of Saudi Arabia, see *The Changing Balance of Power in the Persian Gulf*, an international seminar report by Elizabeth Monroe, the American Universities Field Staff, New York, 1972, pp. 26–7.
8. The usual estimate—there are no statistics—is half a million.
9. In a speech delivered to the All-World Congress of Peace-Loving Forces in Moscow: *Pravda*, 27 October 1973.
10. *Strategic Survey 1972*, IISS, London, 1973, p. 74.
11. The Baltic States: in Lithuania, in May 1972, riots were reported to have taken place at and after the funeral of a young worker who committed suicide by burning himself—see *Strategic Survey 1972*, p. 84.
12. That of a doctor working in a Russian village during the years of the Revolution.
13. Geoffrey Gorer and John Rickman, *The People of Greater Russia*, The Cresset Press, London, 1949, pp. 88–9.

17

CONCLUSION

To return to the findings of this study of Soviet foreign policy since 1962, it is a paradox that, once rough numerical strategic parity with the United States had at last been achieved, Soviet rivalry with China grew more intense than it was with the United States at the height of the cold war (Soviet and American troops have not confronted each other directly for over half a century); that in spite of this rivalry, the Soviet Government entered into a network of agreements with the United States Government which made the stock Chinese accusation of super-power collusion still harder to rebut; that—except where Soviet national interests were involved—little more than lip service was paid by the Soviet Union to its doctrinal commitment to support national-liberation movements; that as Soviet military power, both strategic and conventional, became increasingly formidable, so the Soviet need for Western help in modernizing and developing the Soviet economy grew more apparent; that Western, and particularly American, willingness to provide this help evoked fierce controversy, in the Soviet Union as well as in Western countries; and finally, that so far the only Soviet attempt to explain this series of paradoxes to the Soviet people and to the world communist movement—to bridge the gap between the theory and the practice of Soviet foreign policy—has been to add three words to part of the fourth of its basic tasks. Yet, in reality, the adjectives now applied to the Soviet relationship with the United States—'permanent' and 'irreversible'—and to the two countries' joint responsibility for maintaining world peace—'special'—are a far cry from the Marxist class struggle.[1]

At the outset of this book it was observed that the nature of the new relations between the two super-powers was complex and ambivalent, and had therefore so far eluded attempts to define it in a single word or phrase. *Détente*, the shorthand currently used in the United States, is open to the objection that in the Soviet Union it is restricted (in my view, correctly) to its traditional meaning in diplomatic usage—the relaxation of tension: from the Soviet viewpoint this is a consequence of the policy of peaceful coexistence between communist and non-communist states as the 'generally accepted rule of international life', not the policy itself. Although the governments of both super-powers agree that their relations are special, this description contains a misleading echo of the Anglo-American special relationship of the post-war years. The most accurate, but an inelegant, definition is adversarial partnership, although this also echoes an earlier term—*frères ennemis*[2] —used in the different circumstances of 1961. Among the cluster of metaphors drawn from geometry and magnetism, the concept of bipolarity was useful in the past, because (as the inventor of the term super-power foresaw thirty years ago)[3] it need not necessarily imply the existence of polar opposites; but it has been obfuscated by adjectives—'loose' and 'tight'. Bipolarity has since been contrasted with multipolarity—the concept underlying Nixon's formulation of January 1972[4]—which has given rise to hexagonal and polygonal definitions. Multipolarity was in turn superseded by the passage in Kissinger's statement about the Year of Europe, delivered on 23 April 1973[5] on behalf of the United States President, in which he drew a distinction between the global interests and responsibilities of the USA and the regional interests of America's European allies: interests which were not necessarily in conflict, but in the new era not automatically identical. These words both recalled Fox's original definition of super-power and foreshadowed the conflict between American and European interests during the Middle Eastern crisis six months later. And it was at the height of this crisis—in his press conference of 25 October 1973—that Kissinger described the super-power relationship in two sentences that cannot be bettered:

the Soviet Union and we are in a unique relationship. We are at one and the same time adversaries and partners in the preservation of peace.

At the other end of the spectrum, there are those who maintain that the term super-power has become an archaism: in their view, in the late twentieth century, what determines the relative weight of a state in the counsels of the modern world is not the possession of a vast arsenal of strategic nuclear weapons capable of destroying the globe—no one today, they affirm, will ever commit national suicide—but the scientific, technological, and industrial capacity of the state, set in the context of its geographical position, the size of its population, and its natural resources. Since military power does not, as Kissinger has observed, automatically translate into influence, strategic nuclear power would indeed have little meaning if taken in isolation. (If, by a *reductio ad absurdum*, a government were to devote so much of its country's GNP to developing and maintaining a nuclear armoury that it was left with little or no resources to be used for the other weapons of modern diplomacy—trade, technical assistance, cultural cooperation—this twentieth-century Sparta would find itself in the unenviable position of having only a single international card to play.) On the other hand, if— as in the case of the super-powers—strategic nuclear power is combined with the full panoply of highly mobile conventional weapons and of conventional diplomacy, it means a great deal. As an American journalist wrote thirty years ago: 'even after you give the squirrel a certificate which says that he is quite as big as any elephant, he is still going to be smaller, and all the squirrels will know it and all the elephants will know it.'[6] These words remain valid today, except that the word 'both' should be substituted for the word 'all' before the word 'elephants'.

Rather than attempt to construct conceptual models of a world power structure that is changing before our eyes, it is wiser simply to accept two lessons of the past decade: that strategic nuclear capacity is indeed relevant to the exercise of super-power (or global power, as Kissinger has expressed it), and that the twin centres of such power, and of the decisions that flow from it, will remain Washington and Moscow, until such time as Peking becomes the third centre—a goal[7] which the Chinese leadership seem set to achieve even before their people reaches the 1,000 million mark. If so, what are the prospects for regional power? In particular what conclusions should be drawn in Western Europe, where most countries have, since 1949, been joined in a defence partnership with the Western super-power, and are together still facing not only the Soviet strategic nuclear armoury, but also the massed, and swiftly reinforceable, conventional forces of the Soviet Union and its allies in the centre of the European continent, and increasingly in the Mediterranean and on the south-eastern flank?

Subject to the reservation already made about the dangers of prophecy, an attempt will now be made to sketch briefly three possible paradigms, of which there could be many variants, for the development of super-power relations over the next ten years; beginning with what Wavell, when he was Commander-in-Chief in Cairo during the Second World War, used to call the Worst Possible Case. Whatever the disadvantages to other countries of the super-power equilibrium—the French President and his Foreign Minister suggested some in 1973[8]— it has one advantage of inestimable value: it sustains an international order within which the overwhelming majority of the world's inhabitants can live at peace. If this order were to collapse, under the strain of one or more of the dangers described in the previous chapter, the threat of large-scale conventional war, perhaps developing into nuclear war, would follow. And if, at the moment of this collapse, the Western European states—far from achieving their goal of unity—were still in a state of disarray, too weak to defend their wealth and their cultural and political heritage, Western Europe would then find itself no longer the partner of one super-power but the hostage of both.

Dismissing this vision of a helpless approach to Armageddon, let us next consider an intermediate paradigm. In this case, although the variables considered in the previous chapter may cause periods of extreme tension, the super-power equilibrium is maintained. Rather than see Western Europe united both as a political and as a defence entity, the Soviet Union encourages the United States to maintain a military presence in Europe. Nevertheless, this presence is gradually reduced between now and 1983, partly for financial reasons and partly because America's irritation with its European allies, voiced at the highest levels in the United States in 1973 and early in 1974, develops into disillusionment, so that interdependence—the watchword of the Atlantic Alliance—becomes a mockery in the later 1970s, until a point is finally reached where whatever American troops may still be stationed in the European theatre are either there on sufferance or have lost their credibility as a deterrent against the exercise of Soviet military power.[9] Here again the crucial question would be the state of Western Europe. If this were one of disarray, then each Western European country would have no alternative but to reach whatever accommodation it could with the most powerful state in Europe; and so far from being 'Finlandized', they might—depending on the circumstances obtaining at that time—find themselves so fragmented that their treatment by the Soviet Union would be less favourable than that received by the Finns during the past thirty years.

Lastly, the paradigm of the best that we can reasonably hope for: the equilibrium between the United States and the Soviet Union withstands all the stresses to which it may be subjected during the next ten years, in particular, those arising from the Middle East; both super-powers keep their present military partners and do not seek others; the Soviet Union finds a means of preserving the effectiveness of the Warsaw Pact, while allowing its members a greater measure of freedom to experiment with internal political reforms; the American military presence in Europe is reduced, but remains credible; a Western Euro-pean defence entity emerges, including a nuclear capability, despite all the formidable difficulties, both political and technological, which this would involve; Western Europe, without aspiring to the status of a super-power, is none the less able to exert widespread political influence and to avoid walking 'naked into the council chamber'—in Bevan's phrase.

None of these three paradigms has mentioned the world's fifth strategic nuclear power—the People's Republic of China. Sooner or later the Chinese nuclear force will rise from its present level, roughly equivalent to that of France,[10] to something resembling that of the United States and the Soviet Union. Once this transition has been effected, the scene of world politics will be transformed. The Soviet-American equilibrium could be destroyed and end in a chaotic scramble by each of the three super-powers to secure the alliance of one or the other, for both the United States and the Soviet Union would have important concessions to offer China, if they chose to do so. A world divided between three super-powers is indeed what Orwell foresaw in *Nineteen Eighty-Four*. Historically, the maintenance of a triangular balance of power has been fraught with danger for other, neighbouring, states.[11] Whatever happens, the moral remains identical: 'a choir of contradictory European voices is of no use to anyone'.[12]

It may be objected, first, that the disproportion between a nuclear deterrent force of the size and degree of sophistication which Western Europe (and specifically Britain and France) might be able to afford, on the one hand, and the nuclear armoury of the super-powers on the other, is so great that in practice the Western Europeans would become no better than the blackmailing nuclear guerrillas already mentioned; and secondly, that if this is the best projection that can be offered for the late twentieth century, some alternative machinery for keeping the world at peace must be found before the century draws to a close. To the first of these two objections the answer is that there is an important difference between the leader of a guerrilla group responsible to no one other than a distant headquarters with which, at the critical moment, he may no longer be in contact, and the democratically elected head of a European government, controlling a carefully safeguarded nuclear deterrent; and that the international weight of a government known to possess the nuclear ability to tear a limb from its adversary, even posthumously, must be greater than that of a non-nuclear power.

Nevertheless, if it is indeed unrealistic for Western Europe to aspire to exert anything more than moral influence on the course of world events in the rest of this century, should we turn our backs on history, leave the super-powers to dispose of the world as they choose, and cultivate our gardens—a policy of Little Europe? To this question the reply must surely be: only if Little Europe could be sure of being able to resist the Power of Menace.* True, the machinery of the United Nations Organization is a useful, perhaps an indispensable, instrument for helping to maintain world order, especially so long as the permanent members of the UN Security Council are also the five strategic nuclear powers. But it is rightly called an organization; it is no more than that. A federal system of world government is inconceivable in this century.[13] We are therefore thrown back on an ancient and admittedly imperfect, because human, system of maintaining international order—what the Peace of Utrecht described as a just balance of power, the best and most solid foundation of mutual friendship and a lasting general concord. It is a system that has had some distinguished advocates, across the centuries. As Clausewitz pointed out, it is just the weak—the side that must defend itself—which should always be armed in order not to be taken by surprise;[14] and it was Richelieu who observed that of two unequal powers, allied by a treaty, it was the larger of the two which ran the greater risk of being left in the lurch.[15]

In 1962 Acheson jolted British public opinion when he remarked that Britain, having lost its empire, had not yet found a role. Today no one doubts that Britain and its partners in Western Europe were wise to give up their empires—the relic of another epoch, in which Western Europe dominated the world. It has also become clear that even in the new era of the super-powers the countries of Western Europe have a role to play: a role which they cannot refuse, if they wish to survive.

* This striking phrase is Curzon's, used in *Russia in Central Asia*, ch. VIII.

NOTES

1. For Soviet definitions of the 'basic tasks' of foreign policy, the super-powers' special responsibility, and the class struggle, see ch. 1.

2. Raymond Aron, *Paix et guerre entre les nations*, Calmann-Lévy, Paris, 1962, pp. 527 ff.
3. See ch. 1, n. 14.
4. See ch. 12, n. 1.
5. *Keesing's Contemporary Archives 1973*, pp. 25933 ff.
6. Samuel Grafton in the *New York Post*, 23 November 1943.
7. For an assessment of Chinese nuclear policy, see 'Nuclear Weapons and Chinese policy', Harry Gelber, *Adelphi Papers* no. 99, IISS, London, 1973.
8. Michel Jobert (as reported in the *Scotsman* of 13 November 1973) said that the Nuclear Agreement of 22 June 1973 had set up a 'veritable condominium of the super-powers' and reduced the EEC to impotence. The super-powers' collusion was 'dangerous ... because experience has shown that the direct dialogue between the US and the Soviet Union could lead not only to a *détente* but also to a generalized confrontation. ...' The US and the Soviet Union had committed an error in 'brutally brushing aside' France and Europe while imposing a Middle Eastern settlement. 'Europe, treated like a non-person and humiliated in its very existence, because of its dependence on supplies of energy, is none the less the object of the second battle of the Middle Eastern War.'
9. For Nixon's remarks about Europe, made in Chicago on 15 March 1974, see *The Times*, 16 March 1974, which gives the full text. For a pessimistic view of American military credibility even in existing circumstances, see Taylor, *Foreign Affairs*, April 1974, p. 588, where he describes the US Seventh Army as a 'hostage force' in Central Europe.
10. For this comparison, see Gelber, op. cit., p. 8.
11. In *The End of the Post-War Era*, Weidenfeld and Nicolson, London, 1974, p. 81, Alastair Buchan points out that the price of the triangular power balance in Central Europe at the end of the eighteenth century was the Partition of Poland (a salutary lesson for Western Europe, should its leaders show the same inability to agree among themselves as did the members of the Polish Sejm two hundred years ago).
12. Brandt, addressing the European Parliament at Strasbourg on 13 November 1973: *Glasgow Herald*, 14 November 1973.
13. Indeed 'there has rarely been a less promising moment in modern history to advocate the disappearance of the nation state': Alastair Buchan, Reith Lectures, *Listener*, 20 December 1974, p. 844.
14. Carl von Clausewitz, *Vom Kriege*, translated by J. J. Graham, vol. 2, p. 155 (Bk. VI, ch. 5), Kegan, Paul, Trench, and Truebner, London, 1908.
15. Armand de Richelieu, *Testament politique*, part 2, Imprimerie Le Breton, 1764, p. 41: 'Bien que ce soit un dire commun, que quiconque a la force, a d'ordinaire raison, il est vrai toutefois que de deux Puissances inégales, jointes par un traité, la plus grande risque d'être plus abandonnée que l'autre.'

POSTSCRIPT: 1974

The account given in this book of the way in which the relationship between the Soviet Union and the United States evolved, from the Cuban missile crisis until the conclusion of the Fourth Arab-Israeli War, ended in the autumn of 1973. Up to October 1974—exactly twelve years after the Cuban crisis and twelve months after the cease-fire of October 1973—has anything happened to modify either this account of Soviet foreign policy or the attempt (in Part Four) to consider how the relationship between the two super-powers may develop further? The short answer is, nothing. Indeed, events have served rather to increase the lonely eminence of the super-powers.

None the less, much has happened in 1974. This has been, above all, the year of the world energy crisis and of the inflationary turmoil of the Western economic system. Politically, some of the outstanding international events of 1974 have been these: the replacement of the leaders of the United States and of the three principal countries of Western Europe; the quarrel between the United States and Western Europe, repaired at Ottawa and Brussels in June; the arcane struggle for power in China; the last stages of Nixon's struggle for survival as President of the United States; notwithstanding this, the feats of American diplomacy in the Middle East in the first half of the year; the ferment in Southern Africa, after the overthrow of the old regime in Portugal; the Indian explosion of a nuclear device in May; the United States Government's decision to give nuclear aid to the two principal antagonists in the Middle East a month later; the agreements between the super-powers reached at the third Soviet-American summit meeting in June/July, followed in October by the Soviet assurances[1] on freedom of emigration;

the Cyprus crisis; and the succession of Vice-President Ford as President of the United States.

This sequence must be considered against the Soviet domestic background: under Brezhnev's ascendancy, the authority of the collective leadership questioned less and less; approval of their foreign policy reaffirmed by the Central Committee immediately after Nixon's departure from Moscow; the import of Western technology and capital gathering speed; a reasonably good harvest in prospect; the first moves towards another meeting of at least the European branch of the world Communist Movement; and the voices of the dissident minority within the Soviet Union increasingly stifled—Sakharov cut off by the Russians from American television during an interview which he was giving while the United States President was the guest of the Soviet Government, and Solzhenitsyn living in exile, the first Soviet citizen to receive this punishment since Trotsky.

The change of American leadership on 9 August 1974 left the super-power relationship unchanged. The new US President kept Kissinger, the architect of American policy towards the Soviet Union in the present decade, as his Secretary of State; Ford's assurances regarding the continuity of this policy were publicly accepted in a speech delivered on 25 September[2] by Brezhnev, who said the same about Soviet policy towards the United States; and a month later it was announced that the two leaders would meet in Vladivostock on 23/24 November. Just after Nixon had left the Soviet Union and just before he resigned, the Cyprus crisis erupted. Although the consequences of this crisis on the south-eastern flank of the NATO alliance—in Greece* and in Turkey—affected the national interests both of the Soviet Union and of the United States, neither government became directly embroiled in the crisis.[3]

Chapter 14 offered some reflections on the world scene as it might have appeared to an observer in the Kremlin in the autumn of 1973. One year later, he might find two questions worth especially careful attention: first, the effect on the Soviet Union and on the super-power relationship of the world energy crisis and of world-wide inflation, and second, the value of the agreements reached between the Soviet Union and the United States in the summer of 1974.

The quadrupling of world oil prices at the close of 1973 brought to

* Constantine Karamanlis returned from exile to Greece, where democratic government was restored. Greek forces were withdrawn from NATO, on the French model.

an end the era of cheap energy: one of the basic premises on which the industrialized countries had predicated their unprecedented rate of development since the Second World War. These countries—unless (like the Soviet Union) they are self-sufficient in energy—now face a new dimension in the problem of balancing their external payments; and this has greatly accelerated their internal rates of inflation. This is bad enough. But for the Third World, excluding the oil-producing countries, the effect is far worse. From the Third World a Fourth World has now evolved, whose 'members are those who lack major resources or economic power . . . are more dependent, more deprived, and more aware of it than any large segment of the world's population in history. That some of the desperate nations of the Fourth World now may have access to nuclear weapons only adds to the prospects for tragedy.'[4]

If he so chose, the Kremlin observer could shrug off this prospect as being the apocalyptic crisis of capitalism long foreseen by Marxist prophets: a crisis which must both justify and benefit the Soviet system. This was indeed the assessment that a member of the Politburo and the secretary of the Central Committee responsible for international relations both presented to a conference which had been convened in Moscow to discuss the teaching and the achievement of Lenin, on the fiftieth anniversary of his death.[5] But if the observer took a less superficial view, he would be bound to conclude that the world economic phenomena of 1974 were by no means an unmixed blessing for the Soviet Union. True, the Western countries were at sixes and sevens; and the Soviet Union's own reserves of foreign currency were swollen by the steep rise of world commodity prices, among which the fourfold increase in the price of oil was the most striking and the most significant element. But the observer would also be aware that the Soviet Union's Eastern European allies (themselves all importers of oil) were not immune from the consequences of Western inflation. And he could not turn a blind eye—although so far the Soviet Government seems to be doing just this—on the new problem of the Fourth World, which includes one of the Soviet Union's principal associates—India. Finally, even looking at the purely national interests of the Soviet economy, although he could take comfort in the fact that the Soviet Union can, in the last resort, be self-sufficient, he would also know well that the prospect of rapidly developing the Soviet economy still depended on the import of Western technology and capital, both of which had become much more expensive in 1974.

The agreements reached between the Soviet and US governments during Nixon's second presidential visit to the USSR, which lasted from 27 June to 3 July, were published on the front pages of *Pravda*:[6] among others, the ten-year agreement on economic, industrial, and technological cooperation, signed on 29 June; the Treaty of 3 July banning underground nuclear weapon tests having a yield exceeding 150 kilotons, with effect from 31 March 1976; the Protocol (also signed on 3 July to the 1972 Treaty on the Limitation of Anti-Ballistic Missile Systems, whereby the two governments bound themselves not to exercise their right, under the Treaty, to deploy an ABM system in the second of their two deployment areas; the agreement to open negotiations on environmental warfare; and—in the text of the joint communiqué of 3 July—the governments' conclusion that the 1972 Interim Agreement on Offensive Strategic Weapons should be followed by a new agreement between the Soviet Union and the United States on the limitation of strategic arms, covering the period until 1985 and dealing with both quantitative and qualitative limitations, which should be completed at the earliest possible date, before the expiry of the present agreement, their delegations being reconvened at Geneva 'in the immediate future on the basis of instructions growing out of the summit'.

In their communiqué the two governments also agreed to consider a joint initiative in the Conference of the Committee on Disarmament for the conclusion, as a first step, of an international convention regarding chemical warfare; they favoured an early date for the final stage of the CSCE conference, and they 'proceeded from the assumption that the results of the negotiations will permit the conference to be concluded at the highest level';* they considered it important that the Geneva peace conference should resume its work as soon as possible; and they agreed 'to remain in close touch with a view to coordinating the efforts of both countries towards a peaceful settlement in the Middle East', which should be based on UN Security Council Resolution 338, taking into account 'the legitimate interests of all peoples in the Middle East, including the Palestinian people, and the right to existence of all states in the area'.

In forming a judgement of these agreements, our observer would have been prepared by a good deal that had already appeared in the Soviet press both before and during the summit meeting. Thus, he would have been impressed by the paragraph of the joint communiqué[7] issued on 28 March, at the end of Kissinger's visit to Moscow, in which

---

* It was, at Helsinki, in August 1975.

both sides expressed their determination 'to pursue ... the established policy aimed at making the process of improving Soviet-American relations irreversible'—an adjective that was to be adopted by Nixon three months later. More recently, he would have noted Brezhnev's statement, in an electoral speech delivered in Moscow on 14 June: 'we wish Soviet-American relations to become really stable and independent of unfavourable combinations of events. We are in favour of both our countries and of the whole world receiving the benefit of their further development.'[8]

Unless he was a member of the Kremlin inner circle, he would not have been aware of the full extent of the American domestic controversy that surrounded the departure of the US President for Moscow, although he would have been warned by *Pravda* that the Chinese were seeking to support 'those who longed for the days of the cold war', and that recent invitations to visit Peking were 'no accident'.* And he would have observed Nixon's emphasis, in his speeches of 27 June and 2 July, on the value to relations between the two countries of the personal relationship established between their leaders ('able to meet together as friends'). He might also have compared Brezhnev's warning in his speech on 27 June—that if the two sides could not accomplish the task of assuring a stable peace between the Soviet Union and the United States, then all remaining achievements in the development of their mutual relations might lose their significance—with the remark made in his speech five days later, that although the nuclear agreements reached by the two sides, taken together, signified a substantial advance, this might perhaps have been even more comprehensive.† Nevertheless, he would have been impressed by the language used in the account of the reception given by the Central Committee to Brezhnev's report on the results of the summit meetings, described as 'a massive landmark in the history of the relations between the Soviet Union and the USA' and 'a massive contribution towards the improvement of Soviet-American relations', making possible a further relaxation of international tension.

A Soviet observer would not have known from his own press that the two governments had reached an (unwritten) understanding in principle that the inspection of peaceful nuclear explosions would involve the presence of observers—for the first time on Soviet territory. How much

---

* China was visited in the summer of 1974 by Heath and Jackson, among others.

† Speaking in Warsaw on 21 July, Brezhnev told the Sejm that he would have liked an agreement banning all underground nuclear weapons tests.

else he would have understood about what occurred between 27 June and 3 July 1974 would partly depend on whether he also received foreign reports of the summit meetings, in particular the transcript of the US Secretary of State's press conference on 3 July.[9] If he had read the latter, he would have known that these discussions about the nuclear arms race were the most extensive that had ever taken place, and with a frankness that would have been considered inconceivable two years previously ('indeed with an amount of detail that would have been considered violating intelligence codes in previous periods'); and he would have been struck by Kissinger's personal impression that both sides had to convince their military establishments of the benefits of restraint—'not a thought that comes naturally to military people on either side'. This last remark would have given any Soviet observer grounds for reflection. And another major anxiety left in his mind would have been the doubt whether the commitment simply to 'stay in close touch over the Middle East'* was enough to contain the continuing tensions between the Arab states and Israel, even though these were described in the communiqué of 1974—unlike that of 1973—as of 'paramount importance and urgency'.

In the West, fears were expressed before the summit meeting that it would become the occasion either of a 'quick fix' or of a deadlock on the paramount issue at stake between the super-powers—the future of the arms race. This requires a decision on the part of both governments whether or not to embark on a new generation of strategic nuclear weapon systems. In effect, they agreed in Moscow to defer the decision a little longer—in Kissinger's words: 'in the hope, not the assurance, that if such an agreement were reached next year, we should be talking of a ten-year agreement . . . to gain control of multiple warheads . . . by introducing some stability into the rate and nature of their deployment'. Therefore there was neither a quick fix nor was the third summit meeting merely a Field of the Cloth of Gold.

The excesses of optimism and of pessimism about this complex question have tended to be based both on an unwarranted assumption and on a misunderstanding of the nature of the strategic arsenals of the two super-powers. The assumption, which in the light of the history of the past twenty-five years is extraordinary, is that Soviet technology, following in the footsteps of its American counterpart, would not be

---

* In the event, the Geneva Peace Conference is still in recess, at the time of writing.

capable of successfully testing multiple independently targetable re-entry vehicles and of equipping the gigantic new Soviet ICBMs with MIRVs. The misunderstanding, which lies close to the root of the super-powers' nuclear dilemma, relates to the asymmetry of their strategic nuclear forces: at the risk of some oversimplification, it is broadly true to say that the USA has struck a balance between land, sea, and air, whereas the Soviet Union has until recently concentrated its principal strategic investment on land-based missile launchers.

Given this asymmetry, and given the inevitable Soviet determination to close the qualitative gap between the two systems obtaining in 1972 (the year in which the first strategic arms limitation agreements were concluded), it is hardly surprising that 1974 has not proved to be a year of nuclear restraint. It is indeed something that the two governments agreed on as much as they did in Moscow, including the underground test ban, which—for all its imperfections—may at least do something to inhibit the development of a new generation of warheads. Nevertheless, there is no ground whatever for complacency, especially since the explosion in the Rajastan desert on 18 May: thirty-nine governments have refused to sign the Nuclear Non-Proliferation Treaty.

If we have not reached an agreement well before 1977, then I believe you will see an explosion of technology and an explosion of numbers at the end of which we will be lucky if we have the present stability, in which it will be impossible to describe what strategic superiority means. And one of the questions which we have to ask ourselves as a country is: what in the name of God is strategic superiority? What is the significance of it, politically, militarily, operationally, at these levels of numbers? What do you do with it? . . . We will be living in a world which will be extra-ordinarily complex, in which opportunities for nuclear warfare exist that were unimaginable fifteen years ago at the beginning of the nuclear age. . . .

This was how the American Secretary of State felt the pressure of time in Moscow. Although there were no corresponding remarks on the Soviet side, in 1974 neither super-power could ignore the possible alternative to agreement:

> And yonder all before us lie
> Deserts of vast eternity.[10]

NOTES

1. *The Times*, 19 October 1974. But the Kissinger-Jackson exchange was not the end of the story, since the terms of the US Trade Bill (finally passed in December 1974) were regarded by the Soviet Government as inconsistent with the US undertakings of May 1972. A question mark therefore still remains over the development of Soviet-US trade in the immediate future.

2. *Pravda*, 26 September 1974.

3. The Cyprus crisis began with the overthrow of President Makarios by a right-wing *coup d'état* on 15 July. Cyprus was invaded on 19/20 July. Karamanlis was sworn in as Prime Minister of Greece on 24 July. Although the Soviet Government did not become embroiled in the crisis, it did not mince words about it: for an exposition of Brezhnev's view, see *Pravda* of 26 September 1974.

4. Walter Mondale, 'International Economic Society' in *Foreign Affairs*, vol. 53, no. 1, October 1974, p. 5.

5. *Pravda*, 19 January 1974, reported Suslov's and Ponomarev's addresses to this conference. The full text of Ponomarev's was given in *Kommunist*, no. 2, Moscow, 1974. Suslov spoke of the 'very sharp ideological struggle that is going on in the contemporary world' and Ponomarev of 'a definite qualitative shift in the development of the crisis of capitalism'.

6. *Pravda*, 30 June, 4 July, and 5 July 1974.

7. *The Times*, 29 March 1974, has the English text.

8. *Pravda*, 15 June 1974.

9. *Department of State Bulletin*, July 1974, vol. LXXI, no. 1831, pp. 205 ff. All subsequent quotations from Kissinger's press conference of 3 July 1974 are taken from this source.

10. Andrew Marvell (1621–78).

SELECT BIBLIOGRAPHY

Books

ALLISON, Graham, *Essence of Decision: Explaining the Cuban Missile Crisis*, Little, Brown, Boston, 1971.

AMAL'RYK, Andrei, *Can the Soviet Union Survive until 1984 ?* Harper & Row, New York; Allen Lane, London, 1970.

ARON, Raymond, *Paix et guerre entre les nations*, Calmann-Lévy, Paris, 1962.

ASPATURIAN, Vernon V., *Process and Power in Soviet Foreign Policy*, Little, Brown, Boston, 1971.

BREZHNEV, L. I., *Leninskim Kursom*, Moscow, 1972.

BRZEZINSKI, Zbigniew, *The Soviet Bloc*, Harvard University Press, Cambridge, Mass., 1967.

BUCHAN, Alastair, *The End of the Post-War Era*, Weidenfeld & Nicolson, London, 1974.

BUTTERFIELD, M. and WIGHT, M., *Diplomatic Investigations*, George Allen & Unwin, London, 1966.

CHICHERIN, G. V., *Articles and Speeches*, Moscow, 1961.

CLISSOLD, Stephen, *Soviet Relations with Latin America 1918–68*, Oxford University Press, London, 1970.

CURZON, G. N., *Russia in Central Asia*, Longmans, Green, London, 1889.
Diplomaticheskii Slovar', 2 vols, Moscow, 1964.
Diplomatiya Sotsializma, collective authorship, Moscow, 1973.

DUMONT, René, *Cuba: socialisme et développement*, Editions du Seuil, Paris, 1964.

ERICKSON, John, *Soviet Military Power*, Royal United Services Institute for Defence Studies, London, 1971.

FORWARD, Nigel, *The Field of Nations*, Macmillan, London, 1971.

FOX, W. T. R., *The Super-Powers—their Responsibility for Peace*, Yale Institute of International Studies, 1944.

GITTINGS, John, *Survey of the Sino-Soviet Dispute 1963–67*, Oxford University Press, London, 1968.

GORER, Geoffrey and RICKMAN, John, *The People of Greater Russia*, Cresset Press, London, 1949.

GRIFFITH, William E., *The Sino-Soviet Rift*, Allen & Unwin, London, 1964.

GROMYKO, Antolyi A., *1036 dniei prezidenta Kennedi*, Moscow, 1968.

HAYTER, William, *Russia and the World*, Secker and Warburg, London, 1970.

HOFFMAN, Erik and FLERON, F., *Conduct of Soviet Foreign Policy*, Aldine and Atherton, Chicago, 1971.

HORELICK, A. L. and RUSH, M., *Strategic Power and Soviet Foreign Policy*, University of Chicago Press, Chicago, 1966.

Istoriya Vneshnei Politiki SSSR, edited by Ponomarev, Gromyko, and Khvostov, two volumes, Moscow, 1971.

JACOBSEN, Carl, *Soviet Strategy—Soviet Foreign Policy*, Glasgow University Press, Glasgow, 1972.

KARNOW, Stanley, *Mao and China*, Viking Press, New York, 1972.

KENNEDY, Robert, *Thirteen Days, a Memoir of the Cuban Crisis*, Macmillan, New York, 1969.

KONDRASHEV, E., *Tsenoobrazovanie v promyshlennosti*, Moscow, 1956.

KULSKI, W. W., *The Soviet Union in World Affairs, 1964–1972*, Syracuse University Press, Syracuse, New York, 1973.

LANGE, Oscar, *Socjalizm*, Warsaw, 1973.

LENIN, V. I., *Collected Works*, Foreign Languages Publishing House, Moscow, 1960; Lawrence and Wishart, London, 1960.

MACKINTOSH, J. M., *Strategy and Tactics of Soviet Foreign Policy*, Oxford University Press, London, 1962.

MACMILLAN, Harold, *At the End of the Day*, Macmillan, London, 1973.

MEDVEDEV, Roy, *Kniga o sotsialisticheskoi democratii*, Alexander Herzen Foundation, Amsterdam/Paris, 1972.

MONROE, Elizabeth, *The Changing Balance of Power in the Persian Gulf*, an international seminar report, the American Universities Field Staff, New York, 1972.

NOVE, Alec, *The Soviet Economy*, George Allen & Unwin, London, 1968.

SAKHAROV, Andrei, *Progress, Coexistence, and Intellectual Freedom*, Penguin Books, London, 1969.

SALINGER, Pierre, *With Kennedy*, Cape, London, 1967.

SCHLESINGER, A. M., *A Thousand Days*, Deutsch, London, 1966.

SOLZHENITSYN, Alexander, *Archipelag Gulag*, YMCA Press, Paris, 1973; English translation, Collins, London, 1974.

SORENSEN, Theodore, *Decision-Making in the White House*, Columbia University Press, New York, 1969.

SORENSEN, Theodore, *Kennedy*, Hodder and Stoughton, London, 1965.

TATU, Michel, *Power in the Kremlin*, Collins, London, 1969.

TRISKA, J. F. and FINLEY, D. F., *Soviet Foreign Policy*, Macmillan, New York, 1968.

TROTSKY, Leon, *Moya zhizn'*, Granit, Berlin, 1930.

ULAM, Adam, *Expansion and Coexistence*, Secker and Warburg, London, 1968.

ULAM, Adam, *The Rivals*, Viking Press, New York, 1971.

YORK, Herbert, *Race to Oblivion*, Simon and Schuster, New York, 1970.

ZHDANOV, Andrei, *Essays on Literature, Philosophy, and Music*, International Publishers, New York, 1950.

ZHURIN, V. V. and PRIMAKOV, E. M., *Mezhdunarodnye konflikty*, Moscow 1972.

ZUCKERMAN, Solly, *Scientists at War*, Harper and Row, New York, 1966.

PERIODICALS

PUBLISHED IN BRITAIN

Adelphi Papers   *The Economist*   *Encounter*
Keesing's Contemporary Archives   *Military Balance*
Strategic Survey   *Survey*   *Survival*

PUBLISHED IN THE UNITED STATES

Foreign Affairs   *Foreign Policy*   *Problems of Communism*
State Department Bulletin   *Time Magazine*

PUBLISHED IN THE SOVIET UNION

Journal of World Economics and International Relations
Kommunist   *Kommunist Vooruzhennykh Sil*
Literaturnaya Gazeta   *Mezhdunarodnaya Zhizn'*
Novoe Vremya   *Novyi Mir*   *SShA*   *Voprosy Istorii*
The Working Class and the Contemporary World

PUBLISHED IN CZECHOSLOVAKIA

World Marxist Review

PUBLISHED IN CHINA

The People's Daily

NEWSPAPERS

Frankfurter Allgemeine Zeitung   *Guardian*   *Hoy*
International Herald Tribune   *Izvestiya*   *Krasnaya Zvezda*
Le Monde   *New York Times*   *Observer*   *Pravda*
Rude Pravo   *The Times*   *Washington Post*

INDEX

dispute with, 14, 31, 33, 47, 48; relations with military of, 43, 73; and with local communist parties, 53, 154; New Left criticized by, 87; and neo-Stalinism, 88 &n; *see also* Central Committee; Politburo

CPSU Congresses, XXth (1956), 12, 14, 17, 36, 64, 68, 85, 155, 165; XXIInd (1961), 13, 14, 84; XXIIIrd (1966), 2, 44, 48, 56; XXIVth (1971), 2, 41, 85, 87, 89–91, 111n, 127, 139

Cuba, 4, 102; missile crisis (1962), 1, 4, 10n, 17–18, 22–30, 32, 34–5n, 38, 39, 40, 51n, 138, 144, 150, 151, 152, 174; Bay of Pigs fiasco, 23, 24; Communist Party of, 51, 52n, 53; Soviet aid to and political relations with, 55–6, 90–1, 101, 122; economic development of, 55–6, 62n

Curzon, G. N., 152, 155, 172n

Cyprus, 1967 crisis, 60; Soviet policy in, 106–7; 1974 crisis, 175, 181n

Czechoslovak Communist Party, 68, 70, 71, 72; XIVth Congress of, 73

Czechoslovakia, 9n, 87, 88, 94, 120; Soviet invasion of (1968), 3, 45, 51, 56, 67, 68–75, 77, 99, 126, 154, 164; armed forces of, 42; arms deal with Egypt, 57; economic reforms in, 68; Brezhnev's policy towards, 90, 98–9; Soviet Treaty of Friendship with, 98–9; becomes member of GATT, 131; West Germany signs peace treaty with, 136n

Damansky Island (Chenpao Island), Sino-Soviet fighting on, 49, 52n

Daniel, Yuli, 88

Dayan, Moshe, 106

Defence, Khrushchev's policy, 11, 13–14, 32, 35n, 37, 40–1, 42, 43; Soviet budget for, 11, 41, 86, 89; Soviet arms deal with Egypt, 12, 21, 57; Research and Development, 13, 38n, 41, 151 &n; Sino-Soviet co-operation over, 15, 17; Collective Leadership's policy, 36–44; Vietnam War and, 45–6; and invasion of Czechoslovakia, 68–75; Yugoslav concept of total national defence, 75; Soviet-Egyptian Treaty, 105; Seabed Treaty, 110, 120; Indo-Soviet Treaty and, 111; Soviet-

Iraqi Treaty, 121; US superiority in strategic bombers, 115; and FBS system, 115; banning of chemical and biological weapons, 120; Soviet superiority in conventional forces in Europe, 129; *see also* ABMs; military aid; nuclear weapons; NATO; SALT; Warsaw Pact

De Gaulle, General Charles, 65, 92n, 95

Denmark, 129, 130

détente, 127, 128, 135, 143, 145, 150, 152, 168; *see also* peaceful co-existence

Dorticos, Osvaldo, 91

Dubcek, Alexander, 99; Czechoslovak crisis and, 68–73 *passim*

Eastern Europe, future political change in, 163–6; effect of Western inflation on, 176; *see also* COMECON; Warsaw Pact; individual countries

economy, economic development, 6; Khrushchev's policy, 11–13, 32, 35n, 84–5; Soviet foreign aid programmes, 12, 54–6, 122–3; Indonesian debt to Soviet Union, 54, 62; Soviet-Iranian agreement, 59; and Soviet-South Yemen agreement, 60; Cuban, 55–6, 62n; Romanian independent foreign trade policy, 64; reforms in Eastern Europe, 68; motorcar production in USSR, 82, 84, 98; Soviet economic dilemma (1969–70), 84–6; Stalin's economic system, 85, 86, 92n; the Economic Reform (1965), 85; 1965–70 and 1970–5 Plans, 85, 86, 89; reasons for economic failings, 86; East-West technological and managerial gap, 84, 86, 88, 158–9; and over-commitment of resources to defence, 86; link between political and economic problems in Soviet Union, 84, 88; Soviet cooperation with West, 88–9; 130–1; and exchange of scientific and technological know-how, 89; decisions of XXIVth Congress, 89; Soviet-W. German trade agreement, 94; and intra-Comecon trade, agreement (1972), 114, 116–17; and Soviet-Japanese trade, 118; Soviet

economy, economic development-
cont.

oil imports from Iraq, 121; and
trade agreement with Cuba, 122;
and limited aid to Chile, 122–3;
Soviet-West German economic
agreement (1973), 127–8; and
Soviet-American cooperation, 133–
4, 159–61 &n, 167; and US Trade
Reform Bill, 135–6; and credit-
barter compensation model, 142;
energy crisis and inflation, 159–60,
174, 175–6; 10-year Soviet-US
Agreement on economic, industrial
and technological cooperation
(1974), 177

Egypt, attitude to Soviet Union of, 4,
9n; Soviet arms deal with, 12, 21,
57; and financing of Aswan Dam,
21, 55, 57; and Soviet relations
with Nasser, 54; and Soviet purchase of cotton from, 57; Six-Day
War, 59–60; involvement in Yemeni
civil war of, 60; UN Resolution on
Arab-Israeli dispute and, 60–1; and
War of Attrition, 62; Soviet direct
intervention in (1970), 62, 87, 101–2,
104n; and Jordanian civil war, 103;
Sadat succeeds Nasser as President
of, 103; Soviet treaty of friendship
with (1971), 105–6, 107, 120; Soviet
military advisers withdrawn from,
120–1; October 1973 War with
Israel, 144–5, 147; future nuclear
capabilities of, 162, 163

energy crisis, 151, 159–60, 174, 175–6

EOKA, 106

Erhard, Ludwig, 32

'essential equivalence', American
definition of, 38, 44n, 109

European Economic Community
(EEC), 148n, 151; Protocol on
inter-German trade, 119; cooperation between COMECON and,
120, 131; Britain, Denmark, and
Ireland join, 119, 130

Export-Import Bank, 122, 137n

FBS (US forward based systems), 115

Fiat factory in USSR, 82, 83n, 89

Finland, 98, 164; Soviet territorial
acquisition from 19; SALT talks
in Helsinki (1969), 79–80; Soviet

Treaty with (1948), 98n; 'Finlandization', 98

Fischer, Ernst, 87

Ford, President Gerald, 147, 175

foreign aid, Soviet, 12, 54–6; to Cuba,
122; and to Chile, 122–3; *see also*
economy; military aid

Fourth World, new problem of, 176

Fox, William, 5, 168

France, Suez crisis and, 25, 57; Arab-
Israeli dispute and, 61; withdraws
forces from NATO, 65, 76n; Soviet
relations with, 65, 95–6, 136n;
abstention from MBFR proposal,
67, 76n, 96, 129; Non-Proliferation
Treaty and, 78n; May 1968
students' revolt in, 87; Soviet
industrial cooperation with, 89;
Moscow Treaty and, 94; and Quadripartite Agreement on Berlin, 107,
119; *force de frappe* of, 171

Gandhi, Mrs Indira, 74

Garaudy, Roger, 87

GATT (General Agreement on Trade
and Tariffs), 131, 135

Geneva Conference on Indo-China,
46

Geneva Disarmament Conference, 78,
120, 177

Geneva Talks on Arab-Israeli dispute,
148, 177, 179

German Democratic Republic (East
Germany), 64; Treaty of Friendship between Soviet Union and, 32;
and Khrushchev's initiative with
West Germany, 32–3; armed
forces of, 42; and W. German
Ostpolitik, 67, 81; Moscow Treaty,
93–5; and Warsaw Pact, 97;
Quadripartite Agreement on Berlin
and, 107–8, 119; and treaty on traffic questions with West Germany,
119; and Basic Treaty, 119; attends
MBFR talks, 120; Brezhnev's visit
to, 136n

German Federal Republic (West
Germany), 6, 24, 64; Khrushchev's
conciliatory policy towards, 32–3;
Romania establishes diplomatic relations with, 65, 67; *Ostpolitik* of,
65–7, 81, 93–4; and Hallstein
doctrine, 64, 67; Soviet bilateral

Interim Agreement on Offensive Strategic Weapons (1972), 114–16, 177

International Development Association, 54

International Monetary Fund, 131

Iran, 62n; Stalin's forward policy towards, 57; Soviet rapprochement with, 57, 59, 121

Iraq, 74; withdraws from Baghdad Pact, 62–3; Soviet Treaty of Friendship and Cooperation with (1972), 121, 124–5

IRBMs (intermediate range ballistic missiles), 25, 27, 32, 44n, 119

Ireland, 130

Israel, USA refuses to supply more Phantoms to, 102; emigration of Soviet Jews to, 143, 160–1; Palestinian Arabs under rule of, 63n; Romania maintains relations with, 65; importance in US domestic politics of, 161; future nuclear capabilities of, 162, 163; see also Arab-Israeli dispute

Italian Communist Party, 51, 161

Italy, 129, 162; Fiat factory built in Soviet Union, 82, 83n, 89

Jackson, US Senator Henry, 116; his Amendment to the US Trade Bill, 135–6, 160–1; visits China, 178n

Japan, 6, 13, 51, 91, 113, 151, 154; claim to Kurile Islands, 19, 118, 148n; Soviet economic and political relations with, 88, 118–19, 124n, 131; reaction to Chinese-American rapprochement of, 92n; Chinese policy towards, 140

Jarring, Gunnar, UN Special Representative for Middle East, 61, 102, 106

Jerusalem, Israeli occupation of, 61

Johnson, President L. B., 45, 46n, 60, 78–9

Joint Declaration on Basic Principles of Relations between the USA and the USSR (1972), 116

Joint Trade Commission, Soviet-American, 117

Jordan civil war (1970), 103

Jordan-Lebanon crisis, 17

Kadar, Janos, 71

Karlovy Vary statement (of European communist parties: 1967), 66, 67, 72

Kassem, Abdul Karim, 53

Kazakhstan Soviet Republic, 18, 119

Kennan, George, 100

Kennedy, John F., 7, 51n, 83n, 115, 150; Cuban missile crisis and, 22–30 *passim*, 40; Khrushchev's 'Friday Letter' to, 23 &n, 35n, 154n; and Vienna summit meeting, 23, 24, 25, 46; Khrushchev's 'Saturday' letter to, 30 &n, 35n

Kennedy, Robert, 29, 30, 150

KGB (Committee for State Security), 10n, 126, 143; foreign directorate of, 8

Khrushchev, Nikita, 1, 2, 3, 4, 5, 11–36, 50, 51 &n, 55, 68, 82, 141, 155, 165; his doctrine of peaceful coexistence, 11–12; and peaceful transition to socialism, 12; and attitude to Third World, 12, 53, 54, 55, 56; visits USA, 12, 131; defence policy of, 13–14, 32, 35n, 37, 38n, 40–1, 42, 43; and Sino-Soviet dispute, 14–19, 31; Berlin crisis and, 21, 24, 25, 40; and Middle East policy, 21, 57; his quarrel with Hammarskjöld, 21–2; and Cuban missile crisis, 22–30, 35n, 40; and Vienna summit meeting with Kennedy, 23, 24, 25, 46; his policy of temporary *détente* with West, 31; and 'minimum nuclear deterrence', 32, 37, 40–1; fall of (1964), 32–3, 36, 37, 138, 150; number of offices held by, 37 &n; Vietnam policy of, 46; and economic policy, 84, 85; civil liberties under, 87, 88; Eastern European policy of, 164

Kirkuk oil field, 121

Kissinger, Henry, 120, 123n, 160, 161n, 169, 178, 179, 180; paves way for US-Chinese rapprochement, 91; reaches agreement on Vietnam with Le Duc Tho, 118; Washington Agreements and, 132–3; appointed US Sec. of State, 135; Fourth Arab-Israeli War (1973), 145, 147, 149n; and statement about Year of Europe (1973), 148n, 168; fears of diplomacy in the Middle East, 174; retained as Secretary of State by Ford, 175; visits to Moscow, 177; assessment of 1974 US-Soviet agreements, 179–80

Korean War, 39